MW01644565

An Anatomy of Feminist Resistance

An Anatomy of Feminist Resistance

Rebel in the Wilderness

Henriette Dahan Kalev

LEXINGTON BOOKS
Lanham • Boulder • New York • London

Published by Lexington Books
An imprint of The Rowman & Littlefield Publishing Group, Inc.
4501 Forbes Boulevard, Suite 200, Lanham, Maryland 20706
www.rowman.com

6 Tinworth Street, London SE11 5AL, United Kingdom

British Library Cataloguing in Publication Information Available

Library of Congress Cataloging-in-Publication Data

Names: Dahan-Kalev, Henriette, author.
Title: An anatomy of feminist resistance : rebel in the wilderness / Henriette Dahan Kalev.
Description: Lanham : Lexington Books, 2019. | Includes bibliographical references and index.
Identifiers: LCCN 2018045008 (print) | LCCN 2018046010 (ebook) | ISBN 9781498524360 (Electronic) | ISBN 9781498524353 (cloth : alk. paper)
Subjects: LCSH: Feminism--Israel. | Feminism--Religious aspects--Judaism. | Women--Israel--Social conditions.
Classification: LCC HQ1728.5 (ebook) | LCC HQ1728.5 .D34 2019 (print) | DDC 305.42095694--dc23
LC record available at https://lccn.loc.gov/2018045008

∞ ™ The paper used in this publication meets the minimum requirements of American National Standard for Information Sciences Permanence of Paper for Printed Library Materials, ANSI/NISO Z39.48-1992.

Printed in the United States of America

For my son, Ayal, who missed many hours of my time as a single mother with a career.

Contents

Preface

When Havatzelet Ingbar and Vicki Knafo's rage was ignited and they began to march to the streets, rebelling against their oppressors, they did not imagine that their struggle would become a historical chapter in the struggle of marginalized women in Israel. All they wanted was to improve a little of their income and labor conditions. During that struggle, they learned as well as their oppressors to what extent human cruelty and struggle against it could result in. Indeed, their struggle did not put an end to the exploitation and oppression of marginalized women, but it violated for a short while the oppressors' peace of mind. Ingbar and her friends started a strike that was aimed at putting an end to fourteen years of economic insecurity and repeated dismissal from the textile factory, where they worked. They ended up being the CEOs of that factory, a precedent in women labor history in Israel.

Knafo began her journey marching hundreds of kilometers from the remote town of Mitzpe Ramon to Jerusalem. All she wanted was to meet with the minister of finance, Benjamin Netanyahu. She wanted to explain to him that even the salaries she brought home from working two jobs were not enough to feed her children.

These two women found themselves going through a deep process of transformation that they did not expect to go through. Along their journey, they stood in front of the establishment: one which once seemed to them to be omnipotent but now was revealed to them as made up of a bunch of clerks and politicians that were clumsy, hollow, and limited in abilities. As opposed to that their personal reflection mirrored to them with surprise. The image of the weak single mother, a factory worker who lived on the social and peripheral margins in the remote Desert of the Negev, now looked at them from the media pages and the public sphere as glorious, fighting Amazons. However, as the days of struggle went by, these images transformed as well. Soberness and cynicism poured into their real lives, and these two charismatic women matured politically. Their consciousness transformed, and they widened their minds as to the power relations game the neoliberal rule was playing. They never left the southern desert, and their salary power did not improve much. However, they grew up to be well conscious democratic citizens and well aware women whose children and the people around them are inspired by.

The story which I bring here is a story of consciousness transformation. I had the privilege to know these women as I stepped out of the ivory tower and walked with them for a distance in dramatic parts of their lives' paths. They opened their inner worlds to me, and I wouldn't have marched with them had I not opened mine to them as well. We looked back to the stormy events, sometimes with hesitance, discussed labor options that single mothers have and the differences from women who live in couples, what the talks with the politicians did to them, and who they became after the drama ended. We criticized the establishment and officials, but we sometimes understood the boundaries that modern and complex politics and economy could have. For all of these, I will always be in debt to these women who became model figures for fighting women in a wild era of global capitalism.

TWO LINGUISTIC COMMENTS

The struggles that are presented in this book took place in Israel. The reports in the media and documents in film series were in Hebrew. All the sources I used in this book, as well as the interviews, were in Hebrew. I made all the translations from Hebrew. Occasionally, I wrote words in Hebrew, in most cases slang, which were followed by suggested English translation.

Some of the analytical and academic literature is written in Hebrew. The bibliography list of the Hebrew items is brought in Hebrew with my translation to English.

PERSONAL COMMENT

As an academic, a social justice activist, and a single mother, I have always lived through the dilemma of either staying put securing the food I could bring home to put on my sons table or jeopardizing my job and going public to make a difference by criticizing and subverting power holders when injustices are committed.

I was fired from jobs, and my promotion was hindered more than once. The dilemma was always resolved when ignited with the rage against injustice I experienced. This is what always inspired and motivated my academic and public activism. The moral of this book is that rage has a right and moral side, too.

Acknowledgments

This book tells the story of rebellion by Havatzelet Ingbar and Vicki Knafo. I want to thank them for the nobleness with which they opened their hearts to me and enabled me to explore and understand the precarious life women sometimes live through.

I want to thank the editors at Lexington, especially Holly Buchanan, who patiently replied to all my queries and questions, and to the publishers who bore with me when my schedule kept changing.

Introduction

Women's life story, as personal and private as it could be, is a source of significant knowledge on gender relations and feminism. By learning a life story of a woman, the construct of life conditions are unfolded in front of us. By telling life stories of particular women, alternative life options and power relations uncover various natures of gender power relations and of the ways in which women maneuver while interacting with other people. Focusing on telling one or more central aspects of particular women's lives can shed light on the ways in which deep and hidden social and cultural constructs chain women from within their conscious interpellation. Telling life stories present us with women agency at certain points in their lives. Therefore, discourse analysis of life stories of particular women can reveal ways of becoming a subordinated person, resisting the subordination of a certain woman as De Beauvoir's suggested (De Beauvoir, 1984). In other words, elaborating socialization forces or broad construction of power relations are not enough. It is necessary to search for specific time and space contexts and trace the particular constructs while they are at the making processes to understand how women's lives are constructed. The era and the particular culture are the "flashlight" under which we should search for explanations of gender formation and understand what women do with them. The feminist agenda of women who take action makes changes in their lives may work in particular cultural context but might be inefficient in another. Working agenda for women in the western world does not mean it works for women whose life conditions were modified in Middle Eastern communities. Looking into particular settings that shape women's lives on the way can tell about the challenges they face when paving their road to liberation. Each day, one woman is liberated, and she does it on her own terms under particular conditions.

In the academic work, the researcher had to hide herself until not long ago and had to lay out a story according to academic rigid rules of objectivity and universality (Harding, 1987). This formatting tried to capture the 'un-capturable' and trap the storyteller and the woman-subject of the story in a frustrating relationship because of stiff rules of objectivity that Susan Bordo has formulated as working from an imagined point of view of God (Bordo, 1994). Postmodern critics of science have contested these scientific intellectual principles and pointed out their cognitive and political pitfalls.

The way out of this trap, as both Harding and Bordo taught us, was done first by simply uncovering and re-presenting the researcher who looks through any imaginative lens of the microscope and exposes her political and ethical biases (Harding, ibid.; Bordo, ibid.). The general presupposition, these critics concluded, was that there is no way to avoid power relations, including researcher-researched subjects, be it human, animals, plants, or still objects. Harding and Bordo went all the way to define "strong objectivity" as that which accepts the unavoidable relative point of view of looking from a specific point within space and history. The researcher will always come to the field of study as a human whose socialization involves cultural and psychological constructs that makes her who she is as a human being. When the academic scholar sets the boundaries of her work and position herself within the context of her field of research, she simply reveals what was hidden and never discussed before: the researchers may have unlimited scientific imagination and intellectual abilities but these are delineated by ethical, cultural and political setting from whence they come to the scientific field. Moreover, the reality from where the researchers shape the study is always chaotic and complex, hence the researchers' work is to cut and disentangle very small sections to put under the microscope or philosophical analysis. It is always a re-presentation of just a piece of reality and not the reality itself. This understanding is especially significant when it concerns social and human life stories. The method that develops and unfolds in the form of a narrative clearly lie on the presupposition that the research is a type of dialogue occurring between the researcher and the readers regarding a third party that was searched and studied. The researcher reorganizes the collected data according to aesthetic and ethical rules of narration which are extracted from the field, as Bakhtin suggested (Bakhtin, 1981). A focus on one personal story with a magnifier and the analysis of its concrete details could work similar to looking through a microscope, which provides the tissue and the cobwebs a formation of the entire field of gender relations. These relations, I will argue with not much novelty, always involve power. Although one life story, or a few sections of a life story, differs in cultural and temporal details, when pulled and extracted out of a tangled fabric life reality, it becomes effective for the understanding of similar life materials. In other words, the researcher reconstructs anew, according to her ethical, scientific, and political judgment, parts of the reality through her language and cultural media communication filters. Therefore, what remains of the objective knowledge and of the life story of the researched subject, as has been actually lived, is very little. However, what provides the insights, the feminist and political insights in this particular case, and makes the selected life story from one, neglected corner of the world accessible to the broader reading audience is the analytical work of the researcher. Her familiarity with both the particular settings of the woman at focus and with the professional codes of academic studies, when brought together, may bear the fruits of better understanding of the effective apparatus that it puts in the focus of interest.

In the this spirit, that accepts the inquiry limits of life stories and follow the analytical methods that gender research has developed and adapted to the understanding of women's lives under patriarchy, this text brings hereby sections of two women agents' experience: Jewish women of Middle Eastern origin. The stories center on rebellious actions and existential struggle in the women's sections of lives where they did all they could to carry on with their everyday lives under oppression and exploitation until their powers to survive the burden of life left them. Powers that only, when they told me their stories, had they noticed that they were not aware of having them. Until then, their self-images, they said, was of feeble women. Their struggle, so they have realized, disrupted deep gender patterns and reached boundaries of male/female division of power since their girlhood. Two women of mixed cultural origins—Jewish Israeli but of Arab and Muslim countries of origin—found that Israel as a western state did not always leave space for their profound socialization as women of non-western origin. One came from Jewish Indian origin, and the other from Jewish Spanish-Moroccan origin. They both grew up in Israel, a western democratic country that did not always consist with the multicultural non-democratic socialization. This cultural mixture of roots bloomed and flourished, making them obedient women, different from women whose origin was entirely eastern or entirely western. The fact that these particular women acquired a mixture of east-west gender skills experience mostly passed unnoticed in the study of sociology in Israel. Situations prevail in many other countries. They practiced different patterns as mothers, daughters, sisters, workers, and even leaders, as they became adults. Sometimes richer and advantageous in life skills over women whose origin was either western or eastern. When they realized that they did not believe it could happen to them, the patterns of gender obedience to which they were socialized cracked and led to a feeling of rebellion to "burn it all" around them, which was what they wanted to do. The present study aims at understanding what happens at this crucial moment that raised these women's sense of resistance. Through analysis of these two particular women's resistance, I shall explain why and how it happens that women sail between ports of daughterhood, wifehood, motherhood, and sisterhood, as well as workers, teachers, or disciples, often in unbearable scenes enduring oppressive, almost enslavement, conditions of life and remain mute. On the other hand, how is it that at an unexpected moment, they even surprise themselves by taking a resisting action?

Every day a women is liberated, as I stated previously. I chose to discuss individual women's stories of liberation assuming that this process is always done by women as individuals, no matter how many women underwent it before and how many feminist struggles were carried out, or laws were legislated in favor of women's equality or liberation. Cultural, religious, political, social, and economic rules seem to hold against women liberation movements; legal systems use of effective, long-living subordinating norms and apparatus defeat them in a repeated paradoxical way. Idealistic networks and codes provide for women not only "ideal women" "ideal mother," "ideal daughter," but also "the ideal community," "state," and so on. All these models socialize women from early childhood, locked separately from one another. It is well demonstrated in Plato's allegory of the cave, where he explains of a binding method of [wo]men that chains them to each other with their back to the cave exit, unable to move their necks. Luce Irigaray's interpretation of this allegory in her book *Speculum* (Irigaray, 1985) demonstrates how social and gender relations are living constructs cultivated by women, as well as men, who support these apparatus conservation, as I will elaborate further. If and when an individual woman occasionally makes the attempt to unchain herself, it immediately radiates on other chained women who, as a group, are expected to act in concert with the larger community interest. In such cases, the women's socialization calls upon the deviating woman, pulling her back and calling her to order. In this order of things, which is constructed as patriarchal, male gatekeepers (Walby, 1990), who are often authorities of religion, regime, military, education, and so on, second the call back to order. Family, governmental, legal, educational, religious, political and cultural institutions all employ subtle apparatus in favor of conservative patriarchal order. Until not long ago, even the smallest feminist resistance, at early stage of socialization, alerted most effective gatekeeper's apparatus (Foucault, 1995). Girls participating in football, boys playing with dolls, and attempts by young women to join military service or run for religious positions, to name just a few examples, immediately activated medical, psychological, and educational apparatus to "fix the gender or sexual deviation." Such cases of disobedience exposed the vulnerability of heterosexual order and patriarchal regime rather than the "deviation" of the rebelling girl. An innocent claim of a female child to play boys games immediately challenged deep foundations of private/public gender division of labor.

Women are never "just women"; they are always also Muslim or Jewish, African-American or white women, bourgeois or poor, or properly or poorly educated. In this respect, we can presume that there are no essential women but only culturally constructed ones. This means that patriarchal order is not the only order that organizes human lives. There are other systems of order that intersect with the patriarchal. Gatekeepers who maintain the patriarchal and sexual order operate within subordinating disciplinary rules that apply to particular cultural, class, or religious cases, so that they would effectively work for the specific case of a disobedient girl or woman. Even the lightest attempt of women could palpitate the cobwebs and shake the stability of an entire male-ruling network. When more than one woman shows intention for resistance, it reveals how fluid and fragile that patriarchal order is. Irigaray powerfully demonstrated it in her chapter on fluid mechanics (Irigaray, *Speculum*, 1988.)

The life stories that I bring herein discuss how gender division of labor was palpitated and reveals how fluid and vulnerable its margins are. Two women who managed to tear just a few cobs of the power web threatened the conservative patriarchal gender relation. Women who lived in poverty and trapped in humiliating and subordinating labor conditions stood up and said "Enough!" These women were not motivated by public or political ideology, nor were they equipped with women feminist liberation consciousness. They spontaneously crossed the patriarchal lines guided by primordial senses of survival and rebelled against their prolonging life conditions as mothers—one of them a single mother—under which they finally collapsed a system of prolonged oppression. Being of South-Asian and North-African origin, their rebellion had also involved East-West public debate and revealed problems of prejudice that were not particular to the women's resistance case but exposed deeper roots of tensions between Eastern and Western social categories. These roots intersected with feminists of both origins, which in Israel drained to a larger ethnic conflict of the Mizrahi-Ashkenazi rift. Mizrahi are Jews of Arab and Muslim origin; Ashkenazi are Jews mainly of Eastern-European origin.

Points of resistance are often disclosed as unplanned when analyzing particular life stories; bursting out of deeply rooted primary forms of objection to injustice but difficult to be recognized and to be named as such. Psychological aspects play a central role in generating resistance action. Forms of injustice that endure for long and bring individuals to personal circumstances not necessarily marked as "feminist injustice," "racial discrimination," or so on. Forms of injustice are always experienced as generally unmarked compilation of wronged things inflicted and felt in person but not always conscience. A personal element of injustice is the first to ignite resistance, and then it is framed within certain "feminist," "racial" formulation. Initial motivation is always personal and not always specified. However, in most cases, individuals often bear wrong done to them personally and abstain from joining an existing initiative that acts against certain injustice, even when it concerns sever injustice inflicted on her body and soul on a daily basis. This is more so when it concerns women, particularly women of Eastern origin. Cultural differences play a central role on the way women respond to injustice inflicted on them. However, more generally, women are socialized and disciplined to contain forms of subordination and asymmetrical relationship. It is at this point that Hélène Cixous begins her imperative of "The laugh of the Medusa": ". . . And I, too, said nothing, showed nothing; I didn't open my mouth, I didn't repaint my half of the world. I was ashamed. I was afraid, and I swallowed my shame and my fear . . ." (Cixous, 1976, 876). Sometimes it happens that a stifled desire could burst forth unexpectedly and threaten to destroy the world's orders. "Volcanic" forces, as Cixous continues to describe in "The laugh of the Medusa", embedded within the disciplined woman, after generations of devoting them to self-repression, suddenly "…returns, it's an explosive, utterly destructive, staggering return, with a force never yet unleashed and equal to the most forbidding of suppression." (Cixous, ibid., 886)

The stories told in the following pages are rare cases of expression of resistance and refusal by women, especially those corresponding to Cixous's understanding of the suppressed rage of women. The apparatus of reiteration of patriarchal rules accentuate the vitality and necessity of the acceptance of order as if they were laws of nature to attain women's obedience, rendering coercive force in most cases unnecessary.

Women are often the first to be twice surprised by their own burst of resisting forces that challenges subordination. First, they are surprised to discover that the forces prove to be unnatural and unlike what looked as before bursting against them; and second, they are surprised when discovering that their inner refusal forces are potent and effective, hence to alert gatekeepers' attention. The moment of discovery that order constructs are cultural rather than natural resisting women make their first step towards liberation. It is a moment of moral perception transformation. Values and convictions are transformed, fate is doubted, and disillusionment of cultural defect is now reformulated simply as an injustice. Empowering feelings of liberation and experience of conscious turnover on the personal level and hope for gender and political change on the public level appear in a mixture of the new psychological state of mind. In short, an agent is borne out of a resisting woman. For the rebelling individual woman, it implies a personal stuttering and rebirth of her worldview. It is at this location that a personal story of one individual woman becomes so important to understand. It involves patriarchal structure undermining in person, gender apparatus not just as an abstract notion, and cultural constructions subversion in details, interpersonal relations at real-time reformation, moral transformation, and, above all, consciousness liberation of the individual past-subordinated-women.

The personal stories in this text are the fruits of numerous meetings and conversations with women who underwent the previously described experience of rebellion after years of subordination—on an individual level and a political-public level. My aim is to make an anatomy of the critical moment of experience of rebellion and change that these women initiated, with an attempt to comprehend it with its full complexity, especially consciousness transformation during and after initiating the rebellion. I discussed these experiences with the rebelling women in detail, more than once reviewing turmoil moments of consciousness transformation and liberation.

The mere fact of bringing transformation moments from my meetings with the rebelling women—the heroines of this book—is an intellectual and research experience in and of itself. A registration of the parts of the women's experiences who generously shared with me their unique experience I have put in a broader analytical thesis of gender studies. The women's stories stand at the heart of the analysis, grounded in my world of academic knowledge in gender and politics. They corresponded with theoretical foundations that emerge from discursive fields in which previous experience and stories of other rebellious women. Mizrahi feminists, namely feminists conscious to their non-Western feminist agenda, have an origin of being from Arab and Muslim countries. The insights and perceptions which I bring are of my own point of view. In other words, the contents of the present text are selected from what I chose to put in the heart of this account. The events herein are anchored in thematic foundations, theorized and conceptualized within a critical framework. The questions of "When do women decide to rebel, to act out of resistance?" and "Why do women bear continuous states of oppression and repress until that moment of rebellion?" are discussed extensively, especially from the women's own perspectives. Their view of the social conditions and the economic and political circumstances in which they are trapped and how they understand their personal position within the larger sociopolitical picture is rarely researched. What happens when women bear subordinating conditions, and when do they rebel? These questions are contextualized within Eastern-Western feminist perspectives and require special attention to a particular category of women whose life experiences take from both. What roles does cultural and political mixture play, both in keeping women obedient and, eventually, bringing them to a point where they don't obey anymore?

Another question which I put forth in this text relates to reasons and circumstances in which women's life conditions become obstacles on their way to make a change—that is, why is it that women's femininity, sexuality, body, looks, and so on become time and again an obstacle on their way to generating a change—any change—at home, the office, a firm, or a factory? This question emerged repeatedly from both cases in this study. In the conversations I had with the women and before that from the flow of events as they have been telling them appear to be very important for the understanding of the dynamic of changes they were trying to make.

In the first chapter, I lay the theoretical groundwork for the analysis of the case in the focus of this study.

Chapter One

Feminism

An Unending Project

Many life stories, monographs, biographies, and autobiographies have been written since feminist movements broke throughout the western world. In broad terms, the feminist movement's major success lies in the idea that changing women's lives means all women, in masses. The feminist revolution meant not just that change concerns every woman but also in every domain of women's lives. In this respect, feminist revolution essence is the polarization of every issue that concerns every woman. New frameworks, methodologies, and theories have developed and formed discursive corpus of knowledge we could put under an umbrella called the [feminist] discipline of study. Though the idea that gender studies is indeed a discipline in itself is still disputed among many gender and queer scholars, the accounts and biographies bring extremes of describing women's suffering and victimhood on the one hand and women's successes and heroism on the other. Syndromes such as superwomen, glass ceiling, and queen bee were created, leaving behind the majority of a woman's daily life as forms of survival. Under postcolonial studies, a new branch developed: "micro-" studies, such as "micro-history," "micro-politics," and anthropology, which accentuate women's daily life around the world. These works highlight significant breakthroughs that deconstruct patriarchal order and concentrate on women subordinating within specific cultural, class, ethnic, and religious contexts. Through this literature, how women subvert the patriarchal apparatus is unraveled and shows how particular sexualization smothering indoctrination operates. Feminist studies developed along the lines of critique studies using the same methods of subversive reinterpretation used in postcolonial and post-orientalist critique studies. Therefore, one of the first bitter lessons feminism in the United States learned was that sisterhood was an elusive slogan abused in the hands of upper-class feminists. Lower-class feminists realized that what was good for the women in the United States was not necessarily good for all US women or all women in the world, to use bell hook's critique (hooks, 1984). Feminist liberation cannot be achieved through one universal agenda, and strategy of liberation does not work the same way for all forms of women's subordination. These studies made clear that feminist liberating strategies should be adjusted to specific cultural, political, and religious form and beliefs because women are subordinated differently by particular apparatuses adjusted by the different patriarchal orders. In other words, feminist liberating acts cannot be imitated but should be reinvented time and again to fit specific male hegemonic subordination. Ironically, women joined anarchistic political actions believing that women liberation would be achieved through that support. They were disappointed to realize that the struggle applied to a narrower agenda of liberating the world order as it ran in the public sphere of, for, and by men (Firestone, 1970; Pateman, 1988). It has never invaded the private sphere through socialist or cultural ideology. The history of struggles for democracies, for example, registered fierce activism for equality but as the French and American revolutions demonstrate, patriarchal sedimented remained part of its essence. Moreover, women were welcomed as long as they supported men against old sets of order but not when they strived to make reforms in gender interrelations of that order as well. Hence marriage and parenthood, motherhood and sexual relations, and family structure and division of labor were all conserved structures. Notions of freedom, equality, brotherhood and sisterhood symbolised myth for women. Female images symbolize justice, wisdom, and even brotherhood in the human history, but concrete women are separated from the cultural icons in which they represent peacemaking. In *Lysistrata*, the piece written by the comic playwright Aristophanes, peace is women business opposed to war, being business of men. Aristophanes linked peace to women's sexuality. According to the patriarchal codes, women spirit is glorified not because they rebel and stand for their rights but because they put up with subjugating life through motherhood routine, family, and child carers. Even their sexuality and emotional world are put to the service of this order of things and they are expected to sacrifice desires and ambitions altruistically. When everyday life stories were told within patriarchal cultural context women sacrificial trait is praised. Part of socialization of women to their role is strengthened by glorifying sacrifice as part of their duties. The book of Proverbs in the Bible speaks of "A woman of valour" (Proverbs 31:10–31) in a concise and poetic way instructively demonstrating woman's devotion to her roles, altruistically. It praises the woman who goes out of her disciplined way to initiate commerce, crafts, and living resources as long as she harnesses the enterprise to keep the patriarchal order and allow her husband to take care of the public affairs with his peers at the city gates. The more she conforms, and contributes to that order, the more she is glorified. Women were thought very highly when they brought their nations to victories and saved the believers who followed them in the battlefield. They won high positions when they proved spiritual and intellectual abilities as legislators and judges that followed male-domineering religious paths. Such were Christian Joan of Arc, the Muslim Aisha, the Prophet's third wife, and Deborah, the Biblical Hebrew Heroin. Their lives remained a model to our days within the particular cultural and religious context with many hints that these women were exceptions and women shouldn't follow them unless the nation is at jeopardy. Opening a critical feminist eye on these cases revealed it as complex and dangerous when women get to leadership. All three women, we realize, had no children. All of them ended their lives either being persecuted or accused for bringing civil war and dividing the nation of the believers. Their tragic end was left as a legacy that should warn against women's reign (Dahan-Kalev, Jezebel, 2013). Therefore, reviewing myths and history of particular and unique women such as these suggest that these are no role models for women. Feminist stories that glorify women who made a change in their own lives, left unchanged the male/female and public/private dichotomies, as these cases demonstrate. The history told often consists with religious feminist norms, usually Jewish Halacha and Muslim Sharia'a ethics, as part of patriarchal apparatus. Eventually, reiteration of such instances in history, reinforces old conservative patriarchal order. In other myths, women were often presented as wicked, irresponsible, dangerous, reached the throne by tricky methods, such as the queens Jezebel and Athaliah (Dahan-Kalev, Jezebel, 2011). On a non-religious part of feminist critic, the literature focused for decades on the exploration of middle-class heteronormative women.

A historical genre termed "herstory" engendered history parts and discussed in theoretical terms of subversion that feminist of the middle class led in the west. It took three decades, from the 1950s to the 1980s, to crack the seemingly sisterhood universal liberation of women. An "inner revolt" of women who did not belong to middle class feminists split of the movements claiming that their, race, class, and/or ethnicity were suppressed although they felt these parts of their identity was no less significant and inseparable of the feminist agenda. "Intersectional feminism" was born and contributed to broader academic discourse on politics of feminist identity (Hill Collins, 1990). Feminist politics claimed that a different 'chemistry' forms multi-subaltern identity and it can't be deconstructed just by listing different forms of subordination of women who differ culturally or by their racial experience. It was painful to white feminist activists to realize that women who claimed that their class, race, or ethnic experience was significant more than feminist solidarity. In some cases they turned against upper-middle-class white-women feminist and highlighted loyalty to male counterparts. More generally, these events, which took place in the 1980s by US feminist activists, only illustrated the much broader silence of women who remained loyal to conservative patriarchal communities around the world rather than joining the revolutionary feminist movements. The critique went on accusing feminist activists of hypocrisy for their economic exploitation of poor women along with capitalist men (Ramazanoglu, 1989). The conclusion of this sad aspect of feminism was that better-off women did not really share solidarity with worse-off women, and the latter often preferred to refrain from challenging their cultural patriarchal communities. To the gender blindness argument, feminist studies expanded to race blindness, with class and ethnicity blindness often bundled under subaltern studies, bringing various conflicting cases among women from all regions and countries.

New feminist role models emerged and brought up to the public debate more silenced issues that women suffered from, especially in war areas in the Middle East and South East Asia and Africa. Palestinian women under the Israeli occupation distributed their accounts, at times incorporating them to East-West clash of civilization. Role-model women who survived female genital mutilation and coerced marriage under the age of ten years old became UN ambassadors to the West and reported their dreadful experiences; women who have been raped or took or forced to polygamy held the headlines of the news all over the world. These were always shocking stories of individual women cases. The understanding that change would come only by long and sometimes Sisyphean process was already here, and it took occasionally a single woman's case to remind the world that feminism was an unending struggle and a business that each woman must carry out in her own turn to get liberated.

A new and significant school surfaced in the 1990s and challenged "heterosexual" trends of feminist studies: queer and LGBT studies. Males who had agendas that were not merely of supporting women but also promoting sexual relations studies and relation to the body, emotional relationship, and various trans-(sexual, gender, bi, etc.) activity came about. These studies gave sexuality and embodiment experience far larger attention than ever and corresponded with postmodernism and deconstructionism thought. Silenced and considered shaming issues were reclaimed and appropriated anew as issues to be proud of. However, race, class, and ethnicity relations' differences were replicated in these fields and the same cultural heterosexual defects were carried on to queer and LGBT movements, proving time and again that old class and gender cultural loyalties are not automatically discarded when a struggle for sexual or feminist rights are fought for. Subjects of discrimination became entangled with other issues that concerned individuals. This calls for negotiations and formulation of the common ground that unites them but also reveals disagreements regarding other concerns of the individual. The lesson is that one has to develop intersectional consciousness to disentangle and get rid of multiplied discriminations but also to agree about the interests that will be left out of the agenda. At the end of the twenty century, a larger benefit of these new agendas extended the discourse on gender liberation, and it seemed that bringing up every issue was legitimate. Moreover, many concerns of women were left out because their issues were not always consistent with those that were already formulated. This problem expanded and became the major reason why sisterhood did not spread all over the world. Cultural divisions and civilization differences were the leading cause. The East was criticized for still lagging after the West by feminist and queer activists of Eastern origin who lived in the West. Nevertheless, it took a while, and in the first decade of the twenty-first century, it was clear that things were more complex and, indeed, what was good for American feminists was not necessarily good for the Iranian or the Saudi-Arabian feminist, as will be further explained.

Sexualities and bodies' discourses stimulated the exploration of new fields, some of which were expended into biology, cognitive science, and technology. These were investigated before in a few works, such as Haraway's Cyborg Manifesto (1991). The notion of "the woman" as a universal category was deconstructed, and women were no longer fantasmatic representation created in male minds. A multiplicity of concrete women inspired various discursive platforms: new schools and intellectual debates, along with gender and sexual identities, appeared in the field of identity critical studies, new gender division of labor ideas, and hidden worlds pushed old boundaries of knowledge and made more space for complex conceptualization and theorization of gender and sexuality studies.

As it were, it turned out that writing a theory is always easier then implementing them into the praxis of real life. What made it clear was the common ground on which all these prospering intellectual and scholar knowledge were founded. In practice, gender relations continued to be interwoven with the thread of power relations. Disentangling asymmetrical engendering power relations was found as multifaceted, and the efforts of feminist scholars to disentangle them seemed to be a Gordian Knot challenge. To disentangle it required endless efforts. The writings of Michel Foucault, with regard to his rich theses on power relations, became central to gender and sexuality projects and understanding. His writings echoed from most studies and repeatedly pointed out the centrality of the heteronormative order of things that hold the big structure of gender and sexuality together with the other multiplied power relations in capitalism, religion, medicine, education, and psychology (Foucault, 1982 and 1984). Although it seems that no domain of knowledge in the study of humanities can do without the monumental paradigm of Foucault regarding the dynamics of power relations, feminist issues and women were not particular categories in which he engaged. The moral of Foucault's contribution to knowledge is that there is no social and cultural institution that is devoid of asymmetric power relation and free from asymmetric power relations with other institutions. Therefore, as successful as an effort to disentangle one knot in the complexity of power relations, it cannot guarantee disentanglement of the all other knots. Such effort rather uncovers new forms of power relations and requires creativity in search of new strategies in the aim of being free from the Gordian Knot. To better understand the paradigm of power relations, Foucault suggested that the study of subjectivity cannot be reduced or reframed within the studies of objective knowledge and traditional sciences. Therefore, it should be investigated in a parallel trajectory that discards the effort to "objectify" and generalize the study of subjectivity and the exploration of intersubjective relationships. He devoted an entire division of exploration to what he called "epimelea," or care of the self (Foucault, 1981 and 1982; Dahan-Kalev, 2017). This is where the roots of the problem of freedom lay (Foucault, 1984, 351), eventually including women's freedom. Human freedom and liberation processes cannot be grasped if not through our relation to the world, to the law, and to ourselves and others. To disentangle power relations is to disentangle socialization knots that lay as sediment to make the subject who she is and to place her in her right position in patriarchal power web. The subject is gripped in socializing forced, interpellating as if she acts out of free will, but in fact, she is subordinated to the apparatus of the hegemonic power (Althusser, 1970). Louis Althusser concentrated on the notion of "interpellation" in his exploration of the psychological roots of politics and the apparatus of the state's power. His definition of the notion of interpellation clearly explains how it could be that a person acts out of subordination but perceives herself as a free subject:

> I have called *interpellation* or hailing, and which can be imagined along the lines of the most commonplace everyday police (or other) hailing: "Hey, you there!"
>
> Assuming that the theoretical scene I have imagined takes place in the street, the hailed individual will turn round. By this mere one-hundred-and-eighty-degree physical conversion, he becomes a *subject*. Why? Because he has recognized that the hail was "really" addressed to him, and that "it was *really him* who was hailed" (and not someone else). Experience shows that the practical telecommunication of hailings is such that they hardly ever miss their man: verbal call or whistle, the one hailed always recognizes that it is really him who is being hailed. And yet it is a strange phenomenon, and one which cannot be explained solely by "guilt feelings," despite the large numbers who "have something on their consciences." (Althusser, 1970)

In the case of women, it is patriarchal apparatus embedded in all cultures, religions, histories, or political ideologies in which women "recognize that it is really she who is being hailed" to. Therefore, when reflecting on the possibility of the subject setting free, interpellation practices cannot be cut out in one thread of a sward as in a Gordian Knot. They are interwoven through apparatuses in legal systems, in language, and in believed sets of norms and they run deep in personal intersubjective relation constructs. They are cognitively, mentally, and physically implanted through socialization methods from very early age till they seem to be natural (Butler, 1990). Escaping from the concrete arena of subordination does not lead to emancipation, nor does it lead to general or universal emancipation. Liberation is constructed of a long journey congested with hurdles. As Althusser clearly explained after years of effective operation of ideological apparatus on the subject, she may act first as if she is guilty and has "something on their consciences." It is fear that makes her turn her head to the policeman that hails her, although she allegedly acts as a free person. For socialization, experience consists of fear, sanctions, and anxiety, which are reiterated through lifelong years. Gender socialization employs even more severe sanctions, aiming to achieving obedience through heteronormative order. Althusser's policeman resides in the individual subject conscience and unconsciously manipulates her. Therefore, the power does not have to stick a policeman to every subject, he argues. Nevertheless, in the case of women within heteronormative order, it seems that women are put under personal surveillance. Consider, for example, the universal binary paradigm and its reflection within couplings order of things that sets the family standard on a bi-parent cell under patriarchal order (Walby, 1990). A female subject does not need to be called upon unless she really plots to violate heteronormative order. However, in order that she stands up against it, she first has to experience consciousness transformation and learn how not to turn her head to "the hailing policeman" within herself.

The feminist revolution brought about the gospel of women liberation. The feminist activists demanded reformation of legal systems, legalizing new forms of families and motherhood, sexual interrelations, and the transformation of sexualities and bodied perceptions. Feminist global organizations such as the United Nations distributed the word that women' rights are human rights, based on the World Fourth Women Conference in Beijing, September 1995. However, as it turns out, if it is not practiced by individual subjects, the transformation does not take place, and gender power relations remain where they initially were. In this respect, it always comes down to the insight that "practically every day, one woman is liberated from one knot," so the feminist project seems an unending project that each woman must experience in her own turn. Good examples of this trap are legislation and high court decisions that are aimed at generating institutional reforms in gender power relations but insert sporadic decisions with the logic that often works counter to the broader logic of sustaining the power network. This eventually ends in failing to bring change. For example, the struggle of women for their rights to be drafted to a combatant unit or pilots courses or to top positions of the religious hierarchy and other top positions in governing institutions. I will write here about the Israeli experience and the Jewish cases to illustrate. However, these examples may be valid for other states and religions as well. Even if military service or religious rule would be realms that some feminists regard as domains that women must participate in to weaken or even abolish established norms, as long as they concentrate patriarchal sources of power, women can't ignore them. Women's struggle for power must challenge every patriarchal domain.

In 1995, the High Court of Justice accepted Alice Miller's plea to be drafted to a pilots' course in the Israeli Air Force and ordered the Air Force to include her in the auditions to the pilot course of the IDF (Alice Miller vs. the Minister of Defence, 4541/94.) The arguments against drafting women, which Chief Commander Herzl Bodinger discussed, revealed that the military was not prepared for gender transformation neither economically nor consciously. Economically, Bodinger argued, it would cost the IDF additional expenses in building special facilities and to make changes and adjust the course to female needs. This, he continued, does not contribute to the course quality and, above all, a female pilot, unlike a male pilot, would not return the investment cost, as she probably would serve a couple of years and then marry and bear children, leaving the Air Force after a short period of time or even end her service contract. A broader argument was added stating that long periods of flight might even damage women's ability to bear children. Judge Dalia Dorner, the fifth of the high court on this case, provided an ethical argument claiming that equality costs money, and such a cost should apply to the IDF as one of the people's institutions in a democratic state. Miller was accepted, and at a later stage of the course, she dropped out, but the high court decision set the precedent. However, women were discouraged, and it took more than ten years for the first woman navigator to succeed and be accepted to one of the prestigious and exclusive units of the Air Force that had been ever dominated by men. This, however, did not open all the forces in the IDF to women. Women had to struggle for each and every position in the military power network and to disentangle the knots of the flotilla forces or battlefield combatants to open them for women, one by one. As argued previously, the Gordian Knot must be disentangled piecemeal. However, even after the High Court's Decision, the obstacles that the IDF forces put on the women's way to succeed demonstrate how patriarchal apparatus is deeply interwoven within [militaristic] institutional construct, and despite precedent being set, the patriarchal gate keepers—in this case, the chiefs of the Air Force—objected drafting women. Another implication that can be eliminated from this case is that the transformation of women's status requires concrete individual woman's struggle. The next example illustrates women's lack of knowledge for the rules of the game that prevails in the patriarchal game yard. That is, even if there is found a courageous woman who takes the burden of breaking through, she does not always know or is either aware of the rules of the game in the field that is new to her and, above all, that she plays with skilful actors on that field.

In the high-court decision of Lea Shakdiel vs. The Ministry of Religions case 153/1987, a petition was made to allow women to be elected to the municipal religious council of the development peripheral town of Yeruham. Until that petition, only men could apply for candidacy to the elections. The high court decision was that women should be accepted to the municipal councils of religion (Shakdiel vs. The Minister of Religions, 1988). The decision was carried out but with some minor twists, such as taking the final decision of the council at work outside the meeting hall after the discussion was over, informing Shakdiel "by mistake" of the wrong meetings schedule, distributing the minutes with one significant file missing, or providing her, at the last minute, with the documents for the upcoming discussion. Her efforts to effectively contribute to the council work and to make a change were in vain. Eventually, Shakdiel gave up and the high court decision's words died as many other decisions in the judicial system books because of sabotage or political manipulations. Women such as Shakdiel, who "lay on the fence" for those who might follow as the gatekeepers, register another defeat in the tiring struggle of women to engender the public institutions. Therefore, patriarchal order shows survivability even when reforms are taken to transform it. The aforementioned cases, which will be analyzed in different context further in this book, show the patriarchal gatekeepers working in parallel to the state's (democratic) order as if they exist inside, like a "coat lining" of the state's institutions. The women who challenge them in most cases are part of the upper middle class who can afford various types of resources for the struggle, such as money, education, and cultural habitus, which might include language, embodiment, and social networking. It is completely different when women from the margins make such an attempt. First, they lack necessary economic, social, and often ethnic, religious, and cultural resources; secondly, they move out of deeper and multiplied conditions of subordination, and as we shall see in the following chapters, they challenge the patriarchal order in more than one or few power cobwebs, therefore awakening more powerful gatekeepers. Until the resistance is carried out, women at the margins are paradoxically much less observed by patriarchal order and, therefore, can generate change relatively easily in their lives.

In her book *Methodologies of the Oppressed* (2000), which will be further applied to the analysis in this book, author Chela Sandoval suggested that women who generate change—especially women on the margins, women under occupation, immigrants, women of color, women of minorities, and so on—can't avoid practicing the desocialization process of subordination without refusal, resistance, and rebellion involved in their moves. This oppositional activity develops to become a central apparatus that consciously deconstructs some of the consistence of the cobwebs of the subordinating powers. This experience contains the release of energies and personal resources that women invested before in fear and anxiety from disobedience consequences and now learn to convert to liberating forces. In other words, refusal, resistance, and rebellion are ingredients of which women's liberation is fabricated, even if the struggle fails to achieve the anticipated successful results.

Success and failure are part of engendered notions captured by patriarchal apparatus. Success and failure elide ventures, new mental experiences, and extends personal practices. While these might seem to be trivial and, therefore, often taken for granted as part of homological dichotomies, success and failure, resistance, and obedience and the like are notions that receive new contents when women make transformation attempts. Therefore, in feminist explorations, they are also often elided, and potential lessons learnt from them along with different gender content remain concealed. In the following chapters, I shall elaborate more on the transformation of the notions of success and failure within feminist activism context.

Chapter Two

Gender Conceptual Revision and Methodological Toolbox

What seems to be success and failure is not always what it really is at all levels of social, political, and personal experience. To better understand the complex nature of these experiences, it is necessary to change linguistic lenses and almost entirely give up rigid capitalist, materialistic, competitive, fierce conceptual and dichotomous definitions of the notions of "success" and "failure" and of "obedience" and "resistance." What needs to be deconstructed is the dichotomy and allegedly contradiction connoted experiences of success and failure born in the mental sense. At stake is the need to decode and reinterpret the moment in which the watershed line is redirected to a new path, or at women's turnover point, her obedience forces inverted to resistance. A deeper glance could uncover contradictions and reflect subordination as a rebellious move. Flickering moments of resistance in a continuous state of obedience can be revealed surprisingly as a success and yet be identified as a failure. Changing conditions of subordination, partial removal of the suffering circumstances mark convergence of obedience to mastering relationship. More than it coheres with the Hegelian notion of master-slave dialectics, it merges with Louis Althusser's idea of interpellation where personal agency forces are captured in shared ideological features (Althusser, 1970.) In the moment of change, sediments of refusenik consciousness precipitate converting into adjusting forces and appear as accepting the determined order. It is well demonstrated in the works of the Greek poet Hesiod, who lived in sixth-century BC, and expressed in *Works and Days*. The wisdom of the sages that contested Homer's epic stories of *The Iliad and Odyssey* ethics. A onetime courageous act in the battlefield should certainly be rewarded; however, pertinacious stability under existential conditions that generate continuous suffering and burden are not equally praised. The forces to endure monotonous and repeated conditions of subordination are not considered virtuous and deserving of appreciation. The western world has highlighted the Homeric epos while the Hesiod epos is not praised as valuable for its virtues.

The stories that I analyze in this book highlight the virtues Hesiod signified as praiseful, redefining success and failure within new context. If it was for the consequences, one might have interpreted failure or success according to the results of the events in discussion regardless of the benefit of the process, such as the experience from the struggle against oppression it has carried within it. A victory might demand a price that the investment might be worth it, for which the Pyrrhic victory notion introduces the idea that some victories may cost the ruin of the victorious. A closely examined successful or failure event would better be defined when separating the results of the events from the process. This argument is particularly worth examining in light of feminist struggles. Resistance of women after being continuously subordinated for long periods of time, even if their struggles result in failure in the traditional sense of the term failure, carry within it the experience of resistance. Therefore, it must be separately evaluated to understand the value of the resistance experience that was gained. Refusal to carry on with enduring obedience norms and reformulating them anew as enslavement conditions potentially mobilizes women to take actions. The first steps of refusal become a success regardless of what the consequences would be. Lois MacNay discusses the agency as it first occurs at the consciousness stage (MacNay, 2000.) Taking an agency act and resisting oppression is an experience of consciousness change. In feminist terms, it is the first fraction of becoming aware of material being. These transformations in women's patterns of behavior are embedded within contexts of culture, religion, national, and class differences. East-West settings of the conflict in which women resist, when they do, is of significance in understanding the factors that held women silenced for a long time before resisting.

A puzzling question kept annoying me when I tried to understand the motivations and the factors that played a role in the events and the results of the stories about the rebelling women discussed herein: Why do people continue to bear enslaving existential conditions and appear as obedient and submissive when they experience exploitation and cruelty that continues for long periods of their life? Such experiences evidently stimulate negative feelings against their tormentors. I found it difficult to call it submissiveness in the face of the thunderous silence that women often hold on for long periods of time, such as for years and years. Since the Marx Manifesto, these reflections interested political theorists. Recently, expanding poststructuralist social philosophers have dug into these questions of accepting subordinating terms in search of new answers. These studies are particularly significant to the goal of understanding how forces fixate individuals in inescapable patterns of oppression. Even when women become aware of oppression being social constructs and not natural, twisted patterns, workers, women, ethnic groups, occupied nations, and the like abstain from social agency and proactive political initiative (Charlesworth, 2000; Mansbridge, 2001). The literature in the Western world, however, prefers to cherish heroic resisting instances rather than highlighting continuous survival under extreme conditions of subordination. Reticence and containment are overlooked, as mentioned previously. These result from the ethical foundation rooted in the ancient perception of Homer's moral in the *Iliad* and *Odyssey* rather than Hesiod's *Works and Days*. The fame and glamour are incorporated to the Western ethics of the onetime sacrifice of a hero rather than to perseverance and day-to-day burdened survival. The social suffering of the ordinary citizen has lost its value in favor of political attributes that dichotomies political weight versus social weight. Some critical literature has drawn attention to this divide. The notion of "social weight" was coined by the French sociologist Pierre Bourdieu who laid down the foundations for the understanding of the social suffering of ordinary citizen both in the West and in the East as well as North African countries (Bourdieu 2000). Social suffering, Bourdieu claimed, is as significant as political suffering and focusing on issues such as political freedom of action and human rights granted to individuals in democratic and free societies but suffer from myopia and bring to partial understanding of our modern life in the global era. By leaving out the larger range of issues of social suffering and by splitting the analysis of the social sphere and the political sphere, potential explanatory notions remain concealed and present an unbalanced understanding of the complexity of the sociopolitical life. Practically, political weight dominates the field of studies of violence and social suffering discourse currently.

Being aware of these flaws, I will pay attention to social weight and search for success and failure in a broader sense. Therefore, analysis of the events will be presented in two scenes: The social and political spheres where the facts are more explicit and easy to observe and to document; and the women's internal world of feelings, cognitive, consciousness, and mental experiences. In searching for the impact of rebellion on women who take actions of resistance and their move to proactive agency, I will discuss perceptions, virtues, and values transformation, along with changes in women's mental and ethical notions and their steps to independent activism to a final stage of liberation as women. Finding signs that shed light on puzzling question such as why would workers continue to harry up to their humiliating workplace and obey their exploiting owners in a situation where they seem to "have nothing to lose but their chains" led me to question how the awareness transformation is produced and how does one become aware of her social and political rights. The question of how to do that cannot be limited to simple qualitative research tools. This insight was purchased while I spent time in the field for this study and had to presume that a rebel, woman, or worker is not born a rebel; she becomes a rebel, just like the De Beauvoirian argument regarding becoming a woman. Does she become a rebel overnight? In one burst of anger or refusal act? Or rather is it a long mental process that a resistant woman walks through for years in a patriarchal socialization process to obedience and then to a process of rebel? Is it always alone? I realized that it is a long cognitive and mental process. During this time, rebelling women abide at some sort of mental and cognitive midland, half aware of the intention to take action. Often it is an indefinite emotional state, a twilight space in which the psyche dynamic movement brings women from mental to political from vague and unverbalized sense of injustice to the understanding that they don't want to carry on with the injustice as it is inflicted on them just because they are women. This journey slowly communicates cognitive inner, mental dynamic venture, sometimes a chaotic one, with an external world that is recognized and formulated in the symbolic and linguistic terms of abuse. The interviewed women in the present research reported it all. They felt that their forces and energies deviated, that it changed directions from the usual paths of containment and obedience to what Chela Sandoval termed "oppositional consciousnesses."

Throughout the research plan, I went to the field knowing that all I have as a researcher on an empirical ground where storming sociopolitical and gender events that I wanted to explore. Delicate tools of patients and listening practices helped me collect subtle pieces of data that indicated not just the existence of facts with regards to the events, but also subtle changes in the women interviewee's opinions and worldviews. I revised details in repeated conversations and observations with the interviewees, using my field diary to register words, gestures, actions, sights, signals, and signs that could indicate changes in the women's world and patterns, as well as their thoughts and beliefs.

Eventually, this project puts in focus two stories of women of non-Western origin who lived on the margins of Israeli society in many respects, not just as women, but also as poor, living in a remote town, in a deprived periphery of the state, and being of Mizrahi origin—the origin of Jews from Arab and Muslim countries that were discriminated against since the establishment of the state of Israel. From "the margins of the margins" of Israeli society, these two women challenged the social and political patriarchal order as experienced in Israel. Although according to standard terms of "success" and "failure" the women's agency failed to bring tangible change, their stories break rigid definitions of what is meant to succeed or to fail when taking a resistance act against subordination and exploitation. Looking at these experiences provide new extended ways to understand them. In addition, notions such as "defeat" and "victory," "power," "courage," "fear," and "anxiety" experienced within women's struggle show context and shed new lights on the content of these notions. I will revise and analyze them, suggesting redefinitions when experienced in a feminist context. Psyche and emotional experiences communicate with social and political events to successfully bring about additional feminist meaning to the social agency. These will take place at the discussion stage of the analysis.

Feminism occurs in a heteronormative world where men initially determined and dominated gender relations. This state of affair is in the midst of revolutionary transformation, but the road to complete transformation—where women are equal and free to determine their own terms of life and to share equal accessibility to power—is still far away. In this respect, individual male-experience power relations with women, as a rule, are in a better position. Once a woman makes an attempt to have an impact on this relationship, the power parallelogram is shaken and generates an action that involves tension and struggles over power. Gender different socialization mobilizes males and females to react differently to women's agency moves; more specifically, resistance actions on the women's part do not occur in a vacuum but create commotion within the parallelogram of power. This issue will be meticulously discussed and examined through the specific role men played in the events when the women interviewees tried to bring change in gender power relation. Their contribution to the success and failure within the complex and sensitive power relations at the flow of the events will be explored in light of asymmetry of the power parallelogram structure that almost immediately determined it in terms of a zero-sum game and in favor of men. Therefore, women's attempts to generate change are at once social agents of change that threaten the patriarchal order and that call upon men's response to this attempt. This dynamic of power relations is structured in gender constructs beneath the sociopolitical order of things. Only when the power relations parallelogram is shaken that the "lining like" gender power relations surface and reveals the infrastructure of power on which the public order is founded.

SUBMISSIVENESS, OBEDIENCE, BLAMING THE VICTIM, AND "LAYING ON THE FENCE"

I find it difficult to understand what forces hold women to stay in the place where pain and torture are inflicted on them. It is hard to grasp, for example, what hold women who report on repeated rape or continuous domestic violence to stay in such violent situations. It isn't rare to hear women who suffer from domestic-violence relationships saying that for years they did nothing to stop the suffering. Often, these women describe the horror as paralyzing. The studies of these dreadful problems remain scarce so far because heteronormative perception placed the phenomenon away in the margin, as if it is the particular battered or raped woman's problem. After all, most women do not live through these conditions; therefore, it must be some anomaly that holds some of the women in these living conditions. Only in the last three decades has violence against women become more perceived as structural rather than a personal problem. In other words, it is related to sociopolitical and cultural roots rather than to particular women's deviation of normality. Moreover, its entanglement with other sociopolitical factors, such as economic, class, or religion, that helps to explain these issues as a derangement problem of the community or society as a whole rather than the subject's alone. Larger aspects of the problem that need to be studied get lost in a theoretical void when feminist theorists try to isolate the problem. It results from a void that exits between disciplines and between theory and praxis. A void between psychoanalysis, politics, cultural, religious and the social research One obvious question for understanding the problem of returning women to the violent scene is to focus on the infrastructural apparatus of the problem. The often intertwined social family codes with sanctions ordained by religious laws and heteronormative political socialization, all these a priori design sexual and gender personality of the individual and gender and sexual relations and brings about accepting "light deviations" of implicit or explicit use of force, either as passive aggressive or as in one-time slap or kick instances. These are neglected by state's judicial systems because the systems are adjusted to certain trajectories of action. For example, if a battered woman does not put a complaint against the perpetrator to the police, the judicial system can't provide the woman with protection. In the theoretical aspect of the problem, we don't have enough knowledge regarding "light" instances of sexual violence that at most times won't be considered as pathological because they are rooted in religious, political, or seemingly "normative" grounds. Women recognize and retain such oppressive social relationships even when they personally identify the sick element embedded in them. The in-between hybrid nature of relationships is difficult to study in paradigms that maintain spaces where these instances of violence occur as either "private" or "public." The mind settings that rigidly conserve dichotomous splits in binary paradigms conceal "twilight" spaces, which, when explored and studied, are difficult to locate. For example, there is almost no professional or legal jargon for "murder of honor" of the family that religious codes ordain, but it still exists as a norm. Struggle against the phenomenon still uses the traditional terminology of "honor." The formulation in and of itself contains contradictions. It should be formulated in "either or" terms; either a traditional religious honor of family redemption or as a criminal act. The superficial approach to worlds that are well hidden by contradictions, such as family codes, social norms, religious commands, and criminal acts, by legal systems terms allows such violent relationships to flourish "in between" these fields, both in real life and in exploration within the disciplinary context. The obscurity of sexual harassment is another variation that flourishes in those concealed spaces. I argue that our understanding of the line that divides between the spheres and other binary paradigms are in fact spaces, or thick imaginary lines, which form a third in-between space between the other two. A space where dichotomies fertilize violent relationships that remain hidden from the public eye and bloom within the infrastructure of power relations—what I suggested to regard as lining of the sociopolitical life. This is the space where women often suffer from oppression and violence and are viewed as "either a victim or an accomplice." Women keep searching for ways to march from the private to the public and expose what seems to be personal but is indeed nonpersonal but political. Every problem that feminist activists put on their agenda started as a personal/private issue sterilized of its political or cultural aspects. The task that feminists took upon themselves was to politicize what seemed to be only personal. In this respect, patriarchal dark sites were enlightened to reveal the connection between the hidden-lining power relations and the seemly sociopolitical order, be it democratic or enlightened totalitarian. Feminist research projects, in this respect, are to trace the roots of these double-layered orders and formulate notions that help explore the hidden in-between worlds. One such scholar, Hélène Cixous, demonstrates a successful attempt to meet the challenge. She writes:

> Write, let no one hold you back, let nothing stop you: not man; not the imbecile capitalist machinery, in which publishing houses are the crafty obsequious relayers of imperative handed down by an economy that works against us and off our backs; and not *yourself.* Smug-faced readers, managing editors, and big bosses don't like the true texts of women—female-sexed tests. That kind scares them. (Cixous, 1976, 878)

The prevailing state of affairs still brings to women's threshold conventional perception that rape requires two persons and, therefore, it is the women's responsibility exclusively to make the change. Indeed, women do not remain all the time in humiliating and frustrating scenes of violence. Following feminist lib revolution in the West in the 1950s onward, things began to change. This brings us back to the basic dichotomous perception: the view that women who don't join the women's liberation movements are held as obedient and submissive. Therefore, it is easier for the patriarchal order to point out the few, often marginal, rebellious women as exceptional and hint that they are deranged women, immigrant women to the West included. The majority of women who conform to oppressive regimes in non-Western societies, influenced by their sisters' activism in the West, are more active in bringing change in their lives but often remain within the religious communities where they continue to mobilize change from within.

A quick glance at the history of women's liberation in the West would immediately bring forth the gatekeepers response to pioneers who cried "enough" and "no more good girls." They were driven out of their queenship of femininity and docility and denounced as vociferous, rude, and order violators. They were called to order using disciplining apparatus, as I will further explain on the ground to the case studies brought forth in this book. The gatekeepers, as the study showed, made sure to elide the patriarchal nature of "the order." The problem that arises is that the rebellious women who wanted a change were responded to by gatekeepers that included women who supported the traditional patriarchal order. A backlash support of conservative women—sometimes aware of the backlash, sometimes less—took responsibility of the family and childcare along with other roles put on them in the private sphere and remade the choice of preserving the old order. The public debate around other options is in its pick, but the majority of women still conform to the conservative gendered state of affairs. In this respect, it can be inferred that most women prefer the "freeze" pattern as developed by Walter Bradford Cannon (1915) in his book *Bodily Changes in Pain, Hunger, Fear and Rage: An Account of Recent Researches into the Function of Emotional Excitement.* The majority of women leave out other options of "flying" or "fighting." This may be justified or understood for the high price the last two options demand; that is, there is much to lose and may end in Pyrrhic victory. Deep foundations of the "victimized-victimizer" construct are still rooted in the prevailing sociopolitical order. True, women are seen in the public sphere and hold high-ranking positions, but it is not just the margins of the patriarchal order that maintain the extreme cases. It is the old patriarchal agency that is still alive and reigns through religion, ethnic, cultural, and political infrastructures, which are all patriarchalism in the first place. These infrastructures are well-equipped with the powerful vivid apparatus that is alerted immediately when a "shrew feminist" tries to violate the perceived order. She is put back right away to her "right" place. Women who dare to cry and release a scream from their mouths face normalizing rules that call them hysterical and doubt their sanity. Such women are often treated as lost or depressed and are silenced so they would, eventually, carry their pain muted and accept their worried and beloved view as unstable, just as in Charlotte Perkins Gilman's classic book *The Yellow Wallpaper* (Gilman, 1899). Social-cultural context permits such restraining forces and encourages them at times that feminism is believed to bring about gender and sexual transformations. Radical feminist and LGBT movements protest and release their public cry while at private layers of personal cases of victimizing and victimizers still prevail. The forceful personal relations' space is wrapped with a thick protecting cover that maintains legitimate crumbs that refuse to disintegrate and are allowed other salient order to replace it. Legal systems and norms, conventions and stereotypes, activate apparatus that cultivate order and protect it from chaos. Fears and hopes, desires and promises, stand at the heart of protecting the shield from disintegration of the schemes that maintain the patriarchal order. Even if it is possible that chaos is imaginative and has no real basis, the fear generated by apparatus against it is real. In this respect, psychophysiology is activated by the apparatus as a protecting shield from falling back to a ledgy, chaotic nature condition. The fear of Thomas Hobbes or Jean-Jacques Rousseau from the natural condition, which should be reviewed for our days, however, still nourishes patriarchal order thus infused to the state's perception of order, and it forms the foundations on which it rests. Therefore, patriarchal hegemonic reign is secured thanks to its consistency with the state's order. The state, in this respect, becomes an agent-led institution in the service of patriarchy; therefore, if feminists want to mobilize change, it is the state and its institutions that they must challenge. This is where the feminist idea of the personal becomes political.

Dichotomy is an effective apparatus in the hands of the gatekeepers; order is negated to chaos, and the order violators are immediately separated from "all of us, the obedient." We are expected to do all that is within our capacity to remove threats of chaos that she might unleash on us. This perception lies at the heart of the idea of order. It is achieved by splitting time and again right from wrong, chaos from order, and it classifies all that can be split or separated. Mary Douglas has clarified the need for order to the degree that humanity sanctified it as the source of purity (Douglas, 1996). The cases that I bring in this book demonstrate the firm set of rules and patterns as to how the patriarchal apparatus functions. A complete set of rules supported by religious, cultural, sexual, ethnic, and social apparatus are all interwoven within the states institutions, even in cases of state separation from religion. Functioning officials leave home to go to the public sphere, their work place and the public institutions carrying their gender socialization construct as man. When they put their uniforms on, they perform ideal types of male patriarchal gatekeepers. It is up to the individual official how to interpret the implementation of equality laws and when to carry out affirmative action. It implies, however, that gatekeeping and agency is made by the individual subject. Implicit sanctions deter the violator among the gatekeepers, as well whose gender socialization begins at a very early age, such as at school and on the playground. It is often sufficient for the person to reconsider her intentions to struggle against the powerful gender constructs of the order so that she faces disproportional sanctions that are well adjusted to the nature of a particular infringement. Women's adultery, refusal to coerced marriage, or disobedience to reproduction codes are treated differently in the different religions and cultures of the world, but they are all covered by the reign of patriarchy. In one, the resistant woman is cast out; in the other, she is murdered; in a third, she is shamed; and so on. Mothers who don't stand up to their duties are fiercely persecuted. Violation of heteronormative gender relations are all interconnected to sexuality: female sexuality. Betty Friedan's "The problem that has no name" (Friedan, 1957) and Carol Gilligan's *In A*

Different Voice (1982) were the first to voice extricated buried women's experiences of allegedly obedience. They critically reinterpreted them as subordinating conventions that women unwillingly submit to and re-presented them under critical analysis that uncovered heavy gender prejudices that work as apparatus aiming at "taming" women in the patriarchal mode of gender relations. These were points of breaking up with old interpellation which were critical for women who took the risk of rebelling. There were women who began to move towards liberation of consciousness. This is a move in which women who broke up with the old obedience and subordinating chains and found themselves in chaos where no patriarchal order reigned. However, this exists only in the mental and consciousness inner world of the women. It may reflect on the real world, but the main experience begins within the woman's world that deconstructs her socialization as a female world. The experience of chaos is a personal experience that rebellious women go through all alone. It is a conceptual and psychological breakdown of meaningful relationship, of a gender relationship that needs to be reconstructed anew. The feminist research project reviews it time and again to deconstruct the tissue of power relations, of any power relations. Especially give accounts and report in a reflexive way and accurate interpretation of existential experiences regarding the processes in which women find themselves mentally detained (Kristeva, 2000). The feminist research project is a political project in the sense that it is committed to registration, documentation, and given account of individual woman's rebellion who is prepared to do the move that women before her abstained from doing. When a woman is making the first move of crossing the line between the private and the public and looking to change the order of gender relations, it means that she is ready to be the first "to lean on the barbed wire" so that the followers would be able to pass. This is always a personal decision that has no guarantee to bring about the change. It rather brings sanctions against the pioneering woman who takes the risk and violates the rule of the patriarchal order. She than is marked as a troublemaker on top of often failing and is watched more carefully. These are the ingredients from which women's rebellion consists and should be learnt for our understanding of women's liberation when a woman's cry is heard.

"IN A DIFFERENT VOICE," OR RATHER SILENCING?

Silence is different from "a different voice" and should be explored in the feminist research project on its own merit more critically to study it in-depth when exploring non-Western cultures. Women may have a different voice, but it might be unheard because it is expressed in various ways other than sounds. Within the patriarchal non-Western apparatus, women have developed different strategies of coping with subordinating authorities and patriarchs that silence their actual voices. Gestures of lowering the gaze and of not responding could be interpreted in more than one meaning, such as obedient. A woman's silence could mean anger as well as appeasement and conformity. It could be understood as subversion, dependant on the context. If it is a young or an old woman, silence between her and her parent or her spouse are of deep meaning that in the Western research has hardly been studied or even discussed. In the *Theory of Literary Production* (1978), Pierre Macherey discussed the importance of silence intervals as opposed to voiced texts. The understanding of mute communication, of white noise, may well express refusal and resistance, especially of female resistance, which could be effective in producing a destructive force against an oppressor power, of any oppressor. Women in the non-Western world are articulated to use silence as a feminine force at times of gender or sexual power relations concerns. It is in this sense that the "laugh of the Medusa" is terrifying (Cixous, 1977). It uncovers the arbitrary and unnatural use of force and opposes it to human and individual resistance expression. It puts the other's bare face, with all its force, against the oppressor (Levinas, 1995, 67–68). In this respect, silence is a form of strategy of violation of order, a rebellion against the rules of the game of the oppressor in a way of subversion common to female strategies in non-Western societies. Gender conflict in non-Western societies do not and cannot take the common form as we know it in the feminist's struggles for rights in the West, such as massive movements, legislation processes, and the employment of the rights of speech, gathering, and demonstrations. Not even in countries with more liberal regimes, such as Lebanon and Jordan. Therefore, it is each woman to her own self with her own secret women community assistance that must search for her way out of gender subordination. While roaming in that in-between space, trying to cross the lines from the private to the public, at least in their consciousness transformation, women in non-Western societies employ bargaining strategies in front of their spouses or male counterparts, be it brother, uncle, cousin, or father. One woman's strategy of bargaining repeats itself time and again in different variations and tells the agency story that shows the different possible ways of negotiations. The telling of the plot, even if told before, to different audiences—be it the media, a close family member, a judge, or the police—brings up new details that help to decode hidden mechanisms of action within the interaction that was aimed to bring about change for the individual person. It may not be possible to make generalizations from a particular story, but it does help decipher emotional and intellectual processes that may be found similar to other experience told for the same reason. It may generate reflexive assessments that don't depend on mere facts. A narrative of an individual's experience given in a written account is, in the end, a reconstruction of the real event told through the writer's eyes, which is also committed to research codes.

In a feminist light, women's subversion is quite opposite to scripts from the old sages. In religious scripts, women are often defined as "rebelling woman" if they stand out to make a statement. In the Jewish script of *Mishna Ketoubot* 5:7 and in Mimonides, *Ishut*, Chapter 14, Halacha 8, "a rebel woman" can be forcefully divorced if the husband argues that he experiences his wife's rebellion. The scripts account a wide range of actions within the list of "a rebelling woman": refusal to sexual relations, house and children care, mode of expression and impertinence, infidelity, immodesty, and disobedience. As already mentioned, the opposite rewards the woman as a woman of valor, such as Salomon's Proverb Book glorifies in Proverb 31. To certify women's obedience, this mythological proverb demonstrates how the worlds where women roam are interconnected and expect them to be well behaved. The proverb illustrates her greatness in person, social member, mental, economic initiator, head of family, and mother, and, above all, her husband's assistant. Women who dare to rebel are women who fail to stand up to the woman of valor standard, and they simply lose the chance to enjoy the pleasures that the proverb promises. In this manipulative scene, the options are "either or" without any in-between possibilities.

Chapter Three

Laboratory of Humanities Is the Real Life

Analysis without Amnesia

Writing this book brought up many ethical questions, which I will focus on in this chapter. Methodologically, the analysis requires a special inspection of the researcher-participant of research relations, as these could be crucial to the understanding of the events. Since the researcher is the mediator, and unavoidably not a neutral one, as I explain herein, the relationship and the pitfalls must be discussed that might affect the analysis and should be displayed before proceeding. The reader must be able to assess the part the researcher played in the reporting and the analysis.

Firstly, at the time of the rebelling burst in August 2000 and in July 2003, I had some conversations with the leaders: Havatzelet Ingbar, Avigayle Ifrach, and Vicki Knafo. Two years later, I had a series of meetings over a period of eight weeks with Ingbar, the leading figure of the first case of resistance in 2000, at her home. During the earlier stage, when the factory in which they rebelled was delivered from the owner's hands to the workers, the process was documented by Doron Tzabari and Julie Shlez, two documentary filmmakers, in the series "*Daroma.*" The series was awarded by the Israeli film academy for documentaries as the best of 2003 and was screened on Channel 1. I used chapters of the series for cross-reference of the storming and sometimes confusing events.

The second rebel I interviewed was Vicki Knafo, in July 2003, a single mother who marched 200 kilometers from her remote development town to the capital of Jerusalem to meet with the minister of finance. I also had a previous opportunity to meet the rebel before she began her rebellious journey. She marched in July 2003; I met her by chance only two days before she began the march.

The stories were full of shaking experiences with exiting and joyful climax moments of hope and some sense of victory while simultaneously painful, sad, and saturated in humiliating emotions of failure, which were not easy to be exposed in a straight-forward manner through the research. The stories always mediated through abstract conceptions and theories that aim at deciphering its complexity and its relevance to the academic general thesis framework. Academic and research discourse, however, is always alien and external to the story. The heroine at the rebelling moment does not act with awareness to research. However, when telling the story, the story always includes mental and psychological details that are crucial for analysis, for the insights and the conclusions. Most of all, the implications on women's liberation in the future are borne in the mind of the researcher rather than the heroine of the events. For this matter, the story and the heroines become the means rather than the ends of telling the story. This convergence of focus from the heroes and events to the analysis occurs at the moment of the meeting between the researcher and the heroine, who becomes a more general entity of, as a social change agent is placed in a different context. In the context of research, the time flow turns to look back to reconstruct a memory of what really happened in the past. It is up to the researcher to structure what she hears through the study structure in new motivation aiming at knowledge producing but not immediate social change. This is simultaneously a process of appropriation of the story that constructs new power relations between the storytellers, which in this case are the heroines, and the researcher. The agent in the field of discourse (i.e., the academic) is not the heroine of focus, but it is her story. The story is delivered to and told by a new agent, the scholar.

The researcher is often not just a researcher; they are also other things, such as a parent, a spouse, an activist, or a teacher. These roles may sneak into the story unconsciously, especially when the task is to give "a thick description" as Clifford Geertz has termed it (Geertz, 1973, 3–30). Giving account not only of the dry facts but also of the human moments of experience, such as storming emotions and intimate instances, eventually influence the report and the analysis. Being an activist—of social rights, in this case—I was involved to a certain extent in the events as they have occurred in real time as both an activist and as a researcher. I was interested in what happened to the women who mobilized the rebellion since they were trying to change their working conditions and their abilities to stand up to the responsibility as breadwinners for their children. I witnessed intimate moments in real time, frustrating and embarrassing instances (Cotterill, 1992) for which I asked the heroines permission to report. This comes in addition to the analysis of the power struggles that were built into the relations at the scene of the rebellion and the disclosed moments of becoming aware of power effects as discussed in qualitative analysis literature (Shlaski and Alpert, 1992).

In 1999, the NGO *Achoti* (My Sister) organized an annual conference in the northern Israeli development town of Ma'alot. Development towns in Israel are often populated with a lower-class population and located at the peripheral parts of the country. The agenda of the organization, established in 1999, focused on women of the margins of society, especially women workers who were hit by the globalization policy to which Israel's economy was accommodating its economic policy. The economic transformation policy of Israel will be discussed in further detail in the next few chapters. Historically, however, since the establishment of the state, its northern and southern developing towns were the most vulnerable economically and always the first to be bitten by recessions and unemployment. The population was moving from one recovery from recession to another but always lagged behind the stronger groups, mainly towns in the center of Israel—the region of metropolitan Tel Aviv called Gush Dan. Socioeconomic strata correlated to regional division such that a vast majority of the veteran population, originally Jews from Arab and Muslim countries, was of lower-class living on the periphery or on the outskirts of big cities. This is opposed to the kibbutzim, whose population originated mostly from Europe and consisted in the 1960s and 1970s of no more than 5 percent of the entire population. Economically, they were listed as the top priority for economic support because they were considered as the economic backbone of the state, even when their productivity kept declining for many years. Kibbutzim in the peripheral areas were supported by the government. During periods of recession, the kibbutzim debts to the state were erased systematically. One of the most scandalous instances occurred in the 1980s when farmers in the kibbutzim were exempted from their debts while moshavims—larger farms—which were mainly populated with Mizrahi, went bankrupt and the population in these development towns were lagging behind while the neo-liberal policy was prospering. Therefore, the gaps between the Jewish populations grew even deeper. Arabs, citizens of Israel, were faced with even worse conditions than the Mizrahi, who consisted of the majority in the pro areas, as will be further explained. However, it should be kept in mind that the Arab-ness of both Mizrahi and Palestinian-Israeli citizens played a hidden role in the policy-making, including the economic policy-making, and brought them to the lower strata of the population.

Being one of the NGO *Achoti* founders, I took part in the first Mizrahi feminist conference in 1999 in Ma'alot. I encouraged the projects for the next year to be "The year of women workers." I took the role of raising money for the projects to start a struggle for working rights, such as "mother workers," "equal wages to women at the factories," "completion of elementary education for lower-class women," "promotion of single mothers rights," and so on. Living in southern Israel, in Beersheba, the main city of the Negev

Desert, I planned to invest my volunteering time in development towns in the Negev. There are about seven of them in the southern portion of the country. I then visited the development town of Mitzpe Ramon, and met with the workers at a textile factory, where a majority of the women were of Mizrahi origin along with a minority of Russian women, who came mainly from the southern areas of Russia at the end of the 1980s after the collapse of the Soviet Union and the Berlin Wall. Coming from the south, mainly from the countries ending in "-stan," where a significant Muslim population resides, the Jews who came from such countries are considered in Israel mostly as Mizrahim. I am a Mizrahi of Moroccan origin who came to the country as a child. I grew up in tents and tin sheds in the transition camps early on when migrating with my parents to Israel in 1949. Sharing my life story with the workers that in many of the economic and cultural details were similar to that of the women in the factory, it laid an empathetic common ground for communication and proved to be significant for the coming events. During my first visit, I met with Havatzelet Ingbar, the person leading the first rebellion, which I report on in this book. She was a prominent working woman in the textile factory, but we both did not know that her story was going to become an important part of the upcoming events.

On another instance of my visits to this small town one hour distant from Beersheba, I also met Vicki Knafo, the woman who led the other rebellion. She struggled against the government's economic cuts of single mothers allowance in 2003. This was originally an allowance given, by laws, to single mothers and was legislated in 1992. Again, I could not foresee the coming protests of Knafo, and as she stated later on, she, too, did not plan her resistance ahead of time.

Some activity cannot be feminized or engendered for women's activism. I neglected it in the field exploration, although I give it central attention in the analysis. I kept visiting the women in the remote towns in the coming three years and could expend on the women's needs when meeting the donors whom I knew from my board membership of the Israeli-US funds. I brought up issues of women's sociopolitical consciousness and agency, which I believed were more concrete then speaking of feminist consciousness. However, the process of consciousness transformation was already a labor when I met with the women workers. The feminist nature of rebelling women is a continuous debate among activists in Israel. The debates will be introduced further in the book to reveal the undercurrent tensions of the problematic feminisms, especially those which intersect with class and ethnicity issues. More importantly for me was to pronounce endocentric positions to open up a wider angle that spots the marginality of women from their own perspective. In this respect, the account of women workers' struggle expands the discourse on labor struggle that often entered into male labor struggles but were neglected when concerning women. Women's labor struggles have their specific feminist angle and gender encounters that are insufficiently studied within labor market research.

BRIEF HISTORY OF FEMINISM IN ISRAEL AND MAJOR DEBATED

Historical Dimension: First Seeds of Feminism

A few years before, Israel, in 1967, was in crisis, struggling with security and threats from outside, as well as economic and social difficulties from inside. Growing social and ethnic gaps resulted in a negative balance of Aliyah, which manifested itself for the first time in 1965 in the migration of Jews out of the country. Unemployment increased to double digits, and recessions and enduring political scandals threatened the political stability. During the same period of time, countries in the West experienced youth rebellions against European decadence led by Red Danny and various students, radical resistance groups such as the Red Brigades, "Make Love Not War" protests and the movement against the Vietnam War in the United States, along with the struggle for human rights for African Americans and the women's liberation movement. These all shook the Western world. It took another four to five years for these visions to arrive in Israel.

In June 1967, Israel was attacked by its Arab neighbors, and the war ended in a glorious victory that surprised both Israel and the world. Following the war, most of the crises were resolved when Israel was proven to be an industrious and powerful country with advanced military technology and strong defense forces. Economic contracts and agreements put an end to the recession and unemployment; the security threat was removed, at least for a while. The war victory stimulated Zionist sentiments of Jews in well-off countries, and waves of Aliyah turned the balance in a positive direction again. The Aliyah, which came after the 1967 War, consisted, among others, of young women that experienced and took part in human rights activism and protests against the war in Vietnam and the women's liberation movement activity in the United States, flew to the country, importing some of these ideas to Israel. They began to disseminate seeds of liberal activism and civil rights. In one case, social protest against deprivation of Mizrahim (Jews of Arab and Muslim origin) by the stronger sector of society consisting of Ashkenazim (Jews of Europe and the Americas) led to the establishment of the "Black Panthers Movement" (Dahan-Kalev, 1991). In another case, they formed a left-wing movement, "Shalom Achshav" (Peace Now) (Dahan-Kalev, 2001 and 2009), and in a third case, they planted the first seeds of feminism. Women such as Naomi Kiss, Galia Golan, Marcia Friedman, Marilyn Safer, and Barbara Swirski, along with many other young women, gathered small groups and formed feminist agendas. They called for equal opportunities for women, the cessation of domestic violence, and the granting of equal wages to women. This mixture of issues was mostly expressed through grassroots activities with various types of strategies ranging from demonstrations through networking, legislation attempts, and lobbying. They opened the first shelters for battered women in Haifa, founded *The Women's Voice Journal* in Jerusalem and Haifa, and started "Women to Women," a twin organization to the one in the United States. They founded the "Women's Lobby" in Jerusalem and began an annual tradition of gathering for an annual feminist-movement conference in Givat Haviva, a kibbutz known for its communist ideology. Some legislation attempts took place in 1973, especially against the control of abortion. The feminists who expressed their Zionist sentiments through these initiatives for about a decade made an effort to open women in Israel to feminism, succeeding in motivating mainly women such as themselves: well-educated, liberal, secular or conservative, left-wing feminists. However, as Yemenite-Israeli poet Bracha Seri has put it, they failed on a different level:

> What do they [the Ashkenazi women, HDK] know about what it means to be a Mizrahi woman? A woman with many children, religious? They close their ears to us. They are patronizing. What can one say! How can you even talk with them about our regular harassment—an unrequited love [. . .]. They gave you all the reasons in the world to make you feel a stranger [. . .]. No opportunity to open your mouth. There is nobody to talk to anyway. A club [. . .] of feminist *Neturei Carta* [an exclusive sect of ultra-Orthodox Jews, HDK]—most of the time even the language is different. A club for immigrants where the domain and language is English. (Seri, 1983, 4)

This comment reflects, in a nutshell, the deep alienation most women felt when meeting the young feminist migrants from the United States and explains why Israeli women had difficulties in identifying with the promise of liberation associated with feminist activity. It reveals the birthmark of feminism that will, later on, become a major debate. Engaged with strong feminist and Zionist enthusiasm, the young women failed to see the complexity of the Israeli society and were confident that their feminist ideological messages would swiftly engage the Israeli women into a revolutionary movement. In a sense, this blindness may have been an advantage for the feminists because knowing beforehand about the complexity of the Israeli social structure may have discouraged them from making an attempt to share their feminist ideas. At this stage, the seeds were planted, and women may not have joined the activists, but that did not mean that awareness was not arisen and urged. The first dialectical phase of feminism in Israel came to its end. The revolution may not have occurred, but it was not a bitter failure either. In the late 1980s, the second phase of feminism developed, and we witnessed a slow infiltration and adjustment of the liberating ideas to the various social sectors. Some changes required frontal and conflicting strategies, others required legal means, and yet others needed bargaining. A closer look at the forces acting from within the society discloses how the new feminist ideas affected not only the women but rather the larger domains of civil society, as in the case of the civil-military interface.

SOCIAL DIMENSION, MULTI-FACTION STRUCTURE: THE CIVIL-MILITARY INTERFACE

Alice Miller High Court Decision (Bagatz [Supreme Court Decision] 4541/94 *Miller vs. the Minister of Defense* 49(4) P.D. 94.1994)

Israeli society has been intensely preoccupied with security issues since its foundation. From a very early age, Israeli citizens are socialized to perceive the military in civilian life as central (Dahan Kalev 2006). The Israeli Defense Force (IDF) has always been involved in the educational system; it took part in agricultural and settlement projects, the integration of immigrants, and, thus, has been viewed as "the people's army." This entailed a very high chunk of the state's budget and far too much power and control over civilian life. Ideological justification is fostered by the security threat on the state and keeps the military as the top priority. The law of mandatory service in the army drafts all citizens at the age of eighteen, both male and female, to serve in the IDF. Drafting women suggests that rights and duties are allegedly equal to both genders. However, gender division of labor, as prevailing in civilian life, effects both the division of labor in the army and after the soldiers are released and start their civilian life. Until the early 1990s, most women soldiers functioned mostly as secretaries, in welfare services, and held educational positions. Many professional military and combat tracks were closed to women. This division was valid also to women who chose a professional military career. The access and promotion to the better paid positions were closed as well. Consequently, opportunities to get access and develop professionally were severely unequal between genders. Women could not access professions as pilots, in armor, flotilla, or high-tech positions. The options for men relied very much on the "old boys' networking" that reserved the best jobs for veteran high-ranking male officers. Deprived of these opportunities in the military and the civil sphere, women could hardly progress or run for prestigious positions. At the retirement age, which is around the early fifties for soldiers, men could often develop a second, well-paid professional career. This resulted in multiplying the obstacles that women faced, both in the IDF and the civil sphere. The jobs at the top implicitly require military experience regardless of their training, and almost all high-ranking veteran officers enjoy the fictional credit of being qualified for political, economic, technological, industrial, and even academic positions. Therefore, both inaccessibility to the public sphere and its militaristic nature subordinate women to a masculine social structure where the roles left for them to fill are family care and reproduction. Another dimension of this gender equation is how power relations in every sphere subordinate women to men and bound the equation to an abuse of power. Sexual harassment was for many years a norm in the IDF. When feminist ideas began to disseminate in the civil sphere, abuse of power in the military was one of the first issues that surfaced in public discourse. It infiltrated the IDF, and the military authorities appointed committees seeking investigation and reports regarding gender issues in general. The reports drew a picture of gender inequalities and abuse of power but abstained from describing them as discrimination and harassment. It was when they appointed civil consultants from the academia that the reports were criticized, reconceptualized, and named as such. They related to sexual harassment and power abuse and recommended gender reforms of professional opportunities. Some new professions and rank promotions opened up for women. However, the most prestigious forces and positions did not open up without explicit feminist struggle. Feminists debate the issue of equality of women in the IDF: Should women contribute to the militarization of the society or abstain from it and work to demilitarize it? This debate will be further discussed after I present the struggle of Alice Miller for the right of women to access the IDF pilots' course.

The Alice Miller High Court Decision

In 1995, Alice Miller, a young Israeli citizen, was drafted into mandatory military service. She applied to the IDF pilots' course, an unusual application for women up to that time. She was rejected and took the Air Force to the civil High Court. The Women's Lobby and Naamat Women Labor Organization represented her in court. The chief commander of the Air Force, General Herzl Bodinger, represented the IDF. Explaining the rejection, he contended that the pilots' course is expensive and focuses on the security interest of the nation and the state rather than on individuals' ambitions. Gender equality, in this case, he argued, would violate the principle of maximization of cost and benefit considerations of the Air Force. The chances of the Air Force to maximize the output of the investment in the pilot, he argued, would be very slim in the case of women, especially if the female pilot gets married and bears children before the investment is returned by service. In addition, he mentioned the reproduction damage women risk when spending many hours flying. He concluded by explaining that the decision to draft women will also require expenses for gender adjustments and structural changes, such as regulations for the purpose of logistic gender separation of bathrooms, barracks, and so on. The judges, after weighing and considering the questions of efficiency versus equality, decided with a vote of 3:2 in Miller's favor, with Judge Dalia Dorner's decisive position contending that the army is of the state, the state is a democratic state, and, thus, the equality argument prevails in this case: that is, Alice Miller should be accepted to the course in the understanding that democracy costs money. This decision resulted in some further reforms not only in the Air Force but also in other forces, and for the last five years, the statistics show that the accessibility of women to most IDF positions is increasing. At present, women can achieve any rank only one away from the highest, which is Brigadier General, but not all the positions are open just yet.

The Debate

The public debate regarding gender equality in the IDF has opened a "Pandora's box." The IDF's centrality in the life of Israeli society had been again revealed, but now it also showed how gender issues are complexly embedded in this structure. Semi-military positions that traditionally were part of the IDF vocation reopened and were questioned. On the other hand, women saw the new opportunities promised in realising the rights to participate in the new militaristic professions, both in the IDF and the civil sphere. However, given the complex social structure, new complications arose. Religious mandatory service by males interfered with gender demands for equality, as a condition for the service on the part of the Orthodox draftees consisted in keeping gender separation in the military unit, according to which men and women cannot be trained together or work on the same tank or helicopter. These new issues blended with the persisting old debate and were exacerbated by the controversy regarding the dominating role of the military in civil life. Controversies rose also within feminist factions disputing the feminists' responsibility in Israeli society. When it became public that Alice Miller's motivation to join the feminist NGOs was more personal than feminist, and when she refrained from taking a lead in the struggle as a feminist, disappointed voices began to wonder whether the struggle for an interest of an individual woman was worth the support of the feminist NGOs. There were other voices that argued against the overemphasis of the gender and military debate in general. Other voices questioned the value of the achievements and called for the women's role to take an oppositional stance and struggle against the over-militarization of civilian life. The court decision and the IDF gender reforms may be good for equality but at the same time they enhance the essentially masculine ethos, hence fostering male domination, they argued. Feminist uniqueness lies in the counterpoint as demilitarizing activism. On top of these arguments was the class contention according to which it was argued that the number of women who would benefit from the court-decision precedence could be reduced to a few upper-class women; the vast majority of women who really needed feminist support would not gain much from it. Therefore, the feminist effort should not be wasted on this issue but rather focus on issues that concern the middle-lower-class majority of women.

Alice Miller ultimately ended up failing the pilots' course, but the precedent paved the road for other women who dared to apply to the pilots' course and were able complete it. The dilemma remained undetermined. The voices in favor of equality of access to military positions and open opportunities took the stance that as long as the military is so central to civilian life and that society prioritizes qualifications acquired in the IDF, feminists should struggle to promote women's chances to enter higher positions in the civil hierarchies through gender reforms in the IDF. The opposing view that demanded restriction of militarism, both in the IDF and civilian life, and the extension of women's representation in civilian life stressed the feminist role in the demilitarization of civilian life. The debate continues.

SECOND DILEMMA

Mizrahi Feminism and the "Quarters Principle": Multi-Factions' Intersections

The Mizrahi-Ashkenazi rift in Israel is an intersectional conflict that stratifies the society along lines of class and ethnicity. When feminist winds blew in from the United States to Israel, a very small number of Mizrahi women participated in feminist activities. They were mostly well-educated women whose make up was from deprived segments of the populations on the social margins to the middle class. Operating from the bottom of the social strata, they knew what it meant to struggle and achieve. They were each well aware of feminism and women's rights and were devoted to the feminist initiatives and missions. This awareness was grounded in fair understanding of discrimination not only for being a woman but also for being of Arab and Muslim origin in a country with Western orientation. Along with these women, there were Palestinian-Israeli women who also belonged to the minority makeup. They came mainly from Haifa and Nazareth: women who originated from communist families, who were highly committed to Marxist ideology, and were often Christian. For both categories of women, sisterhood was an empowering message, and they endeavored, in neighborhoods and amongst Arab communities, to recruit women for feminism. However, shortly after they began to do so, they realized that there is an undercurrent stratification going on within the initiatives that subverted their beliefs in sisterhood, just like Seri, the poet that was quoted earlier. Ethnic divide surfaced throughout the activities. Whereas Ashkenazi activists went to the meetings with the political leaders and legislators and traveled abroad to represent the women's movement and the feminists in Geneva, Marrakesh, London, and even at the Oslo negotiations in the mid-1990s, Mizrahi and Palestinian women did the fieldwork, the organization of demonstrations, and maintained the infrastructure of these activities. Ashkenazi feminists dragged social deficiencies and divides from the larger society into the feminist initiatives. Mizrahi and Palestinian activists complained in NGOs such as the Women's Lobby, the Jerusalem Link, Kol HaIsha (The Woman's Voice), Isha LeIsha (Woman to Woman), and many others. No wonder that apart from the handful of Mizrahi and Palestinian activists, the vast majority of women in Israel found it difficult to identify with the movement's ideology and refrained from joining it.

The Rebellion

Feminist conferences traditionally were held in Givat Haviva. Many groups and NGOs participated in an annual conference to celebrate the women's liberation movement. Mizrahi and Palestinian women continually experienced exclusion and feelings of marginalization, and they harbored bitterness and increased tensions until such feelings blew up dramatically at the 1995 conference. On a Sabbath evening in the main session during a discussion on the Israeli feminist future, Mizrahi activists Netta Amar, Ela Shohet, and others entered the stage and demanded that the session be stopped at once to give the floor to another discussion: a discussion about the discrimination of Mizrahi and Palestinian women in "the movement." Similar to the conflict between white and the African-American women, such as Audre Lourd and bell hooks in the United States (hooks, 1984), those in Givat Haviva openly accused their Ashkenazi comrades of oppression, patronization, and discrimination. The Ashkenazi feminists were deeply hurt and accused the Mizrahi and Palestinians of their ingratitude. They disputed and disagreed, ending with some of the Mizrahi and Palestinian participants splitting up. The Mizrahi women who left traumatized began to meet separately and built up their own agenda and forum. One year later, they celebrated the first Mizrahi feminist conference led by activists Netta Amar, Dafna Baram, Mira Eliezer, Avital Moses, and others (Dahan-Kalev, 2007). They gave the movement the name "Ahoti," or "My Sister." It was indeed a significantly different agenda from the Israeli/Ashkenazi one. Almost instinctively, they returned to their past history in an attempt to recover their erased historical narrative. They began to reconstruct the life stories as heard from the mouth of their mothers and placing them next to the Zionist curricula that they had learned at schools. The ethnic rift played a dominant role in this reconstruction and intersected various topics of the feminist debate. The Palestinian feminists who participated in the initial rebellion did not join this initiative. Instead, they turned insular with their community and formed their own agenda, as will be discussed further shortly. The Mizrahi agenda began to form around identity questions and to look for particular issues that concerned lower-class women, immigrants, and foreign workers to where their roots belonged. Today, Ahoti, placed in the south of Tel Aviv, where the extremely deprived women often wander, is one of the few feminist NGOs that open its doors to Ethiopian women, which are women refugees who were smuggled to the country from African countries at war or are sex workers from the FSU. In this respect, Ahoti is still the organization that maintains Mizrahi and lower-class feminist agenda. It continues the legacy of the founders.

The Quarter's Principle

However, not all the women left the main group. Some Mizrahi continued the debate from within until a solution was formed around an idea that they called "quarter, quarter, quarter, and quarter." It focused on securing equal representation of four social groups within every initiative: Mizrahi, Ashkenazi, Palestinian, and lesbian women. This order prevails to this day, and it may be concluded that the event in 1995 was a historical moment that reformed the feminist movement and ensured equality to some of the social groups in the Israeli society. It does so despite the fact that the quarters principle does not guarantee that the best representation for each sector will always be ensured. Moreover, this principle does not ensure that all sectors in the divided Israeli society will be represented. Nevertheless, what was achieved was the collapse of the domination of Ashkenazi upper-class women. The feminist movement never recovered from this split, and suspicion still persists in the discourse. Ever since, Israeli feminism consists of a plurality of NGOs that specialize in diverse issues for diversified populations. Some support lower-class women, and some promote women's representation in small or large businesses, in political parties, or military institutions. Small initiatives and organizations keep appearing and respond to special needs of different groups of women for a limited amount of time. Consequently, when a common goal is identified by a number of NGOs, they form a coalition and join forces to promote it, such as the struggle against the trafficking of women and cooperation for peace and equal opportunities in public institutions. These diverse and vibrant initiatives mostly emerge in Tel Aviv and the center of the country. It does not really reach the periphery, where high rates of female poverty, single mothers, and non-Jewish Israeli citizens struggling to survive.

THIRD DILEMMA

The State's Laws versus the Arab Codes—Al Fanar: Between Loyalties

Israel's Arab population is around 20 percent. They are divided along various factions of Muslim, Druze, Bedouins, Cherckees, and Christians. However, the Jewish-Palestinian rift runs largely along lines of the Israeli-Palestinian and class conflict. Until 1966, this population lived under a military government. They were and still are severely deprived from social and political rights. The state's policy consistently preferred to grant the population rights to be led by traditional Arab leadership of patriarchs, the sheiks, imams, and Kadies. The Muslim Sharia Law prevails for the family law and tribal or extended families' (*hamullas*) customs are common. All these are held within the rule of law of a democratic state and affect the community significantly as a whole as well the individuals. Thus tension is prevalent and individuals are caught within a multi-instances system. The Zionist context and the Israeli-Palestinian conflict worsen the already complicated status of the individuals, both male and female, and the gender relations. This is the scene in which Palestinian-Israeli women find themselves when wishing to take action and make an effort to bring about change. "Al Fanar" (the lighthouse) was an initiative that took this risk.

Al Fanar

In 1994, young Palestinian-Israeli women gathered a small upper-class group from northern Israel and shined a spotlight on the phenomenon of "honor killing." They called it "Al Fanar," or "the lighthouse." This group challenged the traditional custom of murdering women for suspicion of adultery, loss of virginity before marriage, or being the victims of rape. It is not an issue of honor but sheer murder that must be ended at once (Hasan 2002), they argued. Scholar Nadia Kevorkian marked this struggle as the struggle against "dead women walking"(Shalhoub Kevorkian, 2004, 95). The task Al Fanar took upon itself was twofold: first, to break a circle of silence around a taboo concept that kept breeding violent tradition within the Arab society; and second, to break silence around the state's abstention from taking the necessary steps to enforce the law for murder equally within the Arab community as in the larger society. "Palestinian women's lives are cheaper," they contended. The state, on its part preferring to respect the community codes at the expense of the individual rights, counted on the inner institutions' resolution such as blood avenges and ransom.

The Arab street response was one of double condemnation: how dare Al Fanar bring such a shame and embarrassment to the Arab community and tradition; and the other was directed to the disloyalty to the Palestinians who live in the heart of the Zionists (i.e., the rule of the enemy). This was considered almost similar to treason.

From the state's police perspective, things were no less problematic as it turned out that even when the state arrested a suspect for the intention to commit the crime, according to the custom, the responsibility passes on to another member in the family because the redemption of the family honor is the responsibility of the collective. Bringing the problem to public awareness, however, revealed how complex it is for a feminist to make change in the Palestinian-Israeli community. The patriarchal bonds are gripping the desire for liberation, and when women engage in making a change, they risk their lives.

Polygamy

The problem of polygamy in the Palestinian community is similar to murdering for "family honor." Polygamy in Israel is illegal, but women continue to be married, sometimes compulsively, within polygamous families in the Bedouin community. Muna, a Bedouin woman from Rahat, the biggest town of Bedouins in the Negev (Spector, 2013), took it upon herself to risk bringing the voice of women who silently continue to suffer from compelled marriage in polygamy to public attention. The rate of polygamous marriage increased in the last decade due to the increase of the better-educated women in the Bedouin community. The paradox of better-educated women who marry within polygamy is explained by the fact that by the time these women complete their studies, they are at an age that is considered late for them to find a match. Therefore, if they want to stay within the community, they must accept the terms of marriage that the family or tribe offers them.

Muna, supported by the Southern Branch of Itach-Maaki NGO, an organization of women solicitors that helped her in formulating the statement for the campaign, faced the same twofold condemnation like Al Fanar activists: for her accomplice with the Zionists, and for shaming the male members in the community. According to the customs, she was supposed to approach the male sages in the community. After she did and nothing happened, she went on to contact the NGO and the media. Coming from the low strata even within the Bedouin community, and being divorced and very poor, she was desperate and did not have much to lose. She has literally putting her life in jeopardy to speak out. To her surprise, it was proved to be feministically empowering and protecting, and she was left alone by the authorities in the male community. However, the dilemma remains: whether to take the risk at being the first to "lean on the fence" and hope that other women will follow, or remain silent and subordinate. It was the classic dilemma of "to be, or not to be." The cohesive and old custom bonds in secret societies began to crack around the issue of polygamy but the way is still long for Muna and her comrades.

RELIGIOUS REFORMS: SHAKDIEL'S HIGH COURT DECISION FOR THE REPRESENTATION OF WOMEN IN RELIGIOUS COUNCILS

(Bagatz [Supreme Court Decision] 153/87 *Shakdiel vs. the Minister for Religious Affairs* 42(2) P.D. 221 (1988)

Religious Feminism

The religious population in Israel is about 17 percent. The problem with presenting an exact percentage lies in the range and definition of how religion is practiced and perceived. Ultra-Orthodox communities, for example, are heavily patriarchal and tend to solve their problems through inner rabbinic institutions. They segregate themselves from the larger society and lead a very rigid gender division of labor. There are, though, other factions that range on a more moderate religious spectrum, which are more integrated and tolerant to the larger society's order. Gender relations are practiced generally according to Jewish religious laws of halacha in various degrees of flexibility. Religion, by offering value systems for all domains of life, contradicts with feminism that is founded on the idea of transformation and change. Such are the codes of modesty that go against activism in the public sphere or mundane political activity often planned for Fridays and the Shabbat. Therefore, religious feminists founded their own NGOs. Kolekh and Emuna are two of the prominent religious NGOs that set agendas that concern religious women and offer appropriate tools aimed at feminist concerns within the religious community. On the one hand, they identified special ways to cope with "regular issues of gender," such as struggles against domestic violence and women's health issues; on the other hand, they bargained and negotiated with the patriarchs and sages of the religious communities to generate some reforms. The right of women to read the Torah in the synagogue and reforms of the laws of halacha in favor of gender change of relations are two of many examples. Strategies of negotiation and bargaining are tools that enable women to bring about changes without having to leave the community. After two decades of changes in gender relations among the different religious factions, deep reforms occurred that can be perceived as a revolutionary. This case proves that major debates might be managed with strategies other than frontal conflicts or liberal modes of public protests.

Shakdiel's Precedence

I will conclude this section with the case of Lea Shakdiel's High Court precedence of representation of women in religious councils. In 1987, Lea Shakdiel, a woman from the southern town of Yeruham, identified as religious Zionist, has forwarded a petition to the High Court, claiming that her candidacy for the municipal religious council was rejected. Until then, all the religious councils consisted of men only. The High Court that often prefers not to interfere in the religious courts' decisions took the challenge in this case and determined the precedence in favor of representation of women in the religious councils. The High Court decision ordered the Yeruham council to accept Shakdiel's candidacy. Shakdiel carried out the election campaign for the religious council and was elected. However, being inexperienced in politics, she had no idea of how political games are played in Israel. She learned that decisions may be made outside the framework of meetings, and when voting time came, she was always in the minority. Sometimes, she was informed after the decisions were voted on or she was isolated. The lesson of feminism, in this case, was that the court may make justice for women, but if there is a debate that is rooted deep in patriarchal religious tradition, the struggle for representation must also cross experience in political manipulation. The debates on representation not only in the religious councils, but also in all other religious institutions are still raging. Women run for positions in academic, political, and religious institutions. And sometimes, they win.

This history and the major debates in feminism in Israel seemed to neglect the issues that related to really marginalized women. The movement was open to women agents who already had some awareness of their rights as women but had difficulties to attract those women who did not take the first steps in the struggle for their equal rights. Therefore, many women, who were occupied with burning issues of survival and hardly could spare time for activity that didn't contribute directly to their survival, remained outside the circles of feminist activism. Women such as Vicki Knafo and Havatzelet Ingbar were such women. They had to pave their own way on an individual basis, as repeatedly mentioned, one by one.

As this is a field grounded in theory, I accepted the approach of the women rebels and largely used their language formulations of the events as the main version. It was spoken to me in Hebrew, and I made efforts to keep the English translation as faithful as possible to the spirit of those expressions that the women used. This was the basic structure on which I have added other sources, such as media reports, television interviews, institutional protocols and minutes, and politicians' and other actors' expressions and descriptions from the documentary series *Daroma.*

Social structures and processes are dynamic and abstract, and yet, they are held as substantial entities. As such, they part of the major challenges for understanding reality in a time of change as events flow rapidly. In exploring the stories of the women rebels, I will move through four stages of analysis: first, the flow of the story; second, the political and social transformation that the women rebels experienced; third, the dynamics of my relations with Ingbar and with Knafo; and finally, the analysis of personal consciousness transformation under all three previous stages.

In the winter of 2003, I had a few meetings with Ingbar at her home in Mitzpe Ramon, after having met her once in my office in Beersheba. That was about three years after the rebellion at the textile factory. Our meetings took place on Fridays, the day that Jewish-observant women are typically preparing family meals for Shabbat. We agreed to meet and talk while she was preparing the meals, and I assisted her because during the week, she had difficulties finding free time to talk. We had less formal and more relaxed conversations than conventionally structured interviews. Ingbar spoke of her personal life, family, and works in associative flow. From time to time, she went to the children's room, where her two boys of fifteen and twelve stayed, and she answered their call for help completing their homework. She moved from one part of her biography to another without me interfering except for clarifications of one or another detail. Ingbar was fluent, and she communicated vividly. We became closer, and our relations got warmer.

I met the other leaders of the rebels who led the strike in the textile factory, Avigayle Ifrach and Larissa Vinogradov, and about ten of the women workers in the textile factory. They were all Mizrahi. I discussed with them mainly about their own experience in the textile factory. Then I met with Knafo for the first time in July 2003 at a television studio. Since then, I have visited her in the rebelling campaign tent camp opposite the Rose Garden in the governmental city in Jerusalem. In both events that I explored, I paid special attention to the women's experience of consciousness transformation and how they felt during the transition from being obedient women to becoming resistant and rebellious women, and eventually, how they felt to mobilize from submissiveness to becoming fierce social agents. Their cooperation and motivation to share with me their experiences was outstanding. In most of the meetings, I tried to abstain from using a tape recorder, and when I did, I asked for permission for every instance of its use. When I heard the women talking to me, I could see that this was not the first time they were telling their stories. I recognized the exorbitant intimacy undertone that was familiar to me from previous interviews I did with lower-class women; women who had very little to protect when most of their waking hours were spent working out of the home in manual labor for a slim wage.

In Ingbar's home, we spoke while her spouse was present at all times. He did not say a word and was helping in the preparations for the Shabbat. Ingbar's marriage with her husband, Motti, was her second, and her two children were from her first marriage. She referred to the children's education and to Motti's involvement in the educational tasks in the third person in his presence, and he still did not interfere.

Motti worked in the municipality, and during Ingbar's struggle, he supported all her moves. He helped support the other families who participated in the rebellion, providing food and blankets when the women barricaded themselves in the factory and closed it from within, as shall be further detailed. During our conversations, he never interfered, and I got the impression of a family and home life that was in full partnership.

I asked Ingbar if she was interested in reading the transcripts of our conversations when I was done with the thematic report. She said that she did not think it was important and didn't want to read them. I had a feeling of full trust on her part, which increased my feeling of responsibility, but at the same time, I suspected that she voiced fear that she wouldn't understand the "academic stuff," hence gave up such a review in advance. It is difficult to assume how close relations between a researcher and a research participant can develop when considering unavoidable power built into such relations. Neutrality is weakened, and power makes the cushion for the dry facts that will, eventually, become scientific knowledge even when efforts are made to minimize its impact. Moreover, power relations are part of the report context, which contributes to making sense of the flow of the events. Often, power relations make sense as unveiling obscured facts. The considerations of both the researcher and the participant are never "pure" personal or professional. There is always more than one layer: the lining, or coating. They are reconstructed unavoidably at moments of conversation between the researcher and the informant. The report of the facts of the rebellion, in our case studies, already contains epistemic reflection, which is reconstructed as narratives. In other words, the lining beneath the facts designs to a certain extent the impact on the understanding of the events. In our case, the moment of the rebel went through narration more than once, at least twice, via the informant's and the researcher's minds.

TELLING THE STORY MORE THAN ONCE

A rebellion is an event full of details and components. How should the researcher elaborate and chose the details of an event that involves so many components and actors? What makes a certain actors' relationship more important than others? How should the events be reconstructed when taking in the accounts and sequences of events? How do we know who are the real actors and who are the false actors? Who played more, or less, significant roles in mobilizing the plots when acting behind the scene? These are challenging questions to the researchers. Experience rather than experiment is to be employed when the scene of research is not a theater where rehearsals were taken but is instead real life. In human sciences, the laboratory is real life. In the case of a written text that is given and doesn't change each time, the researcher may reread the text, and perhaps find new insights and interpretations, the case of re-interviewing is more complex. It is not the same with a spoken review between two persons. Insights are multiplied, as are emotional and intellectual dynamics. This double movement may keep the dry facts in motion but add new layers to the information and the insights through change of moods, memory, and the recollection of details, as well as the psyche of both of the interacting persons. Nevertheless, the movement of telling the story time and again twirls the story and enriches the research fabric from which the final analysis is made. In the series of meetings in which I collected the information with regard to the case studies in this book, I asked the women who participated in the rebelling events to tell me the story more than once. There were three instances: one before reading the written material reported in media; one after reading the publications material; and one after I met with whom I identified as the escorting figures around the heroines. Sometimes I felt that I had not known the women; sometimes they reported the same events in a very different way. I would have thought that they spoke of different ones, had I not known they are the same people. It seemed that Rashomon should be one of the basic assumptions of the study, even when it was the same person telling the story. In telling the stories more than once, the women had opportunities to reflect and emotionally process once again what was such a stormy experience for them. This was a psychological stage which allowed them to highlight different details of their experience. It is the women's experience and their consciousness transformation I was after; therefore, telling the story more than once became a research tool for analysis. Moreover, telling the story more than once also allowed the women to change positions from a mere informant to a critical informant, sometimes being judgmental, ironic, and, finally, sobering out of the illusions they began their consciousness journey with. I employed this multiplied dialogical technique following the recommendations of James Holstein and Jaber Gubrium on research interviews (Holstein and Gubrium, 2002). They emphasized the idea that the interviewees grow from the events they experience but also from telling about them more than once from the same position. For the researcher who is after social agency and change, these are important insights. Moreover, they influence the power relationship dynamics and move some of it to the women who gain a growing amount of control over what they decide to share. For the researcher, it is a chance to uncover more sides of the events rather than stick to the "dry facts." The nature of this interaction is similar to therapeutic dynamics, although its goal is different. The researcher receives an opportunity to examine what was significant at the different instances for the storyteller and learn more about the impact of the details on her. In accumulating and comparing the information both between the repeated versions of the story and telling it by different participants, the researcher's ability to cross-reference the information promotes the final credibility of the conclusions. Through the systematic registration of the talks I had with Ingbar and her work colleagues, I could see her personality and worldview more widely. I was able to view her perceptions about family and children, motherhood, ethics of work, about partnership and friendship, and about her going through social and labor relations. These were far more productive then laying out a questionnaire, even an open questionnaire, as she spoke in a free-associative mode and was fluent. She had used words such as "responsibility" and "caring" very often, and she talked about kindness of her spouse or need of her children. I classified these repetitions and the context within which they were brought up. I have also noted where she expressed doubts and question marks. I employed this technique to trace the sequence of the events and to be able to point out when and what changes took place at a specific instance of the events telling. I focused on difficult issues that seemed to be a one-time transition that made an inconvertible change in the sequence of things and her identity. As I will present further on, how, for example, does a woman worker appointed to the chief executive officer in an overnight decision change and how does she make the functional moves to adjust to such a change? More critical was to understand the gender element of this transition and the structural transition along this move. Only when there was enough material from the interviews could I select and elaborate expression and references that seemed to be relevant to this part of identity of professional and institutional transition analysis. The conceptualization and formulation that I used were taken in the writing stage along with the presumptions and hypotheses formulation. These precautions were proved to be important to the understanding of the power relations that only rarely are directly and articulately uncovered. Sandra Harding and Kathryn Norberg (2005) suggested that interviewees sometimes experience opinion and even personality change during a retrospective report on the events when discussing them once more. The interviewees assessment of success or failure of the events and their awareness of truth or fault of what has happened in real time are revised and may lead to the confusion and doubts by the researcher of the interviewee's credibility. This risk brings up again the importance of repeated meetings and encounters with the women who generated the rebellion. While repeating the details, the women may fill the gap between the versions with their own reflections and indicate the moments of social agency's view that the researcher may passionately search for.

Rebels, especially women rebels, even women of Mizrahi origin, and even if occurring in a peripheral location such as that of the Negev Desert in Israel, drew the attention of the media and brought the heroines who led them into the limelight. The women are identified by their names and faces, speak their words, and become public figures, even if for a short while. The stories were documented and transmitted more than once in the case of the textile factory and the single mother's revolt. I, therefore, was debating with myself what should be my approach to the issue of names and identifying events. I have also discussed the issue with the women and gave them the choice to decide. In the Israeli collective memory, the women and the event names are still mentioned by their names and subject titles, such as "Vicki Knafo and the single mothers' affair" or "Havatzelet Ingbar and the Atzmaut textile factory" and are studied in the field of the history of the women's labor market. We came to the conclusion—the interviewees and I—that using false names are useless for this case, as every reader, at least an Israeli reader, would immediately recognize the people mentioned and involved. As for the analysis and the insights, it is my responsibility only.

Chapter Four

Two Decades of the Welfare State Disintegration

The Women's Dismissal First

The context in which the stories in this book take place and the order of violation circumstances that the women mobilized are the state of Israel, the Israeli society at the beginning of the twenty-first century, and the labor market reformation. A democratic state, by its institutions and elections, although lacking some democratic culture and, sometimes, failing to stand up to democratic norms, is considered as more or less democratic. However, when it gets to the unavoidable topic of the Israeli-Palestinian conflict, it is impossible to discuss any topic regarding Israel without relating to it and to the occupied territories. Israel, even when relating to its Jews population, may be discussed as the only democracy in the Middle East, but this country is mostly regarded as a Western state that happens to be located in the Middle-East region. I want to suggest another angle through which we should regard Israel: the state and the country. Throughout the years and it's short history, the state of Israel has gone through "Easternalization." First and for most, it has done so from within. The mass immigration from Arab and Muslim countries of the Jews since its first foundation made an impact of Easternalizing the country and society throughout the years despite the founding fathers' efforts to follow the Jewish cultural legacy as it was practiced in the countries of origin in Eastern Europe. In addition to that, the Palestinian-Israeli citizen struggle for their rights to national had also made its impact on the culture and norms within Israel. Lastly, the fact that Israel is geopolitically located in the heart of the Arab and Muslim world in the Middle East finally penetrated the Western walls that Israel was trying to keep high against Eastern influence. Within Israel, there were two populations that reacted to the Middle-Eastern culture; these populations did not remain passive to what was happening in the Arab and Muslim world. This meant that the superior Orientalist approach had to make more efforts to protect the Western hegemony that prevailed in Israel; it only means that while surrounded from without and from within by the Eastern world and culture, the Eurocentric-Zionist founding fathers efforts for over six decades sometimes showed signs of cracking and couldn't be seen as a purely Western country as those founding fathers intended. Therefore, in many respects, Israel may be considered a Western state but an Eastern country and goes through a process of Easternalization that can neither be ignored nor avoided. It should be considered when trying to understand the policy-making with respect to topics that are allegedly irrelevant, such as its inner policies or the various socioeconomic processes. It is within this broader historical context that makes a brief introduction of the scene for the understanding of the Israeli welfare-state emergence and death. It is within this context that Israel should be regarded both as Western, European state, and Middle-Eastern country. Politically, as well, it is neither entirely democratic nor entirely theocratic or totalitarian. The center-periphery boundary lines formed the setting in which the events I will unfold herein received their specific character. Israel is a state where ideological, national, and Jewish religious civilization institutions are intertwined in cultural, economic, and social networks of power. Once again, power networks play the infrastructure role as the lining of the democratic, modern western regime, and this correlates to ethnic and national splits as well as economic and political ones. Until 1966, the Arabs were put under military government, and the Mizrahim mostly settled on the periphery. Both populations formed the lowest classes where Arab citizens were deprived of most of their social and civil rights.

This social structure was covered with ideologies of socialist orientation taken from Zionism collectivist and even communist ideas. This was best materialized in the kibbutzim and moshavim shitufiym (farming communes). This worked for a few decades before the establishment of the state and endured for three more decades until late 1960s. The socioeconomic policies were meant to apply to all the Jews in the cities as well. The Histadrut, the Zionist labor union established in 1920, was the platform on which social rights and welfare services were developed. Education, housing, work, health, and many more basic services were granted to the labor force as part of the ideological socialist welfare. However, this was strictly based on Zionist party political affiliation and membership. The larger the party, the better the services were to the party member. In other words, the young democratic state was run by the powerful labor party, sometimes a reminder of a Bolshevik order where the party is above the state. Within the labor movement, women formed their women worker branches and struggled from within for representation and equal rights, with not much success. They formed help services for working mothers and fought for representation, but only a few of these succeeded, mainly when they did not show solidarity to the from within women's organization. On the contrary, women who struggled as individuals within the party establishment gained more power and influence then women who struggled as groups within the Zionist movement and the kibbutzim. It took three decades for the welfare state to surrender to the globalization winds, which blew into the country and removed every piece of welfare that was achieved by the workers, at least those who were affiliated with the Histadrut. In 1977, a political turnover occurred, and after more than fifty years of reign, the founding party of Mapay (the labor party) lost power. The liberal-national block party took power, led by the revisionist leader of the Liberty Movement, Menachem Begin. Begin was a nationalist statesman. While this political turnover took place, the socioeconomic gaps between Jews of Arab and Muslim origins—the Mizrahim—and Jews of European origins—the Ashkenazim—grew deeper, to the benefit of the Ashkenazim. Mizrahim, which were at this period of time about half of the population, earned 70 percent of the Ahkenazim's income (Dahan Kalev, 1991). The slums, which grew larger all over the country, were populated mostly with those of Mizrahim origin, and the population in the development town was mostly unemployed, and crime ruled the streets. Prisons consisted of 80 percent prisoners of Mizrahi origin (Dahan Kalev, 1991). In the next two decades, the center (i.e., Tel Aviv) and the area called "from Hedera to Guedera," or formally the Gush Dan Metropol, was developing economically, giving in to the world capitalist ideas discarding every piece of welfare policy or the initial communist ideology and equality. The kibbutz ethos began to crack down as inner crises showed that human nature works better on the basis of personal interests rather than on solidarity. The kibbutzim ethos was now based on their ability to form the central government and send their delegates to be part of the policy-making.

In the small development town of Mitzpe Ramon in the southern portion of Israel, a phenomenon that is difficult to explain took place. Remote from the center, in the desert area of Israel, an area that has never caught up with the Israeli economic temperament rhythm of development, women began to stand up and challenge the economic policy of the state. They swept other women from all over the country to join their rebelling against the economic cuts policy. The economy that hurt specifically feeble groups in society and gave way to wild capitalist globalization, opening the gates of the state to foreign investments and international economic forces, took over. It is important to understand the economic ground in which the rebellious seeds germinated; in the beginning, it was a hidden process, sometimes only conscious to the resistance against the subordinating order that these women grew up in and in the public sphere and acted for many years. Ingbar and Knafo, the leading figures in two separate affairs of women's rebellion, in three years separate from each other, never coordinated their resistant actions. They have neither been familiar with struggles discourses nor to the feminist history in Israel or out of it. Nor were they aware of the struggles or ideologies of the women workers who sprouted up alongside the Zionist labor movement during the establishment of the state. Their stories unfold in front of us as a loge snaked process that lays out broader questions that feminists and socialist feminists are troubled with: questions of long-living obedience and subordination, of lived experiences of humiliation and oppression that women experience with silence and that are nesting slowly into a mature drive towards resistance. An experience that swept public support and, eventually, wrote a historical page of women's revolt in Israel. As mentioned previously, whether they were successful or failed political and personal lessons, they were feministic in the true sense and scholastic definition, and the Ingbar and Knafo affairs beg for interpretation and placement in a broader and interdisciplinary context, which includes worker's worlds and women's workers worlds. It is for this impossibility to place their struggle under a clear, definite category that makes these stories significant and worth exploring. However, first the structuring, economically and politically, and the social scene of the state of Israel must be explained for the purpose of giving a broader context to the rebel events.

THE ONLY (LIMITED) DEMOCRACY IN THE MIDDLE EAST

Israel is often referred to as the only democracy in the Middle East, as mentioned previously. It is possible to stand between and see it as neither entirely democratic nor non-democratic. Like every democracy, its regime took form under specific historical circumstances that eventually made it a Jewish democracy, read, a democracy mainly for the Jews. Thus, Israel's democracy is limited to the green line of the 1948 UN ceasefire boundaries, and there are still four crucial problems that resulted from the region political conflict with the Palestinian people that contest Israel's retention to be the only democracy in the Middle East: unsettled agreements over boundaries; refugees of 1948; and the Jerusalem and the Jewish settlements in the occupied territories on the West Bank captured since 1967 war. Within these limits, Israel runs democratic institutions that include separation of three powers of the legal system, elected representation house, and executive institutes of ministries and a relatively free press. Elections are taking place, and the judicial system serves as a high court for civil rights laws and the basic laws of human dignity and freedom. Since the establishment of the state in 1948, a small part of the Arabs who remained in the state following the declaration of independence of Israel, which was for the Palestinian people the Nakba (the dire or the catastrophe), Israel has controlled the population within the state through the military government for eighteen years. Through this regime, the state granted the Arabs in Israel special mobility and work permissions and some representation through sheiks and reverend representing figures in the public institutions. They were not granted equal citizenship for the next eighteen years when the decision to remove the military regime from the towns and villages where they were concentrated in was made. The population grew much larger following the war in 1967 and the annexation of the Sinai Desert, the West Bank, and Gaza. The Israeli government of the Arab population was now occupied on Sinai, the West Bank, and Gaza until the Peace Agreement with Egypt in 1979 when Sinai was returned to the Egyptians. In 2005, as a one-sided act, Israel withdrew from Gaza only, led by the late Prime Minister Ariel Sharon.

At crucial moments of decision, the High Court of Justice often prefers to abstain from interfering in political decisions when it regards issues that concern the occupied territories and Palestinian human rights (see, for example, *The Rule of Law*, a 2011 documentary). Moreover, the democratic institutions tend to apply mainly to the Jewish population. Religious issues that regard all three monotheistic religions, and especially the Jewish religion, are in the hands of the religious leadership that runs separate courts for family affairs. In this respect and with regard to the legal system, the state is defined as Jewish and democratic equally. At moments of conflict between the two, it seems that the Jewish aspect always overcomes democracy. This has implications for issues that allegedly are irrelevant to the question of Jewish and/or democratic but seem to have some reflection on it. Such are often economic allocations of social and civil resources and privileges that are granted to the stronger groups in the population, which in Israel have always been mainly of Ashkenazi origin.

The affinity of the Mizrahim, the Jews who migrated from the Arab and Muslim countries, mainly at the end of the 1940 beginning of the 1950s, was never viewed or taken as part of the conflict between Israelis and Palestinians. It was tacitly accepted that the Mizrahim where Jews whose Arab-ness had nothing to do with the Palestinian enemy or the Arab culture. More importantly, the assimilating authorities didn't spare any effort to separate them from the Arabs on the way make Israelis, ala the Zionist model. Nevertheless, the fear of the affinity between Jews who lived in the Arab countries and the Palestinians, who were viewed as the enemy from within Israel, was meant to be torn from each other. This approach constructed a conditional expectation according to which if a Mizrahi Jew wanted to better integrate within the melting pot of the Israeli society, he or she would have to Europeanize themselves, or, in the Israeli slang, to "Ashkenazify." Mizrahim should get rid of their Arab-ness—get rid of their traditions, religious customs, legacies, histories, and memories and get modernized, read Europeanize. Most Mizrahim cooperated with this doctrine, which was, at the time, very aggressive and included cutting headlocks and erasing the history of entire communities from the Arab and Muslim countries from the curricula. On the part of the Mizrahim, who wanted very much to integrate, they made specific efforts to remove themselves from the Palestinians, manifesting Jewish-Israeli (read Ashkenaziation) solidarity. The Zionist ideological ethos developed special apparatus aimed at the indoctrination of young children of the Mizrahi immigrants, including technologies of medical psychological and educational methods practiced in biopolitics. The school curricula reported of retardation and primitivism of the Jews when in the Arab Diaspora in the little chapters that they were telling about the Jewish history in the Arab and Muslim world. The immigrants sent to the peripheral parts of the state had schools that were of a very low level, and in fact, two parallel systems of education operated the "melting pot" policy. Eventually, the society was constructed into three sections: first, the Jews of Ashkenazi origin and the second generation of Mizrahim, who were educated under an Orientalist system, deprived from most civil and social rights; second, the Mizrahim first generation of immigrants who lived remote from the resources and representation centers; and third, the Palestinian-Israeli citizens who were discriminated against and were made up the lowest marginalized sector of Israeli society. In the 1970s, this was the social profile of the Israeli society, which, when looking at its political agenda, reflected two platforms: one for the inner affairs that concerned only the population that lived within the green line, and another for the larger affairs that ran the occupation of the West Bank and the Palestinian people that lived there. In a weird way, the settlers that lived outside of the green line enjoyed the government of the inner policy and, through the fine surgical process of creeping settlements, they kept growing at the expense of the peripheral and the lower-class budgets. As the governments encouraged the Israeli citizens to settle in the West Bank, those who rushed to respond to the intensive encouragement, led by allegedly left-wing politicians such as Yitzhak Rabin and Shimon Peres, were mostly people of a lower class of Mizrahi origin who searched for housings, labor, and educational solutions. Many of them lived before with their parents in small apartments. They were about two-thirds of the settlers in the late 1970s. The settlers who came out of the ideology, the nationalists, were mostly of religious Ashkenazi origin, and they founded and indoctrinated the second generation of the houseless and unemployed Mizrahim who came to the settlements questing for personal solutions to their economic problems. By the 1990s, the third generation of Mizrahi in the settlements was youngsters that were educated by the ideological settlers and the growing number of mixed marriages. According to right-wing ideology and due to this policy, the second and third generation of Mizrahim settlers became the faithful carriers of the right-wing ideology. It is, therefore, understood that the Israeli democratic state grew to become alien to the Middle-East region rather than integrated within the cultural and historical development of the Middle-East region's legacy. Even the language, Arabic, was rejected as the "enemy's language," and those who wanted to study Arabic did it for reasons of being accepted into military intelligence service. Ironically, in religious terms, the Jewish-ness of the Israeli democracy developed in radical directions, and new fanatic groups cultivated religious-political ideologies that, at times, promoted nationalist agendas and consisted of the settler's political ideology. In conclusion, Israel became a democratic state in the formalistic institutional sense, which means that it became a state that runs according to democratic institution lines but lacks democratic culture practices, and its citizens are mostly democratic when it concerns the Jewish population. It is a state that is bounded to legal systems but only partially; it applies to its population, but only partially; and to its territories, only partially. Its religious and nationalistic culture and civilization dominates the democratic values and sometimes diverts them away from democratic culture. Its potential of being the only state whose citizens form the real democratic culture in the Middle East is therefore yet to be formed.

THE ISRAELI VERSION OF THE SOCIALISTS WORKER'S ETHOS

Opposed to the ethos that surrounded the historical socialist worker's ideology in the world, and seldom around the women workers, the history of the worker's struggle in Israel differed from that of the European or American workers. The British and American history of the workers provides us with stories of worker's struggles that, in the end, left legacies that led the countries to form a welfare regime that allowed the construction of a working class. These classes grew stronger and formed an economic and political power that was able to stand up against the other two economic powers, the state institutions, and those who owned the capital, the capitalists that formed the private sector. The workers legacy eventually became the working class's backbone for generations to come; the heavy technology industry of Western Europe, the coal mine, steel, and automobile industries, all these branches developed effective labor unions through struggles and strikes. Years of struggles from which the working classes made up the legacy of workers pride and rights, immersed in the history of resistance to exploitation and oppression, protest and class division. Although they now form the middle class and sometimes assimilated with the bourgeoisies, the historical memory of the workers' unions is embedded in their legacy. The Israeli legacy of the working class is different. In Israel, the workers who started the labor-class legacy began with the founding fathers, the socialists in their initial orientation as acquired in the Bolshevik party from the early days of the USSR but motivated by nationalistic ideology. The first pioneers who came from Eastern European countries held communist ideas that counted mostly for political party's organization. The pioneers struggled over Hebrew labor competing with the Arab workers, whom the Jewish landlords exploited for cheap wage during the First Aliyah in 1882. The chapter in the Zionist history against the Arab worker was one of the most significant struggles towards the national revival and was characterized regarding class struggle, although it meant working groups struggling over the right for work. In other words, the struggle of the workers against the capitalist exploiters involved nationalistic motivation, and they finally won, but it was far from the class struggle in the Marxist sense of the matter.

In this respect, the pioneers were owners rather than workers, as they have also founded organizations that aimed at land appropriation and other institutionalization processes. The legacy that they developed had no ruling-class opposition as in the Eastern-European world, from where they came. In many respects, the labor party of Mapay functioned similarly to the capitalist class. When, in the late 1940s, immigrants began to flow into the country from Middle-Eastern countries, Mapay was already the ruling party since 1933 and had welfare institutions that could provide for its members in return of the members' political loyalty. The workers were organized in the Histadrut—the labor union organization that was founded in 1920. The Histadrut was the working organization of the Mapay Party. Those who did not have the "little red book" of Histadrut membership could not enjoy health, education, occupation, housing, and working services. The political system, which was based on party-politics membership, became the exclusive source of the welfare services. Therefore, if one didn't register as an apolitical party member and didn't show loyalty to the party, he (mostly men) wouldn't be able to enjoy welfare rights. The immigrants that came in the 1940s and 1950s came from counties that were not familiar with this communist idea and the Bolshevik system. Working-class consciousness and the militant working class in the classic sense were alien concepts to them. They were more similar to the immigrants that came to Europe after World War II from Turkey, Pakistan, or North Africa. The immigrants who came from the Arab and Muslim countries and joined the labor union, the Histadrut, became automatic Mapay Party members. In this situation, those who didn't want to become the ruling party members had to compromise with smaller parties that were religious, nationalist, and ethnic and who were always dependent on coalitions with the ruling party. However, because of a party principle key, which allocated budgets according to the size of the parties, the largest party of Mapay could preserve its power, control the resources, and even expand them. As a result, those workers, the new immigrants, realized that political party membership was the condition to enjoy welfare services. By the time of the declaration of independence in 1948, what was meant to be the working class formed from pioneers and kibbutzniks, they became the bourgeoisie and the national capital owner's classes.

In the 1960s, it was already clear that the lower working class and the ethnic origin of Arab and Muslim countries correlated. This correlation has, eventually, ended in bitter feelings as the Mizrahim experienced discrimination since they migrated to Israel. In the 1960s, Israel developed its own model of class struggle, which merged with ethnic discrimination marks: Yhoshua Peretz, a working leader of Moroccan origin, who worked in the harbor of Ashdod, registered one of the most significant chapters in the history of working-class struggles in the Histadrut and in Israel. He started a strike demanding improvement of labor conditions and better wages. The authorities and Histadrut leaders who considered themselves socialists were surprised to be accused of being exploiters and oppressors. The ethnic component of the strike merged with the economic exploitation. This combination was made since the immigrants from the Arab and Muslim countries came to Israel, a reason for panic on the part of the founding fathers. They endeavored to achieve national unity and equality, and here came Peretz blowing in their face their failure (Grinberg, 1993). His struggle was against the Histadrut, which he argued cooperated with the Mapay Party, the ruling party, at the expense of the workers. Although Peretz was an uncompromising labor leader and was arrested for taking violent actions, he was the first to bring to the public discourse the idea that the Histadrut' s does not fulfill its vocation of protecting the workers' interests and instead serves the ruling party. Peretz continued to struggle and became a symbol of the worker's leader. The harbor workers' union became one of the strongest unions in the country and registered a labor union turning point in labor market relations. Following this struggle, other struggles in major industrial concerns formed strong labor committees, such as the electric company, transportation, water, education, and hospital nurses (the last two divisions consisting mostly of women), and formed committees that registered as an effective power that showed an ability to protect workers' rights. They all deepened their power within the Histadrut and became the ruling unions with strong leadership.

The Zionist idea of a melting pot and of equality, of national unity and socialism, were now decaying in front of the eyes of the founding fathers. It also marked the shattering of the national unity myth and enhanced ethnic divides. Thirteen strong committees survived to the present, even after laws of privatization legislated in 1979 and a reform dismantled much of the Histadrut power. The committees integrated within the economic system and managed to secure the veteran incomes. Those are now one of the highest salaries in the country. The privatization laws began to be carried out through the 1980s and 1990s, and what was left of the welfare ideology went through being dismantle as well. The power equilibrium of the economic forces of the government and the private sector owners began to accept the international financial institution's investment in Israel. Once again, the thirteen labor unions proved their power to stand against and protect the labor rights, even when privatization and free commerce policy began to shape the Israeli liberal economy. The Histadrut, eventually, became one of the three arms of the Israeli economy, in the triangle of the government, the private sector, and the workers. Thanks to the strong unions, the Histadrut could negotiate for the workers, but sadly, they did so only for the workers who were organized in those thirteen strong unions that were mainly running the states' infrastructure, such as the shipping, the air transportation, and the electricity and waters companies. The rest, as we shall see with the textile branch, couldn't enjoy the Histadrut's power advantages and protection and were on the decline. A closer glance shows that unions that represent heavy technology industries, high tech, the state's infrastructure, and natural resources had enough power to put pressure on the other economic organs, the state and the private sector, and the owners of the production means. Many of the entrepreneurs were affiliated to workers in the military-civilian industry, national resources, and chemical and pharmaceutical production. In this respect, they control their firm's capital investments and influence those investments and development companies' policies. Industries that consist of female workers, such as textile and food, are led by weaker unions and often are not allowed to form their own labor representatives due to employment by contractors. They have no power to impose negotiations or struggle for their labor rights. These industries employ female workers who can't gather without risking being fired. For the last four decades, the stronger labor unions have established new forms of workers' legacy that begin to look similar to organizations in Europe where workers of Turkey, North Africa, and Far-East countries joined large concerns after World War II. It was a legacy of a working class that remained the only support force of the worker after the decline of the welfare state and aggressive economic policy led by Ronald Reagan in the United States and Margaret Thatcher in the United Kingdom in the 1980s and 1990s. The world market opened, and wild global competition destroyed the working class and labor market in favor of a liberal economy and privatizations. How did it happen in Israel that a socialist by ideology and Bolshevik by its party ruling system declined all values of the welfare state?

GLOBALIZATION ECONOMY

The global economic policy was not possible without violating workers' rights, and if the states did not partake in the globalization process, their competitive ability would have declined along with their political ability to maintain their policy amongst other countries. Many countries in the West faced economic recessions from the 1970s onward. In the triangle of the government, the private sector, and the labor power, the first to be hurt were always the workers. Commercial trends transformed from export of goods and raw materials to export of means of production, such as high-tech knowledge and men/women power migration. Row material was moved from the country of origin, where it was dug, to the target country, where the product was planned to be manufactured. Often, third-world countries or margined and remote towns offered chip labor. The products transferred to countries where the consumption force was stronger often concentrated in central cities in the West. As states participated in this globalizing economy, governments had to contribute their regulation forces to maximize economic utility. Eventually, they became accomplices to the wild, capitalist world economy, which extended the gaps not only between workers and stronger social classes but also between rich and poor countries. The next process concentrated on the import of knowledge and higher technological forces from poorer countries to stronger countries, which, in turn, enhanced their economic entrepreneurship. The developed countries concentrated exclusively on developing high technologies and applied hard sciences. Investments in advanced industries developed professional labor forces that enjoyed better salaries and better-off labor conditions. A new workers status developed in the better-off countries different from that which constantly worked for survival in third-world countries. The gender division of labor widened from the family to the local market and from the local market to the global. In the low-income industries in the poor countries, women were the majority while in the more-developed economic markets, men led in numbers (Martha Nussbaum, 2000). The formula of center/periphery worked in globalization so that industries and institutions that were located in the center submitted more to the rule of law and the remote ones submitted to force and were easily violating the laws, including laws that protected workers. This economic reality bred various reactions, often fear and subordination, and, in rare cases, cultivated resistance and rebellion, as the cases in the south of Israel demonstrate. A long process of the welfare-state death in Israel proceeded to that, and it took a modern enslavement version to bring poor women to revolt in desperation.

THE DYING WELFARE STATE OF ISRAEL

The textile factory in Mitzpe Ramon development town was a small factory which was founded as part of the textile manufacturing industry in the 1960s in Israel. This industry has provided living resources to thousands of families mainly at the north and the south of the country, at the periphery. The small town of Mitzpe Ramon, one of the dozens of towns that the state had built up in the 1950s and 1960s, was one that suffered from chronic and severe unemployment. Similar to other towns on the periphery, Mitzpe Ramon became a symbol of poverty, and its population was economically victimized but also accused of an inability to step out of misery. The state dismissed its responsibility to the fate of the town and added to the prejudice of the Mizrahi being incapable of catching up with the rest of the immigrants; they were joined with two new groups of immigrants in the mid-1980s. In 1985 and 1990, new waves of immigrants made Aliyah to Israel from Ethiopia in two waves. They were sent to the remote areas of the country. Then came the Russian population after the Iron Wall fell, and the Jews who made Aliyah were distributed to different areas of the country. However, a few years later, it came out that those who were sent to the remote towns where the immigrants who came from the southern regions of Russia, Ukraine, Georgia, Kazakhstan, Bukhara, Caucasus, and Ethiopia. This population aforementioned was classified in Israel as Mizrahim, as most of them migrated from countries of Muslim populations. On the other hand, those who came from Belarus found their place mostly in larger cities and centers of the country.

In 1977, the political turnover and loss of power of the labor party seemed like an end of a historical phase that began in the 1930s when the state made its first steps of settlements in the Palestinian region of the Middle East. The winning block of Gahal, made of the Liberty Party of Herut led by Menahem Begin, a revisionist founding father, came to power only to discover that the real assets of Mapay, the losing party, were still owned by them through real estate, which they were accumulating in Israel and abroad and continued to own even after the loss of power. Moreover, the directors and the CEOs were all faithful electorate of Mapay and were networked within the major corporations. The ruling positions—the firm's managers and representatives in the governmental ministries and national manufacture and industry—were all in the hands of Mapay Party members. The financial, media, industry, natural resources, and air, sea, and land transportation were state-owned and in the hands of the Mapay founding father's generation and their heirs (Bichler and Frenkel, 1984). The immigrants' ministries and establishment, the Histadrut, the Health services, which was under the government of the Histadrut, and the Jewish Agency, which were of the most powerful institutions, held network fundraising and investment connections with fundraising centers in the Jewish communities all over the world. The winning parties and Menachem Begin, the Liberty Party leader, realized that winning the election did not necessarily imply winning the political power. Begin had to start shifting the ship of the state to new political and economic directions to make an effective change of the ruling power. He did indeed make a few changes; they were sometimes changes that he wasn't fond of because he had to effectively move the government into his hands. This was sometimes at the expense of the lower class and the labor force of the people.

The economy, which twenty years earlier had invested in national assets and ran a welfare policy of a charity state assisting mainly people of lower social standing, the needy, and the disabled, did it through a Ministry of Charity Affairs until the 1970s. The workers' rights and allowances, as well as pensions and health services, were in the hands of the Histadrut, the labor organization, which, again, was ruled by the Mapay Party (Grinberg, 1993). The welfare state, which was making its first significant steps through legislation and transformation to the state's responsibility of some of the labor and social rights, now faced economic difficulties resulting from its closed market and mostly nationalized economy. The reign of Mapay over most of the national infrastructure and resources supported by the powerful trade unions and labor associates ran a static market with economic stagnation and recession until 1966. The state faced a severe process of economic crisis while the world economy transformation began to move on faster and in diverse forms of monetary and financial reforms, the transformation of production markets, and international trade relations. International capitalist globalization and world trends of privatization accelerated in the late 1980s. Prime Minister Begin had to make an irreversible decision to join the world's economic trend of neoliberalism and to open the local market to international competition. This meant the dismissal of tens of thousands of workers and transferring the infrastructure of the large national companies from the state's hands to private hands and foreign investors, first and for most privatization. Begin promoted economic legislation of privatization laws in 1979, which brought reforms to the welfare rights of workers. Privatization laws were unavoidable as Begin had to open up the competition and liberate economic forces from the tight affiliation with Mapay. The social rights of the labor force were the first to be cut, and national firms and companies were encouraged to hire services through contractors who hired the workers. This enabled the contractors to employ workers for cheaper wages and with minimal labor rights. Unemployment rates rose dramatically, and exploitation labor conditions soared (Bichler and Frenkel, 1984; Bichler and Nitzan, 2001). In ten years time, Israel became the state with the highest income gap between rich and poor in the Western world. The gap was 1:11 in the early 1990s. The semi-socialist economic state market, which suffered from stagnation but provided some security to its workers, had now lost almost all its cooperatives, and in many cases, those who were able to present attractive offers to purchase national companies came from old money holders, such as Mapay Party heirs and foreign money. The older national firms, which invested overseas, had real estate that now was open for sale, particularly international transportation companies. Roads and ships, military force and technology, airports and harbors, national housing, and communication were all struggling to remain in public hands and had until then realized that recovery plans were being streamlined. Scarcity and crisis turned off the old aura that radiated around the Zionist project of national revival, and the atmosphere was of the failure for the project. This was, in a strict sense, a sobering moment in which Israeli society looked at its image and realized that it was not an equal society, that its democracy was not so democratic, and that the state separation of religion was far from what was being strived for through modernity and secularity. It was divided ethnically, nationally, and religiously, and to that was added the political camps, which were split between right wingers and left wingers that aligned with and the upper and lower classes, the religious and seculars, and formed monolithic cultural and political camps. The melting pot failed. Baruch Kimmerling described these divides as showing the hegemonic ruling class in Israel as a composition of Jewish, Ashkenazi, secular, male, left-winger, and bourgeois (Kimmerling, 2001).

The end of Mapay's historical foundation era brought Begin to the forefront of the political arena along with many deprived and excluded groups that revealed the bitter failure of the Zionist ethos and of theirs too. The phony democratic image of the Israeli society seen from the economic and national reflections of inequality and social gaps surfaced and became a component was necessary in order to study the Israeli sociology, politics, and culture, and to delve into critic analysis of the pitfalls, not just a documentation of facts. The privatization process moved to the more aggressive legislation and allowed relocations of factories and entire industrial branches to third-world countries. Part of the peace agreement with Egypt since 1979 was an opening of new economic opportunities and the globalization for Israeli entrepreneurs to relocate to low-tech factories in Egypt starting in the mid-1980s. In the late 1990s, when peace was signed with Jordan too, the process was accelerated, first to countries in the Middle East, then to the Far-East countries, such as China, Singapore, and South Korea. It served political interests of Israel in the regions at the cost of severing the process of unemployment and making the already feeble social sectors at home even poorer. Capitalization and Israel's aim to enter the Organisation for Economic Co-operation and Development (OECD) forced policy-makers to legislate laws for hiring foreign workers and lowering wages for heavy-duty manual labor. Unemployed Israeli citizens preferred to receive welfare allowances, as little as they were, then to earn the same amount of money for manual jobs, as the foreign workers did. The employment option for foreigners was valid for a limited term with almost no welfare conditions and social rights protection. At the beginning of the 1990s, the Knesset (the Israeli parliament) passed laws allowing foreign workers to enter Israel and be hired for periods of no more than five years. This allowed thousands of foreign workers to flow into the country, especially from China, Thailand, the Philippines, and Romania. The system promoted the economic gaps between the non-professional workers and the economic elites. Two labor classes were constructed: those who were protected by the old laws and had secure jobs, and the new labor force, which from that legislation period worked on contracts that allowed firing workers on the spot without any compensation or other social rights whatsoever. The first to be hit were the weak sectors consisting of elders, the disabled, and single mothers. Children of larger families moved up on the social scale under the poverty line. The poverty rate went up, and ironically, but according to strict principles of neoliberalism, the economy, in general, and the gross national product (GNP) began to increase. The prosperity of the national economy left the workers without any tool for defending their rights, not even allowing them to strike, as the private sector was not regulated by labor rights laws and any striking group could be fired on the spot, with foreign workers being hired as replacements. The state went through welfare regression, and the union and the right to organize was prevented. The welfare state was making its last dying steps, completing the process that started in the 1980s. The era of Mapay Party exclusion and discrimination of various groups in Israel had ended indeed, but its legacy was already running through the state's systems and institutions. As for the kibbutzim, there was a drill during the Mapay era in which they received financial aid and loans from the banks when they needed, and occasionally, these were dismissed from their debts under governmental recommendations and treasury ministry decisions. After the turnover and Begin's reign, this drill stopped, and many of the kibbutzim fell into a severe economic crisis for the first time. With the globalization process, their situation worsened; the young generation left the kibbutz in growing numbers, and a few of them bankrupted as the collectivist ideology and materialistic modesty that was the heart of the kibbutz's ideology came to an end. It would take another decade until the kibbutzim realized they had to move to capitalism and privatization and to discard communist collectivism and socialist ideology. That was now happening gradually. Along with the economic decline, one would expect that the kibbutzim hegemony would also decline, but it seems that to be a kibbutznik remained prestigious. The fact that they consisted mainly of people who were Jewish, Ashkenazi, left-wing, better-educated, and secular, as Kimmerling suggested, their habits protected them and preserved their status. As opposed to this sector, those who lived in the other geo-social margins—the development towns—were hit hardest by the neo-capitalist economic policy, being thrown into the street and having nowhere to go if they missed paying even one month of rent or mortgage. In most cases, they were either Mizrahim or immigrants from the former USSR or Ethiopia. A growing number of foreign workers would join them less than a decade later in 2000. The development towns consisting mostly of these sectors were populated with relatively larger families that were mostly traditional and religious Jews, second and third generation, poorly educated, and, oftentimes, right-wingers or religious party electorates that were blamed for lagging behind. With this socioeconomic profile, they were clearly distinct from the dominating elite, which consisted of second- and third-generation Ashkenazim who lived mainly in the larger cities and better-off neighborhoods.

WOMEN, FEMINISTS, ISRAEL

The competitions went wild; blue- and grey-collar worker dismissals escalated; low-tech industry and light-mechanic industries transferred to third world countries. Agriculture and farming moved to high-tech systems and mechanization and also dismissed workers that were then replaced by automatic machines. This acceleration down the slippery slope, specifically in industries, afflicted women in massively growing numbers. In the late 1960s, women were 45 percent of the market labor force and were, systematically, the first to be fired. Despite the feminist struggles that arrived in Israel at the beginning of the 1970s, women were almost absent from decision-making positions let alone economic decision-making, and their percentage in the labor market did not grow significantly. Most women had to accept part-time jobs since child-care provider solutions were hardly provided. While in two-parent family structures women's wage were considered secondary, the same was considered as primary for single-parent families, mainly consisting of women.

The feminist movement in Israel that started early in 1970 was founded by new immigrants from the United States together with upper-class women of Ashkenazi origin. The social structure inspired the feminist agenda with issues that interested young, well-off women with higher education. The few women of Mizrahi origin who tried to enter this activity reported that they felt alienated. Even the language spoken amongst the feminists was English and not Hebrew—a language often used by Anglo-Saxon immigrants, who were well-off and well-educated. The first and main issues in those years concentrated on an agenda that looked very much similar to the liberal agenda in the United States. The feminists strived to put an end to women's dependence on public committees for the right to abortion, called to end beauty pageant contests, struggled for sex preferences, called for equal wages for upper-middle-class positions and political representation. In the eyes of the Israeli women, all lower-middle-class women, this agenda was very odd. Considering that the women in these sectors came from traditional and religious legacies that preached to large families according to Jewish laws, the struggle for the right for abortion went in the opposite direction and kept many of the Mizrahi women away from the feminist organizations. In addition, working in heavy-duty jobs with hardly an elementary education, the idea of political representation and election of women to public companies' directors was fantastical and remote. Career and sex preference may have been important, but they were so far behind the list of these women's priorities when everyday survival and providing for the families extracted all their energies. No wonder they did not communicate with the feminist activists; the feminist activists did not make an effort to understand them. Like in the United States and Europe, the crisis that would finally cause the splits in the feminist movements between black, Hispanic, and Asian immigrant groups was yet to occur in the 1990s in Israel.

In the meantime, the wages gaps remained valid to women of different classes. In the late 1980s, in a distance of eight meters from the Bedouin unrecognized village of Abu-Caff and a well-off suburb of Omer, there was the largest gap of income between women in Israel (i.e., poverty and abundance lived next to each other without dissonance). The women in Omer earned the top income while the women in Abu-Caff earned the lowest (Svirski, 1987). Signs of growing rates of bankruptcy marked new trends of growing investments in risk venture capital funds. Small businesses and industrial factories merged by the investors and new opportunities opened for capital markets opportunists but hardly provided anything for the feeble classes. Various heavy-duty, low-tech industries fired women employees and reduced their production volume; paradoxically, the Israeli economy showed only signs of growth. This has happened as the decision-makers pended the local market to international competition, which lowered some of the prices and injected power to the consumer market at the expense of smaller factories and industries. The state removed subsidies and protecting taxes from imported production and small manufacture businesses where the majority of the employees were traditionally women closed down their businesses. Once again, lower classes of women were the first to pay the price of the economic changes. Single mothers who had jobs and constantly lived on the verge of poverty were now below the line.

SINGLE MOTHERS

After the fall of the Berlin Wall, a wave of one million immigrants from former USSR came to Israel. As a result, the Israeli population grew by a factor of more than one-sixth. A large number among them were single mothers. This was a significant group that required the government's attention. The women had to cope both with the difficulties every immigrant would normally face as well as being tasked as the lone breadwinners for their families. Problems of housing, income, education for children, occupation, language, and cultural misfit pushed many of them over the poverty line, although the right of return for Jewish immigrants granted them with some support in the first five years. The women took every job offer they could. The immigrants extended Israel's labor force along the entire scale of occupations, be they academic, white-collar, blue-collar, or grey-collar. The national economic policy began to improve in large steps towards globalization by the labor force the immigrants made. The Shekel—the Israeli coin—immensely strengthened. Israel, for the first time, made agreements that allowed its stock market to enter the US stock commercial with the Yankee bond. All these changes came along with talks for peace with the Palestinians, and a new spirit blew into the region. It entailed new investment agreements, mainly in the Israeli industries of security, chemicals, pharmacology, and high-tech. The Israeli economy was now accepted into the strong European markets as a candidate for the prestigious OECD club. However, there were two problems: first, the gap between the local and the global consumption force as the population's household was not strong and large enough to contain all the changes. The state provided mortgages, but the state's capital revenue was still in difficulties. The state was required to stop subsidizing the lagging small industries, which began anew to fire growing numbers of employees. The other problem was the security situation with regard to the Israeli-Palestinian conflict. While Oslo talks continued and investments were on the line of contract-making, the Israeli entrepreneurs began to mobilize trading at an accelerated speed. The case of the textile industry illustrates how cruel the globalizing policy could be inspired for the hopes for peace winds blowing in. The private entrepreneurs fired their employees in Israel and searched for a cheaper labor force abroad in third-world countries but also opened the gates for Palestinian workers, masons, and service works in Israel. The state encouraged this attitude by subsidizing the entrepreneurs who wanted to move to countries where no social welfare conditions prevailed and loosened the control over the entrepreneurs who didn't follow welfare laws. More factories moved to India, Thailand, and China. In combination with the peace process, Israel enhanced its economic relationship both with Jordan and Egypt by moving more of the textile factories to those countries. The Israel-Turkey relationship warmed up and was reflected in more factories pushing the prosperity of Turkey one step forward. The owners of all these factories where investors of risk venture capital funds who took on textile experts as advisors. In other words, capitalization was the name of the game, not textile production. "Delta," "Sabrina," "Gibor," "Kitan," "Bagir"—these were prestigious logos since the 1950s in Israel, which were located on the periphery and provided employment options to the lower-middle-class populations for decades but moved to other countries living behind growing unemployment problems. As mentioned, the number of women, single mothers amongst them, was large. In the globalization spirit, one could ironically argue that the lives of Turkish, Jordanian, Egyptian, and Chinese women employee's, also single mothers, were now tremendously improved. The International Labor Organization, the International Monetary

Fund, and the World Bank could now use these facts and data to prove how great the globalization and OECD policies were. However, the ethical problem of strengthening one group at the expense of the other remained unsolved.

Chapter Five

A Woman Employee in the Textile Factory

This chapter comes in addition to the rich field of feminist studies about women who contest norms of submission to uncompromising demands to obedience of women as workers. The chapter puts a magnifying lens on one woman, one employee in a textile factory, Havatzelet Ingbar, to explore what the global economic trends did to her. I shall enter questions of emotions, consciousness, and even subconscious in certain aspects. Her personal life and interrelations with the people surrounding her, family, colleagues and subordinators will be explored. I shall explore how political institutions and sociocultural authorities affected her world and her views, how she survived under years of economic uncertainty, and how she and her fellow employees dared, at a certain point in time, to buffer long years of oppression and transformed the decision to close a factory, which was, for her, the only way to make a living in the small town of Mitzpe Ramon, where she lived with her family. In search of stories of women resistance, I was motivated by the puzzle that I unfolded: Why do women accept cruel subordination for long periods of their lives, and in the few cases that women show fractious and resistance, what is the material of rebel it is made of?

One of the globalization effects on working women is that many of them became slaves in a modern version. Economic exploitation is essentially oppressive, as Louis Althusser explains (Althusser, 2003, 36). Only when women make steps toward resistance are there chances that the modern slavery mechanics of subordination become revealed. The vicious mechanics of subordination target the reaction to the heart of potential resistance. It identifies the resisting woman and makes her look like it is a problem that pertains to her as an individual. In the early days, such rebels Were tackled with isolating forces and signified the rebel woman as deranged. Enslavement was allegedly abolished, and economic exploitation is perceived as non-identical with enslavement. In the "sweatshops" similar to the one involved in our story, new versions of enslavement were revealed as multifaceted. Women are subordinated not only mentally and physically but also politically, psychologically, culturally, and in gender and sexual respects. Their human existence as people is twisted along years of subordination, as are their emotions, senses, passions, consciousness, and world outlook. Under hard conditions of subordination in factories, working day in and day out, gritting their teeth with rage that cannot be expressed without risking losing their jobs, their soul is sealed off. A person's abilities for intimacy with oneself and with others are disrupted. This process does not stop at the factory threshold when the worker woman steps out and goes home. This is an overwhelming process that does not undress with the factory uniform and the evening shower. It stays with the woman worker when she is at home, in the marketplace, or at her children's school, and it influences her social interrelations. The irony is that this women's enslavement occurs simultaneously with the revolution that many have perceived as a success—the feminist revolution in the 1980s and 1990s. Historicization focused on success rather than on defeats and failure of feminism. The reconceptualization of what was a success is still defined through androcentric perceptions, according to the results achieved regardless of the processes of lessons learned along the way. This was the setting in which the resistance story of sixty-seven women occurred.

Sixty-seven women were enslaved in a small forgotten factory in the Negev desert in southern Israel. This small group of modern slaves in the small factory mobilized all their strength, targeting at to one thing: to cut off their heavy chains and defy the traditional oppression they were chained to. It was not a struggle of blood and fire, and neither was it planned ahead of time nor did it carry heroic slogans. It was a spontaneous burst that almost surprised the rebelling women themselves. It all began as a Cinderella story with suffering and humiliation followed by a seemingly happy end, consoling, and a victory of the weakened. It was an allegedly trivial story of long years of exploitation of women who got fed up with the extortion of their dead-end economic situations. They rebelled a moment before one of the many dismissals rounds when they were to go home. When looking deeper at the revolt details, different factors unfold, and question marks surface. What exactly had the weakened, enslaved women thought at the moment of the rebellion? How would they defeat a strong factory capitalist owner that truly believed that the women were granted with a job thanks to his generosity, for "if you don't like it, you may step out; there are dozens of Russian women waiting outside the door," as he more than once put it when the women made protesting sounds. As remote as they were from any center, they were aware of their scant abilities to violate the iron rules of global modern slavery, especially in third-world countries. Moreover, this story didn't take place in a third-world country but in Israel, seemingly the only democratic and modern country in the Middle East.

In the first of three rounds of interviews that I conducted for the study of this research, I met all of the women who worked in the factory at the time of the rebellion. Then I met the women leaders and interviewed and documented it all in field notebooks. I met, apart from Havatzelet Ingbar, also with Avigayle Yifrach, Larissa Vinogradov, Smadi Levi, Yaffa Kalimi, and Miriam Berzen. They were the leading figures at the time of the rebellion and the works who were the most outspoken. The first thing that stood out in the initial moments of resistance, as I noticed time and again when meeting each woman, was the power they had to amass in order to abstain from taking an action of resistance and for showing persistent submissiveness and obedience. They spent most of their waking hours in that factory. To keep the job, they had to retrain themselves, to learn to shut up and learn methods of maneuvering between the humiliating conditions and their dependence on the humiliator.

PEPCO, AN UNFULFILLED PROMISE

Michel Foucault clearly introduced power functions in prisons and madhouses, from which he generalized that power is the infrastructure of every relationship. If one wants to understand how the abstract notion of power and discipline works in human institutions and maintains authority as a central rule, she must go to the margins, to the areas where enforcement of the law and governability functions are done so with physical force and with violence. A law that stems from the rule of democracy is enforced in the end through the police and military through violence inflicted on the resisters. Violation is taken care on the margins of the society. On the periphery, far from governmental and legal eyes, physical enforcement of law and order do not hide or camouflage their use of violent methods (Power, 1978).

The Pepco textile factory was founded in Miztpe Ramon in 1972. Based on contracts and the consumption force, the factory employed between sixty and one hundred workers, of which 57 to 70 percent were women. The main production contracts came from the Israel Defense Forces (IDF), which ordered uniforms, and from hotels, which ordered linen and towels. More than 85 percent of the women occupied the production at sewing stations, which included dressmakers, ironing ladies, button machine operators, and women creating cufflinks, sleeves, tags makers, and packing. The little number of men who were employed in the factory held mainly positions in management, as shift directors, and as mechanic maintenance persons who took care of the building maintenance, the machines, and the operation of the production instruments.

In the mid-1980s, when the privatization process began, the future of the factory was often considered. The factory, right from the beginning, shuffled with the privatization process, but the option of moving it to other countries was never a serious consideration. However, the gender division of labor began to blur when the manager had to cut the number of the more expensive employees, which were mainly the men. Women began to replace men as shift directors and at the maintenance stations without a raise in their salaries to be on part with the men's wages. The women who worked at the same stations until the 1980s now moved from station to station and learned new skills for more than one production station. At times, the women moved in the same day from the secretary table to the dressmaking station and ironing ladies took the tasks of the production machines operation. Ten years after it was founded, the textile factory in Mitzpe Ramon entered a constant situation of "almost bankruptcy." During the fourteen years since the factory was founded, Moshe Partook, the owner, developed various methods of production power management and marketing and financial management. In hard times, he would take with him two women employees to meetings with potential buyers. The women workers' mission was to assist him in convincing the buyers to sign the contract. They had to describe the advantages of the factory. In the beginning, the women told the buyers how professional and precise the production was and how quality was the first priority. However, as the economic problems for the factory began, the owner instructed the women to not refrain even from begging for the contract and bring their personal stories up so that the buyer will be emotionally moved. The women were asked to describe their living difficulties and their poverty, to speak words of mercy, and even mention their little children. The women reported that they had no choice but to do that since the alternative, the owner explained, was for him to dismiss them for having no contract. To do that, the women had to overcome their feelings of humiliation. At the same time, being of marginal living in a remote town, these meetings gave them a rare opportunity to see how business and finance negotiations worked, even if in a distorted way. As lower-class employees and as women, they admitted that they were fascinated by the power relation to which they were exposed on these occasions. After a few times, the strategy of begging lost its effect; there were fewer contracts, and the production was reduced as debts grew larger for the factory. First were the suppliers of the raw material who did not receive their payments. Then the maintenance of the factory, such as the electricity, cleaning, and water bills, were neglected. In the next stage, the salaries to the employees were only paid weeks after due time. Then the salaries were paid in parts, with perhaps 75 percent of the payment given with the promise that within a week the rest will be delivered. The women who were involved in the factory problems and knew that the alternative was to go home with no job even showed empathy. They worried about their working place and carried on anyway with the knowledge that there was nothing they could do.

The manager began to beg for more subsidies from the government and the Histadrut, asking for loans in order to pay the workers and other debts. The loan fund of the Histadrut and the government required that the factory show that it is a profitable enterprise. The factory negotiators claimed that it would not have come for the loan had they not had debts and production difficulties not only of the Pepco factory, but also the entire textile branch. The situation deteriorated, and the women began to receive dismissal letters. Periodical renovation of nonfunctional facilities and equipment, such as sewing machine scissor irons, stopped, and everyday work became even harder than before in physical terms. The factory lagged behind deadlines for the small amount of orders they still received. Another round of dismissal letters reduced the already small number of workers to half of what it had been. The number of the potential buyers declined dramatically, the factory competitive force weakened, and some of the social and welfare rights of the workers were further cut. The women understood that their weak position and the factories economic problems could not be met even if they were taking active steps to demand their rightful payments. The factory was doomed to be closed. This sad picture of the factory dramatically increased the unemployment rate of the little town of Mitzpe Ramon. Other peripheral towns were similarly affected as globalization reached the most remote areas and poor places, just as in other areas of the world. The textile branch deteriorated, and unemployment rates increased everywhere. The Investment Center in the Ministry of Commerce and Industry streamed subsidies to the textile branch knowing there was little chance of seeing the loan returned. These growing subsidies, along with some contracts from the IDF, functioned as an artificial respiration as on the other hand the IDF was encouraged to begin to sign contracts with Israeli textile factories that had moved abroad—there the contracts where beneficial since the labor work was cheaper, hence the lower production costs. The economic insecurity of the women workers in Mitzpe Ramon exacerbated, and the future looked dark. However, the workers noticed that despite all these difficulties the owner continued "business as usual," but they couldn't explain it. He kept coming to the factory, drove the same expensive cars, and kept a standard of life that included holding an apartment in Tel Aviv—the highest and most expensive rent area—and doing all the same as he did for the last ten years despite the economic difficulties. In 1999, the factory was dying, and the cruel working conditions that the owner inflicted on the women worsened. There, in the remote small town far from the eyes of the authorities in the center of the country, the women were gripping with their nails to keep their jobs. Witnessing the fancy life of the owner and losing their wages by contrast, the women were trapped, as they couldn't afford to complain. The owner felt free to violate any labor rights he pleased. The CEO and the VCEO were always the owner's friends or relatives, regardless of their professional abilities. They also lived in Tel Aviv or in towns in the center. The women mentioned in their talks with me that there were occasions when the owner showed enthusiasm to the possibility that the factory would be closed. They suspected that insurance compensations would have been paid to him in such a case. During the years before 2000, he reduced the numbers of days a month that he arrived to the factory. Two of his brothers-in-law supervised the work of the factory. Yaffa Kalimi, one of the workers said:

> Partook [the owner, HDK] arrived here [the factory, HDK] once a month, only when the supervisor of [the] Ministry of Defence was coming. Otherwise, he has put here his two in-laws—one was the accountant and organizer of the workers' transportations, and the other functioned as the alleged manager. However, they did nothing [but] slept in the office. They treated us as workers from Gaza [exemplifying inhuman treatment, HDK]. We, the women, did all the work. (Sinai, Ha'Aretz, 25.6.2001)

Arriving in their fancy cars every morning to the peripheral factory or technological plant from Tel Aviv or any other center in the country (or coming from rich kibbutzim, as it happened later on) was a pattern for the white-collar workers, which was etched deeply in the labor market in Israel. Its economic effect was that the higher salaries were taken from the working place on the periphery and invested in the center towards better housing conditions, better public and private market services, welfare, and education for the younger generations. The gap between the center and peripheral population all over Israel was fabricated from these materials. The worse-off citizens had no chance to improve their living conditions as long as they were in the peripheral areas. It was a vicious circle for them, as they never had the chance to earn enough to live closer to the center. The capital, mobilized by the well-off salaries from the periphery to the center, left the poor stuck where they stood. Better housing, better welfare conditions, and better cultural opportunities moved from the desert to the north and made life in the center dynamic and prospering. Eventually, after years, the gaps became part of the social structure and divided the population as if it was two separate countries. Capital and investments generated the economy in the center even when the factories on the periphery did make some profit. This pattern caused the periodic dismissal of the workers and rehiring of them after periods of months of unemployment. Consequently, they could not enjoy the workers' welfare right of seniority and compensations and were rehired anew each time, losing their potential promotions and better payments. The capital flight and the repeated dismissal of the workers prevented from the women workers the force to organize, unionize, and elect representing committees that would stand up for their rights and talk to the manager, let alone seeing him and claim an explanation for violating the labor rights laws. There was in Mitzpe Ramon a small representative of the worker's committee. However, as the situation was so poor that they could not even organize a strike or protect themselves from dispute and arbitrary dismissal. The owner knew that the women would return to the station at the factory every time he would call upon them to come back since the alternative for them was to remain unemployed. At a certain point in 1999, the old equipment did not work anymore. Many of the scissors did not cut anymore, and the chairs in front of the sewing machines were unstable, and the workers had to balance their sitting positions. The stitches would come out deformed, the shift directors were not satisfied, and the atmosphere was tense. The workers' health was deteriorating as well. As Yaffa Kalimi remembers:

> …there were no windows in the factory; the air-conditioning didn't work. We brought ventilators from home, and each one of us placed it next to her machine. In the winter, we brought heaters.

Some of the machines were out of order for a while, and when there came along a buyer with a contract, the owner had difficulties in standing up to the deadlines. At a certain point, the women took the initiative and tried to mend the tools. They learned how to fix sewing machines, to fasten the chairs, and to sharpen the scissors. Miriam Fellus, one of the workers, said that she learned how to fix electricity problems. Rachel Barzan learned how to order row material and equipment. Later on, she learned how to take care of the payment of salaries. Yaffa Kalimi said, "In fact, for the last fourteen years, we [ran] the factory."

The physical conditions damaged many of the women's body. After so many years of technical defects and functioning problems, after long hours of sitting daily on old chairs and ragged furniture, the women learned how to stabilize their sitting positions, but in the end, it affected their bodies, and they started to feel pains in different areas of the body. Upper and lower backache and arthritis were common for all the women. After years of bad working conditions, their hands had deformed, formed bleeding blisters, and cuts had appeared on their hands. Their sight began to weaken in the unlighted halls, "and when we stepped out of the factory, the daylight dazzled us in the eyes" (Sinai, 2001). Ironically, what saved them was the fact that they were fired from time to time, and this enabled the women to recover from the pain and to loosen up their aching bodies until they were called again to the factory when a new buying order came in.

Brian Turner studied the connection between social necessity and physical situation and looked for the reasons that push the body to take action.

Social conditions are operated on the body and tell the body which turns matter. The body is the first to be pushed to the forefront when social conditions and existential necessity are operated on it (Turner, 1996; Turner 1995, 144; Heckenberger, 1995, 312–17). The bodies of the women workers, in this case, materialized this situation. The women knew and felt the pain in their bodies. The question that repeatedly flickered stubbornly in this reality was, "What is the limit that the subject can carry on physically and emotionally in such subordinating conditions without responding in some way?" If these conditions are not a major force and they result from other human beings treatments, when, if at all, would the subject upon whom these conditions are inflicted show resistance and refuse to carry on? Would this be a spontaneous rebelling reaction or planned revolt? After all, in this case, cruel treatment is committed by humans to each other. It is not a major force; it is not an epidemic, nor is it an earthquake. Moreover, at any minute, the subject on whom the cruel action is inflicted could stand up against the abusing person. The point is that this is a situation that originates from a human relationship, and the fact that it stems from these relationships means that it can be reformed and changed. I heard from Ingbar and her colleagues the reports on their working conditions and wondered: How much energy did they need in order to wake up every morning and go to the factory, enforcing themselves to self discipline for long hours under dehumanizing conditions? How much power did they have to recruit to restrain themselves from bursting out, reacting to the humiliations they experienced, to survive the suffering, and stay in the factory when they could simply walk away? I discussed these issues with Ingbar and her colleagues in the factory. The women lived within a cobweb that the factory was only one thread that was interwoven with other threads that they were chained to their daily commitments. Schools and children, family duties, household and bill payments, elder parent care, and many other lines in the web that tied them to enslavement labor conditions would refrain them from abandoning it all. They invested their energies in self-discipline and were interdependent so that if the debts are not paid or the children did not go to school on time, the cobweb could breakdown on them, and sometimes, it did.

Moshe Partook, the factory owner, was an owner that could only be described as a heartless person who tyrannized his workers, especially the women workers. He exploited them economically, but the ways he physically and mentally treated the workers made it unbearable to conceive: "The most depressing were the working conditions…it was like entering a women's prison every day," said Yaffa Kalimi. These women had to lean down over the sewing machines, eight to nine hours a day, sometimes two shifts in row for a total of sixteen hours, with only two breaks of fifteen minutes in the morning and at lunch: "Exactly the time to wash your hands, eat the sandwich that I brought from home, and have a few words with my friends. On the fifteenth minute of the break, the manager used to knock strongly on the door of the dining room and scream 'Yallah, Yallah, get back to work.'" In 2001, the workers earned 15 shekels and 90 agorot for an hour of work. This was the minimum payment allowed according to the law. They also received payment for two weeks a year for vacation (Sinai, 2001).

Rachel Barzan, the person who filled the role of a secretary and did clerk work, said:

> He didn't know us by our names . . . Partook knew us by the number of the station [that] was on the production line: for example, ironing was14, callings 23 . . . when I called to remind him that it was time to make an order of raw material or cleaning stuff, I had to tell him, "It is Rachel speaking; Rachel the clerk."

Havatzelet Ingbar added:

> Even coffee he did not provide; we bought it from home and organized the coffee corner . . . if we stayed home on the cases that the children were ill, he called and threatened us that he [would] fire us.

How could women be treated as if they had no identity? What happens to their souls and bodies when referred to as figures that mark their production station only? What echoed in their chalked minds when the owner's voice hit them? How much power did they have to invest in overcoming these traumatic conditions? They told me that, over time, they felt they wanted to raise their voices and protest but heard inside their heads the owner's voice echoing the regular phrase: "If you don't like it, you may go; there are dozens of Russian women waiting on the threshold to replace you." The submissive workers, restrained and disciplined, made their voices heard only when they were alone. However, this didn't lead them to be organized or deciding to express their complaints about the humiliations and the terrifying threats the owner poured on them. The most sacred thing was to keep the living source as long as the buyers' contracts streamed to the factory. This was a powerful valve that kept their raging mental steam from bursting out. They all behaved without exception, no matter how different they each were in character. When one of them showed loosened nerves and spoke of telling the owner what she thought of him and to resign, her friends did all they could to calm her down and have her surrender to the forced conditions in which they were trapped, just to prevent her from making something she couldn't reverse, which was to lose the only job she could have where she was living in Mitzpe Ramon. The women empowered each other in the direction of keeping their jobs rather than protecting their human dignity, and these two things didn't consist together. In the situation they found themselves, dignity and employment contradicted each other in a zero-sum game, and what seemed similar to surrender was one more day of keeping their job, which was in itself a victory. There was no verb in Hebrew for the description of a characteristic such as self-surrender, but the women invented one—*hitcanut.*

Some of the workers lived in neighborhood development towns in the Negev, outside of Mitzpe Ramon, in places such as Dimona and Yeruham, which are about thirty to forty minutes travel from the factory. These towns also suffered from problems of scarce employment and from poverty.

> We would gather and go out in the morning from Dimona or Yeruham in the transportation bus early in the morning, when the kids were still sleeping, and wake them up [using a] mobile phone. Then we would give them instructions to get up, go to wash their faces and brush their teeth, and dress and take the sandwiches that we prepared for them the night before, then call again to make sure that they were on their way to school, enter the class . . . ill children, too, [were] left alone at home and got instructions [on] how to take medicines [over] the phone.

The women did that for fourteen years, all for a failing textile enterprise and insecure job in which they were dismissed a few times a year if buyers did not make orders. Oftentimes, the owner organized the production program in double-shifts so that the workers would finish the production quota in shorter periods of time, which allowed him to save money on double salaries. The workers believed that the double-shift plan was for deadline reasons until they realized that the owner simply wanted to save the money on the labor force by doubling the shifts and cut down the numbers of production days; he often earned almost double the profits, as they realized in one instance.

Being a worker is an existential matter. It contains images of the self and a viewpoint of the world, altogether. There are ways that the woman worker perceives herself, is perceived by other male and female workers, and is part of the working corpus in the development town, all while on the verge of the year 2000. These existential contexts were very far from the ethos of the worker's history, as briefly described previously. It was for the workers in Mitzpe Ramon an internalized and animated picture through which the workers understood the world in long years of subordinating socialization. They developed self-reflections not just of workers but of oppressed women and not just within the factory but as oppressed subjects. Their lives, thoughts, actions, and relations were all painted with oppression experiences. Their images as oppressed workers leaked out to their other roles and images of being as mothers, married or single, daughters and sisters, and some of them were even grandmothers. Subordination construct overwhelms all possible images the women could develop. In the children's schools, the municipality and establishment bureaus, the grocery and the supermarket, and the reflections that looked back on them all identified the subordination from their face and body postures, their feelings, and their minds—they seemed defeated and precarious. Eventually, the daily encounters with people around them seemed to replicate the subordination only by a responding gaze. The bank or the health services or any other site they walked into embraced them with an expectation that they be the same docile, submissive person, being devoted and silently conforming to any demand. Moreover, they responded to that as expected; they were nice and submissive. The remoteness of the small town, its constant high rate of unemployment and the personal poverty that most of the population suffered from were complementary to each other. Most of the population was of Middle Eastern origin or from the southern part of the former USSR, and in a sense, their affiliation was with the Middle East rather than with the Western ambiance of Israel. This was the image of a marginalized population that lost confidence in itself and had hardly developed beliefs and hopes for their children.

After the women finished a shift or two in the factory, they would go home to begin a "second shift" of household tasks that their family-life required. Sometimes this shift was no less demanding than the first, as the couple relationship was open to ups and downs, usually always around economic stress. On the extremes, violence was occasionally inflicted on the women. The scarcity of elementary food supplies and the daily search for ways to respond to new demands that the children brought from the school teachers made the women have to think creatively. The women ran around, moving from one thing to another, left with nothing and no time to themselves. Hardly having the chance to rest or stop and reflect on their lives, or ventilate the anxieties or intimately discuss them with a close soul, they sought ways out of the burden. In general, their social, gender, cultural, or political relationships were framed within their being first and foremost textile workers at a factory. They fulfilled their duties as mothers, spouses, grandmothers, or in-laws through their functions as workers, be that in a silent and docile way.

FIRST CRACKS AND RESISTANCE SIGNS

In the little factory of Mitzpe Ramon, a worker's committee was elected to represent their interests when negotiating with the owner. This committee functioned since 1994, led by Havatzelet Ingbar. As a worker's representative, her main tasks were to negotiate the working conditions with the manager and improve as much as possible the physical conditions while staying in the factory hall. Occasionally, she mediated between the manager and one of the workers to resolve a conflict. The communication between the worker's committee and the textile branch council, which represented all the textile workers in the Histadrut, was minimal, and later on, it was found to be manipulative, as Ingbar described it. On an occasion about eight months before, a big dispute burst out when the workers demanded, for the first time, to sign a working agreement. After many years of employment without any written agreement and repeated dismissal, the women dared demand what seemed to be a basic legal right of labor, to sign a working contract, but it was never asked before. They made it conditional to their returning to the workstations. The manager, who knew all the time that working without a contract is illegal and that the women meant it this time to insist on the demand, agreed in order to prevent negative publicity. The effect of signing the contract was much beyond the act itself. This demand was a first sign of the women breaking their silence and symbolized their attempt to shake the balance of power. They included in the contract minor changes, such as: "…a present to the workers before holidays; a premium for production that surplus the quota and a seniority increment." This was in 1999, after long years of unclear or rather pirate working conditions. The feeling, Ingbar recalled, was empowering; they felt that they broke the ice. For the first time, they could believe that there was a hope to change something. The significance of this event was rooted in the event itself, in the experience of making their voice heard and forcing the other side to respond. Their agency began to roll.

Dani Chetrit, the council secretary of the Histadrut in the Mitzpe Ramon office, was supposed to represent the interests of the workers, their working rights, and the laws of labor enforcement when negotiating with the employer on behalf of the women. His salary was paid by the Histadrut, so he wouldn't be dependent on the employer. He was the representative of the textile branch in the factory, so his loyalty would be given to the labor union only. However, since he was far from the central bureau located in Tel Aviv and closer to the workers and the owner on the periphery, each time there was a conflict between the workers and the owner, Chetrit could play the arbitrator's role and be the go-between for the parties. This gave him an enormous amount of power considering the disempowered workers. There was also a gender factor, since he was a man who represented a majority of women workers. This added to the symbolic powerful position of a man who was placed there "to protect women," and as we shall see, he made the best out of it for his own interests.

The Histadrut in the late 1990s lost much of its power and was much less committed to the initial ideology of protecting the workers' interests. It became one of the sides in the economic national triangle of the government, the private sector, and the worker's labor organization; in fact, it was a political arm in the grand politics rather than the ideological organization of the workers. It embraced the globalization economic policy and often neglected the weak workers sector. Through the years, the Histadrut became independent and powerful, and it was still identified with the old ruling party of Mapay. To protect its power in the triangle balance, the Histadrut occasionally sacrificed workers interests, allegedly in the name of the interests of the national economy. The workers in smaller and weaker enterprises and factories all over the country became the bargaining chip that the Hustadrut played with and often compromised for. The paradoxical result was that the Histadrut became stronger while the workers' interests grew weaker. Chetrit was part of this matrix; he understood the power constellation in the spirit of the Histadrut, but as we shall see, he never shared his insights regarding power games with the women at the factory. In a sense, Chetrit chose to be the Histadrut delegate to the factory rather than the workers representative in the Histadrut. His interest, as he often presented it, was the factory as a working place; the important thing was the fact that workers come and go as long as the production continued. It was, after all, the place where he made his own living, and he had to play according to his best interests. It was useful for him, however, to convince the workers that it was worth firing some of the workers rather than bringing the factory to a final closure, even when he already knew that the closing was a matter of time. He waited for the Mitzpe Ramon factory to close down, but in the meantime, Chetrit enjoyed the Histadrut and the governmental subsidies.

In 1999, globalization progressed safely closing small industries and failing branches remaining with strong industries and branches in high-tech, transportation, communication, heavy technology, infrastructure, and capital and financial firms, such as insurance companies, bank and stock managers, the telecommunication companies including television and broadcasting unions, the national water company, electricity company, the airports and the harbor, which included two ports unions, the warfare industry company, including the air force industry, the Dead Sea national resources chemicals industry, the teachers, and the nurses. These branches were in the midst of the privatization process, some of them in private entrepreneurship, with others still in the state's hands but going towards privatization. This fact made an impact on the manner of the struggle of the labor unions and the power relations in the globalization era.

The government supported these trends because it was invested in them or had national commitment to the public service. Moreover, through the strong industrial and financial concerns, it secured the pension allowances. Therefore, they were very much invested within these corporations. Most of them were founded in the pre-State or early State era by the founding fathers, which originated from the Mapay Party. Strikes that embraced the entire countries economy now were hooped by collective labor agreements, which required opening the agreements anew and negotiating all over again. This negotiation over articles involved in the collective agreements risks that the powerful unions wanted to avoid. Since a strike in favor of the women in the Mitzpe Ramon factory meant one more step towards the unavoidable collapse of the textile branch, supporting the women's struggle, as the Histadrut considered it, was out of the question. At this point of time in the history of the labor union in Israel, it was clear that worker's solidarity did not play any significant role among the worker's unions, and the weak sectors of workers were sacrificed for the stronger unions. Most of all, the strong unions were blind to women workers since collective agreements were sacrificed at the expense of solidarity. Keeping the triangle balanced and stability became the name of the game. Dani Chetrit, having no authority whatsoever with regard to the thirteen strong labor unions in the Histadrut, had no choice but to cooperate with them. Moreover, on the rare occasions when he took the initiative, his position came out almost misogynistic. Chetrit seemed to enjoy playing the political game and being involved in public affairs. He learned the Histdrut's establishment maze of power and the complexities that the women had no clue of. When the rebellion began, his loyalty was put to the test, and as we shall see, he was hesitant with regard to the women's interests.

Under these circumstances, loyalty to the workplace was far from being achieved, and solidarity became an archaic, Zionist myth. To be a woman worker in Israel was now to work and live under constant economic scarcity conditions with a minimum wage of 3,000 NIS (Israeli new shekel) a month or 24 to 30 NIS an hour. Along with that, only one social right was granted: a yearly recuperation pay. The families were always in a struggle to cut down on expenses. According to the welfare laws in Israel, a worker who earned below the minimum wage was entitled to complementary payment up to the minimum wage paid by the national security authorities. This was offered as an alternative to unemployment and was aimed at the encouragement to take any job offered to the unemployed. Many employees preferred this option over the unemployment alternative, understanding that work was not just about money but also about self-commitment and dignity. There were also many others who got desperate of working and still remained below the poverty line. They reconsidered wage security from the government rather than working income. This was an easy solution for the government to secure the working backbone of the national economy without breaking the delicate triangle balance. All the actors of the triangle were satisfied as the weak party—the workers—kept silent.

SILENCING AND THE POWER TO EARN MONEY

The concept of silencing is discussed in feminist discourse mainly with regard to the postcolonial discourse and conditions of women in the third world and amongst immigrants entering the Western world. As discussed in Chapter 1, women developed practices of expressing their opinions and emotions in various forms of silent communication, as their voices were silenced. I brought up this idea when I spoke with Havatzelet Ingbar and wanted to hear her opinion about women's silence, especially because I kept asking her why did it take her and her colleagues so long to express their resistance. She smiled and said nothing. We both burst out laughing half a second later, realizing that she affirmed their silence as a default by saying nothing. She agreed that women of non-Western countries relate to silence and to making their voice heard differently than women of Western cultures. Pierre Macherey discussed the issue of silence in the Western world more generally as interpreting the cultural role of silence in the West (Macherey, 1978). Ingbar and I went on discussing the experiences of female silence and types of silence, as she elaborated, as including: choked silence, burning silence, choked cry, painful silence, and raged silence. She said:

> What we needed here was that we make special efforts in order to think differently, to make an effort to think little, to repress our dreams, to control our rage. [These are, HDK] sentiments of living through injustice and wrong-doing [of the other, HDK], to think hard that you mustn't respond [to] the employer when he scolded you, even if you would like to slap him on the face, you must shut up. (First interview with Havatzelet Ingbar in the conference on Society and Welfare, Sapir college, 2005. In following extracts, this will be cited as "first interview")

Even though the women workers were not part of a socialist movement and were not decedents of the Zionist founding fathers who were hardly exposed to the labor ethos or history, they were well-aware of labor surplus value. The power to earn money constructed their identity as women workers, in their case beyond and despite of the daily dose of humiliation they were getting in the workplace. Their mission was "to preserve their sanity," as Ingbar once said, to work on their self-discipline, to concentrate on how to hold their body against the sewing machine and their soul against the bosses insults; not to lose it, but to keep silent. For Ingbar, it was meant to preserve her humanness, as she has put it. The interesting thing was that she believed that she must keep all her energy in resisting herself, of going against her desire to break the silence, to say what she thought of the boss and the entire situation. She had to swallow her pride within herself and to bite her tongue and carry on leaning over the sewing machine.

This confession from Ingbar and other workers at the factory shed light on the silent experience that becomes political in a sense. It consists of the power to earn money in the era of modern slavery. The abstract economic analysis and neo-capitalism become concrete and substantial. The human element of the labor market is producing without making a sound. Human powers of emotions, desires, and opinions regarding the person that holds the workers fate in his hands are forcefully repressed. These workers return a gaze to the oppressor but say nothing. The oppression expends the space that exists in-between the mental state of the worker and the social position where she stands as a worker, or should it be as a cog in a factory machine, as part of the production forces in the labor market. She is a real being that embodies an existential entity, not just a labor force that, after long years of exploitation, is distorted, her body and soul ready to deposit the most precious thing, her humanity, in the hands of an employer, and for nothing more than scant pay.

I inquired about the topic of false consciousness, debating the topic first with myself and then with the workers. My questions were: To what extent were these women motivated by false consciousness? Are they blind to the exploitation and oppression? If not, what makes them wake every morning and rush to the factory, to meet their boss and obey his orders? It must have been their self-respect, their sense of value, their feeling of worth when having a job as opposed to when they are fired and have nothing to wake up for every morning. This is apart from simply accepting the allowance paid by the national insurance for the unemployed. The women understood that as poor as the workplace was, coming back home after a working day was the reason why they kept returning every morning to the factory. There was nothing that could replace the feeling of self-esteem, as Ingbar once put it. It felt as if they paid for this feeling of self-esteem, that it was something they purchased in the factory. Ingbar remarked:

> You learn how to love the workplace with all your might. You learn how to organize and how to plan your body motion so that you will reach the maximal quota of collars to the shirts. You make only the necessary gestures to be efficient, economically effective, and, when ironing, you learn how to straighten up the fabric in one slide so that your body won't twist too much, and still you don't reduce the capacity so that you don't miss the premium. The premium we got made our salary over the [minimum] wage, otherwise we had to apply for complementary payment at the national insurance bureau; and besides, who had the time for that in between the home and family and the factory? (first interview)

The woman, Havatzelet Ingbar, who was reified by the factory owner, became a cog, faceless and identity-less, and who had a stormy life, which above all demanded her to struggled to keep her self-image as human and sane.

The women desiccated their frustration by choosing optimism. However, I kept being troubled with the urge to understand where did all the anger, pain, and frustration, which I would have had if I had experienced their life conditions, get pushed. Where did the experience and perhaps the urge to respond to the suffering and humiliation go? Did it evaporate? Was it gathered? How strong could be the sense of self-esteem and self-control? Did the women stand it again and again despite the fact that it was etched on their souls and twisted into their lives? The myth of Sisyphus comes up to my mind time and again. The woman "pushed the stone," almost literally, every morning or every term of employment up to "the peak of the mountain" knowing that it would slip back down the slippery slope of dismissal. They couldn't plan the future or promise a change to their families. However, this is what these women workers kept doing—pushing up again and again and taking each day on its own.

THE STORY OF THE REBEL

Havatzelet Ingbar was born in India in 1958 and came with her family to Israel when she was three years old. She grew up in the neighboring development town of Dimona, married, had two children, and divorced. She came to Mitzpe Ramon in 1980 with her two small children, and when she first began to work in the factory, she did so for five years until her first dismissal. "[Those] were the last five good years in the Peppco Factory in Mitzpe and the textile branch," she said.

> When I first came to the factory, I didn't know how to thread a needle…when the factory closed for the first time, I had a diploma of a seamstress. (The second interview with Havatzelet Ingbar in 2006; in following extracts, this will be cited as "second interview.")

Ingbar taught herself fabric cutting and fashion design in an autodidact way and learned all the production stages, passing easily from one station in the factory to the other. She learned how to operate the machines and provide maintenance on the tools, the sewing machines, the ironing table, and the big machines that operated the production line after the cutting and design stages. She bitterly commented: "Only when I finally became a professional seamstress was I fired." When rehired, she started all over again at the basic stations, unable to negotiate her ability to start from the more progressive professional stations. "I never took relief allowance, never applied to the National Insurance Bureau for complementary payment" (second interview). Her voice divulged her pride, although for her, being a factory worker was not a glorified myth of a tragic heroine but simply existential being. All that was known of the textile history and the textile market, from its glorious days to the present dying time, folded within it the unique material from which the coming rebellion was made of. This was what made the allegedly negligible struggle of a small group of workers at a remote textile factory worth studying. All they wanted was to improve their employment conditions; at least, this is what they thought they were doing when they first stepped into revolting action. The only thing they wanted was to not be fired every time buyers did not send merchandise orders, or at least to have the owner's promise that they will be the first to be hired in the next round. Even when they knew that even if they will not receive any seniority promotions and were going to be fired without compensations, they still had to excel to be rehired in the next one. This kept their hopes alive even in the unemployment intervals.

Working in the textile factory formed the women's social identity just as it did their personalities: personalities as mothers and wives and as Israelis and even as Mizrahi. I discussed with Ingbar the topic of Mizrahi origin. She explained that she developed self-discipline and behaved according to concretization norms, which she needed for what she termed as "the real life," and she was well aware that this was only one part of what could be "the real life." She and the other workers reflected very little on their identity as women of Arab and Muslim countries of origin who lived in Israel—a very Westernized country. Ideology and conceptualization of their practices remained outside their daily being and critic of their situation. "Who am I, what does it mean that I am an Israeli citizen, a worker, a Mizrahi?" these were questions for academics, for journalists, for politicians, and for the people in the center of the country, not here in the periphery where surviving was the first, and often only, priority. This was what stood between existential life of the workers and its manifestation in worker's ideological programs, which could mirror the sense of "being a worker," the sense of "being a working woman," the sense of "being a working mother," even perhaps leading to a worker's agenda. Did they live in a false consciousness, or did they ever give it any thought? The idea was strange to them, and when asked about it, it seemed to not trouble them. I thought that there existed a separation between ideology and its practical apparatus, the way Althusser defined it as previously discussed (Althusser, 2003). Subjects, as Adi Ofir suggested, play the role of being part of the political apparatus, yet they are not familiar with its consciousness dimensions (Ofir, 2015). What occupied the women's minds was the question of what they would bring home to put on the table the next day. What would the children have in their sandwiches? Would they manage to pay the electricity bill the next month? Eventually, these were the problems that occupied their consciousness, and they had no mental space to move on to their abstraction and intellectual formulation. However, it seems that they were "cooking in," as they finally ignited a revolt. Another question was the question of time. When and why did the revolt ignite after fourteen years and not before? Why not after? Why in Mitzpe Ramon, and not in similar textile factories in Ma'alot, yet another textile factory in a development town in the north of the country that suffered from very similar conditions? I raised these questions after all the events were over—a fait accompli. When the events were over, and Ingbar swung between being a worker and a person who experienced political resistance and consciousness transformation as a woman worker, she realized how the entire subordinating system to the last details operated. Once this process began, the burst of revolt rapidly came in.

THE BURST OUT OF THE REVOLT

It was one of those times when the women were going to receive another round of dismissal letters. There was something else this time that made it different, though. Just before the month of July, they received dismissal letters, but this time "the dismissals were final," as the boss had put it. It meant that the factory was not going to be reopened, and the women would not be rehired again. The woman didn't get to enjoy the fruits of the agreement that they signed just eight months earlier. The regular work schedule organized in two shifts for each worker, knowing that they would have to complete the production in a decline of six months, but incidentally, Havatzelet Ingbar overheard that there was no commitment on a fixed date, so the double-shift arrangement was not necessary:

> In a conversation I had with Israel Gam, the CEO of the textile and clothing department in the Ministry of Defence, I realized that we were [being] exploited. I realized that we had to produce the quota in six months because the owner thought he could save money, not because the Ministry of Defence demanded it. We were forced to work in shifts and earn less money, work six months, and be dismissed again. The labor union committee, led by Dani Chetrit, did not bother to inform us and took the owner's side [as usual, HDK] for the last eight years . . . time when I heard about this manipulation, I came to my colleagues, and we decided to complete the production but to not allow the boss taking the merchandise on time until they find a solution, either in the Sewing Workshop [this was the term Ingbar referred when talking about the factory, HDK] or elsewhere, after all these years of exploitation and now of deception . . . I was furious at the boss, the owner, the decision-makers in the government, [all who were] accomplices with this arrangement . . . [all of a sudden all, HDK] was clear to me. I finally realized that this was the reason why the textile workers were in so bad [a] situation. Even the government cheated us. (first interview)

In the eyes of the Ministry of Defence, the effort that Partook made to squeeze the production to six months was exactly what they wanted. They all wanted to get the payment and the job done as quickly as possible. The profit from chip wages was higher, and the labor pay was lower.

> We earned half of what we could get and [worked] half of the employment term . . . on the same day I [had] learned that this was the situation without any planning ahead or coordination, we decided spontaneously to begin a strike, a wild [unlicensed, HDK] strike. We were blinded by rage; we didn't care;

> whatever was going to happen, let it happen, we have nothing to lose. (first interview)

". . . nothing to lose but their chains," says *The Communist Manifesto*. I have learned to be suspicious of this slogan, which so many times failed since it was coined. I personally, in the political activism part of my life, have experienced it more than once. However, this time, I was surprised to find out that when Karl Marx coined it, he didn't elaborate on the spontaneous part. Could he mean that the workers will revolt because they have nothing to lose but their chains, and that they will revolt without being conscious to the revolution they will mobilize? The workers' rage brought the women to the verge of their self-control, and the burst was the result of an enormous amount of rage that sedimented and was repressed for years, unventilated. This was the moment the burst broke all the restraining forces and broke out through all the cobwebs that the women made efforts to stretch during those years of enslavement. It was not a rational thought or planned-ahead program but a force that now changed direction, and instead of investing all their energies in repressing their frustrations, they lighted their rage with fire. The manifest's slogan called for the strike assuming that there must be a moment of rage ignition. However, as it was spontaneous, it couldn't be anticipated or planned, of course not resulting from cold conscious considerations. The workers who had no time to read the manifest did not consider the strike and then the revolution, which Marx foresaw, in the light of this state of affairs. Marx focused on the insight that the workers would have and marked it as a force that would move the workers from false to "correct" consciousness, which is a consciousness transformation that conditioned the strike and then the revolution that he thought he foresaw. As Ingbar said:

> During those years of exploitation and humiliation, many thoughts of revolt and resistance come to your mind, sometimes in the form of dreams, even fantasies that you play with. You want to tear out the oppressive burden to take revenge [for] long years of practical enslavement, to stand up against repeated violence. But what you are conscious of is the opposite, the forces that you have to find in you in order to shut up and carry on, knowing that this is what will keep the job and bring that scant salary home. Your feelings are in constant tension; you are dying to slap the boss on the face, but you go against yourself, as if you are deceived by your own sentiments. (second interview)

This monologue reflects a person who is very much conscious of the entangled situation in which she is trapped. Ingbar felt that, in light of the deception, she could now prove the old explanations had collapsed. No more "the hard situation of the state economy" or "the textile branch crisis" or "the globalization." These excuses sounded weak and arbitrary and the sentiments moved on to rebellious mental points from where she couldn't go back. The forces within her, Ingbar recalled ". . . were stronger than us." They were so strong that they eventually echoed all over the country, and for a short moment, they shook the entire public. It was a short moment, but not much beyond that. That was the first lesson for the women who began to walk through new experiences of breaking their silence and of speaking up. Right away they learned that it is one thing is to burst and ignite a moment of public empathy with their innocent rage and it is something completely different to maintain the upheaval momentum manifested in that rage. To carry out a revolution and destroy exploitative institutions of the state, once the rebel was ignited the challenge, just like it stood in the heart of the Marxist debates between Lenin and Trotsky was the maintenance of the rage on which the upheaval could be carried out. *What Is to Be Done?* was Vladamir Lenin's little book in which he discussed frustration regarding ignition and then maintenance of the upheaval. There he brought up the notion of "the constant revolution" (Lenin, 1902) with Leon Trotsky. However, in our story, it was not clear; maybe the women found the lost sentiment of sisterhood, a version of the solidarity sentiment from which they could derive some belief that agency and pro-activism pays. Ingbar's colleagues decided to join her. Was it the result of an ideological consciousness transformation? It was an incandescent matter. It was a release of suppressed rage that blew up from somewhere in between space that blocked resistance forces from burning out and forced discipline living no room to critic and reflection. This time it seemed that their rage transformed from a mental state of suppression to a forceful burst. The direction of investment of their energy was exchanged, and instead of suppressing anger, they let it out. The feeling of freedom was indescribable. It felt like releasing all restraining ties that chained them to a world fixed by rigid gender, political, ethnic, and class rules. The act felt like cutting off the Gordian Knot and disrupting gender and working fortressed order. Practically, the fact of knowing for sure that the owner depended on them for the deadline played the role of the ignition that strikes the revolt. In this respect, they held some power in their hands they could play with for a short range of time.

> We went out the sewing workshop, burned tires, made a lot of noise, and everything was transmitted by two radio stations—'the voice of the south' and 'B network'—and also on TV, they reported the news for two minutes; it was also reported in the newspaper under the title "One More Textile Factory Was Closed In the South." We realized that the tires burning impact was up, and we decided to entrench in the sewing workshop. (first interview)

At the end of the day, the women closed the factory gates and stayed inside. They took the decision to stay the night, and in the morning, they blocked the manager and the owners from entering. They called their families and informed and asked them to bring in the babies and toddlers that needed their mothers, as well as bring some provisions and blankets. Some of the spouses joined their wives for the night. They had no clear plan, and the entrenchment was as spontaneous as the burst of rage was. The hard feelings that were built up after years of rejection and lack of respect now found a way out as the women expressed frustration and embraced "for not doing it earlier," as Ingbar expressed during one of the quite reflexive instances of the second interview, as if she was speaking to herself. She recollected the shame and painful moments that she felt in front of her family, the children, the creditors, and the grocer, all of whom knew her. The anxieties and fears from what the future holds and the uncertainty, however, did not disappear. Since the women released forbearance, they felt lighter, which allowed them to reorganize their thoughts and retune their worldview to be free and independent people. The fact that they knew that in the coming days they would be either fired or rehired and this time not because the owner wanted but because the women workers made an agent move, which was significant to their self-consciousness. This has intermingled with the understanding that the grocer might be unhappy because they would again have to use a system of credit for their shopping needs. The grocer, a significant figure in their lives, wanted all debts to be paid, that's all. The bank clerks too. The bank will stop the credit and cancel credit cards as they reach their limits, and who knows if they were going to get paid at the end of that month. Before all these creditors, the women will see the children faces, the mouths they have to feed, and their teachers and the afternoon enrichment classes. Each similar encounter, either with the grocer, the school teacher, the municipality authority, or the bank clerk, added more tension and worry to the dilemmas the women debated now at the stormy moments of the revolt. How would they pay the electricity, water, cooking, and gas bills in the next months if they don't acquiesce now and not have their salaries paid as a result. These were problems the women had always had, and they solved them by taking each day, each week, and each month at a time.

In small and poor towns similar to Mitzpe Ramon, the municipality taxes were paid irregularly as a rule, all over the country. The people were so poor that they couldn't afford paying. The municipality knew that enforcing the law meant fining or imprisoning masses of people who would not be able to pay anyway. For this reason, the mayors of the towns were involved and had a stake in such affairs. The mayors were not as networked as were the ones in the bigger metropolis. This situation had advantages and disadvantages, as knowing someone personally could cut short bureaucratic processes and allow human encounters that were less alienating. As for the cooptation and corruption problems, these were more transparent and committed very far from the enforcement of law authorities. The municipality functioned inefficiently but also had very little resources to lose. It seemed that the residents apathetically accepted the situation. As Ingbar noted:

> One month and a half, we entrenched in the sewing workshop together with the Histadrut representative Dani Chetrit. We were determined to block the way and prevent the owner and the manager from coming in. We kept merchandise that [was] valued [at] 200,000 NIS and demanded that the full salaries would be paid to all of us. The salaries were only partly paid, and the owner always promised that as soon as the buyer pays, we would get the rest of it. We knew he lied [as he always did, HDL], but [we] could do nothing. (first interview)

The women entrenched in the factory for more than a month were receiving support and empathy from the public in the little town. The local youth hostel provided mattresses for the night, and the families brought supplies and food, along with toys for the children and clean clothing. The months of July and August in Israel are the school holiday months, and they were the hottest months of the year. The factory was located in the remote part of the little town in the industrial area, empty of entertainment or shopping centers and surrounded by desert wilderness. However, during this period, the area woke up, and next to the factory gates, there were small heaps growing up slowly with plastic toys and plastic swimming pools for the children, which were delivered to the women so they could bath the children and they could play. When the school began, the elder children went back to school, and the small children stayed with the mothers, who now arranged a schedule of three shifts so they could keep their households and still keep the strike going.

The power to earn money day by day was the thing for which the women struggled. They were surprised at the amount of free time they had for themselves now during their sit-in—a privilege they forgot about. Sitting and waiting for long hours for the owner and manager's moves, it gave the women a chance to sit together and talk about things that were not just the hustle and bustle of the factory and stress at home. Reflecting on life issues was an experience that they had forgotten when moving around the base of making a living, taking care of a household, or providing factory maintenance. The time pace was shuffled, and the women felt that there was space for them to breath and think. New words came out of their mouth and gave form to thoughts they had not express for a long time. In the long nights at the factory, they suddenly had time to clarify and elucidate the tangles and went again and again over the circumstances that brought them to the current situation and to the burst of their resistance. They could now begin to consider the possible outcomes and what could they make out of it. The understanding that they were going to be fired, with or without the rebellion, simplified for them the situation. Part of the time, they spent cooking and urged the visitors that curiously came to see what was going on to try their food. The spirits were high. They made some Moroccan dishes famous for their being delicious and offered it to the visitors: "Eat, eat; this is the entrenchment moufleta [a Moroccan pancake], Shula has made it" (Sinai, 2001).

> During the entrenchment, we contacted the media, and after the article of Sagi Bashan, the reporter of Channel 2 in the south, people began to arrive to Mitzpe Ramon from the center [i.e., Tel Aviv, HDK]. Reporters, journalists, entrepreneurs...business people, they came, got the impression, left, and didn't return. The one that showed interest [to help the factory stay open, HDK] made the condition the Ministry of Defence [made] a commitment of buying merchandise of at least three million NIS for the next three years. No one responded [to] this offer, and so he disappeared. (Sinai, 2001)

All the years, Ingbar showed leadership qualities, on both good and bad days. As the weeks went by, two of her friends joined her in the leadership: Avigayle Ifrach and Larissa Vinogradov, who stood out in those days. They formed around them a supporting ring of women and began to discuss the next steps. They began to travel to the meetings with officials in the ministries and government and Histadrut headquarters in Tel Aviv and Jerusalem. They also met with NGOs and social justice activists and returned to the factory full of hope from an enormous empathy the public showed. They were ready to meet anyone who showed even a little will to listen to them, to share the experience, or to give advice. Ingbar heard mixed opinions regarding how weak and failing the factory was and how it should have been closed long before because it wasted the public money in subsidies in vain. However, she had also heard details of how the system should have been operated and how the political establishment should have taken responsibility for the situation. The gaps between the peoples' images of the affair were sometimes huge. For Ingbar, these were the first steps in the world of politics and public activism. Her imagination played a crucial role in the media and went from the ugly-duckling story of forgotten and powerless women to a story of the courageous heroines that the public wanted to embrace. The media work produced magical tales from Sisyphus grey, emphasizing on the hard and boring working material of the women's lives. That forgotten corner of the world was lit at once, and the public talked about the textile branch issue not just as a crisis but as a catastrophe. The women were interviewed and made strong impressions with many leaders. No serious attention was paid to the real problem of the future of the textile branch within a globalization context. Instead, an idea was proposed to make out of the situation something sweet, Ingbar said:

> [. . .] and then, in one of our visits to the ministries, we went to MK Amir Peretz [who held the post of the Histadrut secretary, HDK]. While we were looking for someone that would be prepared to purchase the sewing workshop,

> he [Amir Peretz] suddenly asked me: "Wait a minute, why won't you take the factory [in] your hands?" (first interview)

Amir Peretz was one of a few successful Mizrahi politicians in the labor party who made it all the way from another small poor town in the south, Sderot, to the Knesset. He was at the time of the strike very powerful and led the labor union with much political wisdom, facing complex relationships of the triangle of government-private sector-workers. His reputation was that of one who always took the workers' interests side, although it was not always so. However, he certainly knew how to play the field when it came to political business. His idea that the women take the factory in their hands was wild, creative, and daring. It was convincing, as in the tangled situation all the parties stood at a dead-end alley. For Peretz, it had pure political value from which he could add to his prestige as a popular politician that cared about the fate of the weakened women workers. He was already exposed to the public critic and had nothing to offer after weeks of the women sitting in the factory with the children, and the media kept reporting on the engraving situation.

The first public reaction to his idea came from the media, which reported with skepticism and cynicism. It sounded as if the spontaneous idea was not examined, and it was irresponsible to gamble with the women's lives. However, Ingbar, Yifrah, Larissa Vinogradov were the women to whom Peretz suggested to consider his idea, and he, as the head of the Histadrut, would help transfer the factory to their hands with the Histadrut escort providing advice and financial loans. The women were alone in the room with him, and at first glance, they were shocked. They asked to leave the room and think about it. It was so shocking that they burst out crying with excitement, confusion, and fear. Their desire to be relieved of the deep anxiety where they were standing for the last years and the hope they drew from the entire struggle brought them to seriously consider the offer. The "hallucinating idea," as they put it, at first glance reflected an absurd image of their being the factory owners and managers of what was the enslaving site where they have lived for more than a decade. For a short while, they were taken to the realm of imagination and allowed themselves to toy with the idea. Their responsibility to the other workers that waited for them back in Mitzpe Ramon brought them immediately back to reality. The feeling that there was nothing to lose, as they felt in the first moments of the strike, came again, and now, after weeks in the dark, the idea seemed to be worth considering. They would be the employers of the factory in which they would continue to be the employees, a cooperative enterprise in which the employees are also the shareholders. However, what did it mean to own the factory if they didn't have the money to buy it? Moreover, where could they take the money from to buy the stocks? And what about knowledge in business, finance, management, marketing, and so on—where would that all come from?

> [. . .] we entered to Peretz's meeting room where he was waiting for us and asked all these questions…he promised that professional supervisors and advisors will escort the process and that we will definitely have to take courses while working and learn simultaneously while on the move . . . (first interview)

Going through this dramatic moment once again in the second interview, Ingbar, who seemed to suppress these thoughts on the first interview, said:

> There were more voices on my mind: "Were there left any chances to the textile branch? And how could we even consider adding more tasks to our heavy-loaded daily schedule? Aren't we naive to believe in the success of such an initiative?"

Going back to reflect on the first interview, she said:

> …but the need to survive seemed to be stronger than any of these voices. The workers that waited to hear from us, the families that were desperate and tired but still dependent on us, we wanted to believe in this option, and so we decided to accept it. It was easy to believe then in the values of justice and social change…and so we went out to take the most adventurous journey of my life. When looking back, it was the practical experience in the field and the political maneuvers from which I have learned [the] most and [are] now bitterly sobered. (second interview)

For the first time in her life, Ingbar sat as a businesswoman at the table with the Histadrut secretary Peretz.

> Before leaving Peretz's office, the arrangement we reached was that the Histadrut [who would] give us a loan, which we [would] return in the long run. This loan was meant for purchasing the sewing workshop from the owner, Moshe Partook, and we discussed the employment conditions. (first interview)

The Histadrut had a fund called "The Momentum Fund," which was for use in precisely such cases when factories went through difficulties and needed rescue support. The fund was used this time to loan the women workers one million NIS to purchase the factory. Another sum was provided to each woman who wanted to have a share in the factory's stocks. Each share was valued at five thousand NIS. The loan was meant to be returned by the women in person. One-third of the women took this option, showing trust in the initiative, while the others were more reserved about the future. They mentioned they were already in debt, and they feared not being able to return the loan. This was the first decision since the beginning of the rebellion on which the women were split.

Ruth Sinai, a journalist of social affairs, published in her article in *Haaretz*:

> the negotiation continued all the time when the workers spread butter and honey on the moufletas pancakes. In the factory office, Ingbar sat with the other friend's representative and the committee's chair. There were also delegates from the hotels association from the city of Eilat, who came to check for options to buy bed linen for hotel bedrooms and uniforms for the cooks and other employees. The negotiation was successful…but the Histadrut did not show interest in the existential drama that shared the worker's lives and their families' fate. . . . The sewing workshop Atzmaut [Atzmaut means Liberty, the new name given to the factory after the act of transferring it to the women's hands, HDK] saw good and bad days. In the last summer, the owner decided to close it down, but the women employees entrenched in the factory, objecting the owner's decision to dismiss them. The women [were] stimulated by the Histadrut secretary who suggested [helping] the women purchase the factory and reactivate it as a cooperative. In last October, the renovated factory opened, but the optimistic waves broke down when the old brand of Kitan canceled its orders from the factory. (Sinai, 2001)

Immediately after the deal was done, the women workers, now owners, discovered that one of the old owners in the deal was a fraud. Even then after all those years of cruelty and humiliation, he did not refrain from a last act of deception. He demanded one million NIS for the factory. The Histadrut, without checking much on the price and the property, was ready to provide the loan to the women and the women, who knew very little about how to check the price, signed the agreement. The women trusted that if the Histadrut was willing to pay, then it is OK for them to sign. The women went back to Mitzpe Ramon to begin the restoration of the factory. They made a list of the inventory, the machines, the old equipment, the production stations, and the supplies. The estimation summed up to 250,000 NIS, one-quarter of what they paid the owner. Therefore, immediately after the deal was done, the women found themselves forced to invest in new stuff, requiring them to take more loans from the banks and almost doubling their debts. At this point, the women were so busy renovating and preparing the big day of the factory opening knowing very little about the management and business aspect of the deal. That was the day in which the "ugly duckling was turning to a beautiful swan"—the subordinated employees turn to the factory managers and owners—and this was a victorious day that no one wanted spoiled.

On the opening day of the renewed factory, in the limelight with sparkles in her eyes full of hope, Havatzelet Ingbar cut the ribbon. The excitement was enormous, and hearts were full of joy. The people that came to the ceremony were not just the Histadrut and the media but also many NGOs from all over the country who heard about the happy ending of the revolt, many of them feminists and volunteers. All NGOs promised to offer their help in sharing knowledge on management, fundraising, public relations, marketing, and the like. The women workers were overwhelmed with advisors, professionals in marketing, pricing, human resources, and economists who offered courses, but first of all, love and excitement was shared. Everyone wanted to take part in the story, which for that moment looked similar to Cinderella's end—extremely exploited women workers who became managers overnight. Business cards transferred from one hand to another; telephone meetings and appointments were arranged. Women organizations offered emergency help, including new chairs for the production stations at the factory and sharper scissors. However, these basic needs hinted at the beginning of the sobering path in which the women had to begin marching from that moment on. The very idea of "turning from a textile factory worker into its manager and owner overnight" began to mirror its fantastic, abstract, ridiculous, and, above all, pathetic side. Would the women succeed in preventing the end of the factory and make it to a management position?

WOMEN'S COOPERATIVES

In the economic history of Israel, there were only a few cases in which failing enterprises were transferred from private hands to the workers' hands. One of them was the Harssa Factory, also located in the Negev Desert. Instead of closing it down and firing the workers when faced with economic difficulties, it was transferred to the workers' hands. This decision turned out to be a success, and the enterprise began to make profits after a period of recovery. It is still in working order today and provides for its workers profit and stability. Women's enterprises, since the 1990s, have also become a phenomenon that was expanding, having begun in 1975 after the UN Declaration of the Women's Year in Mexico by the United Nations. It took twenty years for women in the middle-lower class to join this trend. Until then, only well-off women who could afford investments and economic risks in the well-off countries entered the all-patriarchal controlled economic and entrepreneurship fields. It was not until lower-class women struggled against their sisters of the upper class in the mid-1990s that the year of women workers was declared by the Mizrahi feminist organization in Israel. Cooperatives and associations began to be initiated, despite the fact that the globalization era ran rampant in the 1990s. The socialist idea of the workers managing their workplace and being the owners that share the enterprise maintenance as well as share the dividends refused to die. It began shortly before World War II and survived afterwards, especially in Germany and Sweden. In Israel, it had ideological infrastructure as the Zionist movement, which was based on socialist ideas of the commune from which the kibbutz emerged. Cooperative farms worked and shared their production income in the pre-state era as part of the Zionist settlement project. When the welfare state began to disintegrate in the 1980s, the cooperatives system went through the privatization process and put an end to most of the cooperatives. The cost was a severe increase in unemployment. Small cooperatives were bought by big concerns under the state's initiative of joining globalization and became trade monopolies. The feminist movement initiated new activist strategies that were aimed at lower-class women in third-world countries. Their uniqueness resided in the bottom-up emergence idea. Often, they were poor, lower-class feminist activists who became conscious of the fact that the well-off feminists forgot them and, sometimes, even exploited them (Ramazanoglu, 1986). One of the most famous and successful initiatives was the women world banking and the initiative of microfinance banking for women in poor countries, known as the Rotating Savings and Credit Associations initiative, or ROSCA (http://www.investopedia.com/terms/r/rotating-credit-and-savings-association.asp). This initiative shared with women who saved a few dimes every month in order to loan the savings to one woman for the purpose of business entrepreneurship. This was happening particularly in the southern hemisphere and in poor peripheral sites of better-off countries. European feminist coalitions, together with the World Trade Center and the World Bank, were the first to establish such aid initiatives, and they were extended to manufacturing and small industrial branches. In Morocco, for example, a small cooperative developed following the Argan Oil manufacture of the 1980s. The Argan tree, which is known to grow only in Morocco and has been known to have health and cosmetic qualities, was taken from the traditional commercial mode of production. Women who handled all the process, from picking the nuts from the trees through the final stages of bottling and packing, or producing cosmetic creams and soaps, did it in the traditional mode and began to export the products beyond the local boundaries. In the second phase of this initiative, also still in the 1980s, a chemist woman initiated a move from manual production to more modern technology. She opened a line that included chemical laboratories and machines for mass production (Argan Oil, 2012). She began to distribute the product abroad using modern marketing methods, public relations, and advertisement. This was done in cooperation with feminist businesswomen who put on their agenda commitments to sisterhood in the form of helping women in third-world countries. With hard work and persistence, this initiative conquered the European market and developed an industry of hiring economists, accountants, and public relations that are all women that joined the women workers. However, the production line still was dependent on the traditional labor of picking the Argan nuts from the trees and cracking them by the same women in South Morocco, women who were illiterate and transferring their traditional rich knowledge to the more modern actors that were involved in the initiative. The cooperation between well-educated women and poor, "uneducated" women yielded an enormous success. Belgium and France were the largest markets for the product. Today, Argan oil is a world-famous product that developed mass production and other various sorts of product. The tree is still very rare, as it grows in Morocco only, and attempts to make it grow in other places of the world are failing so far. Business people control the market, mainly male entrepreneurs who depend on the women in Moroccan villages to do the work of collecting, classifying, and cracking the nuts. The small cooperatives, which were at first independent, were purchased by larger companies, and the gender aspect of it got lost. This process in the story of the Argan industry symbolizes, in many respects, the phenomena in which women contribution is appropriated by men and remains not being discussed in feminist circles.

In the desert of Negev in Israel, the Bedouin village of Lakiya, an exception of the above examples has occurred. A workshop was opened based on the traditional skills of women embroidery and weaving. The women produce handmade textile products in the traditional way, including carpets and blankets made of sheep, goat, and camel wool. Next to the workshop there is a shop, mainly for tourists, that sells the products. The visit includes a tour and a demonstration of the production process. In the same village, another cooperation produces handmade Bedouin traditional embroidery. The same pattern of marketing and distribution are used as in the weaver's workshop. The tour includes traditional explanations of cultural symbols of Bedouin embroidery. The women work at home, and they are able to combine their work with the household while providing some income. They bring their products to the center where it gets the finishing touches of tagging, pricing, and packaging. In addition, the women also try to market the merchandise abroad. Women's legacy, which was never discussed or explained before and was, in fact, disappearing, is thus reconciled. The additional value of this project is that the women who participate in the project from the beginning to the end also experience a conscious awakening and self-esteem for their legacy that was always taken for granted. Through that, they gain self-confidence and become social agents. What was a young woman's task, to contribute to her dowry, has become an ornament for pillows, bags, purses, and similar. However, at the same time, this makes a strong impact on family and couples relationships. In other words, old traditions transform to fill new needs by way of transforming the Bedouin women's status. In other small towns in the Negev, Yeruham and in poor neighborhoods in the outskirts of the big cities of Jerusalem, in Kattamonim and in Tel Aviv, in the Old Bus station area, other initiatives of this sort were established by women: catering and cooking projects, called "women cooking a business" (Tabib-Calif, 2007); and in Beersheba, there are two initiatives which organize and make the pricing and marketing of handmade, genuine Ethiopian traditional works, including Mezuza covers, small traditions sculptures, and purses. All these initiatives are small businesses initiated and supported by poor, lower-class women of Mizrahi, Ethiopian, Palestinian, and Bedouin women. None of them are of Ashkenazi origin. This is a clear indicator that draws the class and ethnic division in Israel. While women of the upper class are mostly of Ashkenazi origin, the poor women come off the peripheral sectors of social economic and geographic sectors.

Ahoti [My Sister], the Mizrahi women NGO, opened a fair-trade shop in the heart of the city of Tel Aviv where women's products from all the peripheral sectors and areas are sold. In the north of Israel, family businesses of traditional manufacture of Arab women products made of olive oil and herbal cosmetic products are distributed. The above-mentioned initiatives are the successful ones, and they continue to prosper and even grow. However, in many cases where there is a success, it is found time and again that men join the initiative and make it a family business. This fact indicates the centrality of gender in these enterprises, showing that when men are involved, the business takes another path and grows along different lines of agency for the women. Sometimes it is a negative factor, which ends up with re-subordinating women who began with the attempt to become economically independent. Returning to the starting point reveals the androcentric nature of the public sphere that men are dominant and are still very much patriarchal agents. The repeating trend of woman's work of low value is very difficult to be dismantled.

The entrance of women to the public and economic spheres is a process in which two realms and two different sets of rules prevail. The tangles of each cross the other and produce a disentangling knot. The rigid gender division of labor cannot tolerate women's movement to the free market sphere, which is dominated by patriarchal rules. On the other hand, the free market rules played by women who enter a priori as constraint actors do not immediately grasp that the freedom required for such open game is still ruled by some legacies and codes that are patriarchal. They experience difficulties in getting assimilated within this playground. A woman does not automatically become a manager and an agent because she lacks the education or the skills in business and marketing, but especially because finding her ways in the public sphere, she must also discover and purchase the public sphere legacies, business, politics, and culture, altogether. As I will show in the lesson learned from the case studies discussion, there are no shortcuts for the formal education of women who dare take the initiative to enter the public sphere. They must discover the secrets and codes according to which the games in the public spheres are played and which men usually grow into from an early age. Sometimes women make a change in their lives simply because they didn't have a choice. They may have found out at a later stage that they changed radically and there was a turnover in their lives in respect to purchasing masculine patterns of communication and of interrelations. They also find that the changes had an impact on the other women around them. This experience is not always felt when occurring and was not implemented according to some conscious feminist agenda, but it simply was out of constraints. When women make it to spheres where men are dominant, such as the public arena of the business world and the realm of economy, eventually they do have some influence on the rules of the game, and they do leave some footprint on the playground of the gender struggle. In the end, this is how feminists make their progressing steps—one by one. In a sense, it may look absurd that in the cases where women only wanted to be accepted to the sphere dominated by men they eventually changed it. After all, the solid economic rules of supply and demand seem to be blind to gender distinctions, and the rules are successful for those who know how to play.

The intersection point of gender and economy affect each other because these are living systems where living people are constantly busy creating new strategies, whether by way of confrontation or negotiation. Feminist movements suggested ways for legal gender reforms, but reforms, when formulated in abstract terms, are difficult to be implemented and take time to be concretely applied. In most cases, the option for women is to imitate male pattern in order to "survive the male world," as the previous citation by Audre Lorde suggested. When the two systems conform, no change would be achieved if women simply join men in their world and imitate their patterns. The domination of women by men would never come to an end if this continued to be the sole strategy, and the women who join this world only extend the boundaries of patriarchy such that they cover women's experience in the public sphere as it does in the private. The subversive attitude of radical feminists has led to open gender confrontation, or in the common term the "sex war." The good side of the process is that whenever women started a struggle, some men were involved in various degrees of support or cooperation. In the eighteenth century, when Mary Wollstonecraft wrote her piece called *The Vindication of the Rights of Woman* but it was her husband, William Godwin, who published it with her other memoirs after she died. Then, in the nineteenth century, the work *The Subjection of Women*, written by J. S. Mill, was developed with his wife, Harriet Taylor Mill, and published after she had died as well. It seems that without the exceptional assistance of men, prominent men, at least in the beginning steps of the feminist journey, women could not progress much. These cases of men providing assistance and support to published feminist works of women are worth considering because the pattern still prevails today. With our example of Bedouin women in Israel who struggled for their rights for education, report in the majority of the cases that it was their fathers (not the brothers though) who stood behind them to push their struggle for education forward. Even when their mothers supported them, they still didn't have enough power to push the initiative forward. This is true for Jewish orthodox women as well. The patriarchal order of things must, at the end of the day, be broken by individual patriarchs, by the fathers and the husbands who dared to stand up along with the struggling daughters or wives for their rights, even against the clans and the tribes. The confrontation was done within the patriarchal gender relations order not between the sexes. This moral of the process is that women better succeed or fail in generating change in gender relations when men are involved (Dahan-Kalev and Lefevre, 2012). In the case of the factory in Mitzpe Ramon, there was no exception. From the first minute of the struggle through the entire process of transforming into a cooperative, it couldn't change a thing without the involvement of men, powerful men. The men, however, were also those who failed the project, as we shall see in the following chapter. The women of the Mitzpe Ramon factory were the only case known to purchase a bankrupting factory and operate it as a cooperative. In this respect, it was the only case to start a cooperative from a non-profit enterprise.

Chapter Six

Can a Factory Worker Become a CEO Overnight?

The most distinguished challenge the women workers faced when they accepted Secretary Peretz's offer and began the transformation of the factory to a cooperative was the gender factor. For the three leaders, Havatzelet Ingbar, Avigayle Yifrah, and Larissa Vinogradov, the move from worker status to CEO was a move from manual worker to women CEO. They were going to experience a course in political business that even if they studied politics they wouldn't have found in the books. How could one teach power relations in regards to gender? How could a woman worker turn into a manager and save a failing factory without previous professional knowledge and practice? Experience, in every respect, demands time and space for trial and error. Even if they could guarantee that they were quick learners and ambitious enough, which they were, how would they bring a failing factory success while the entire branch of textile progresses towards its end? The decision was made, and the women committed themselves to taking the risk. Now they had to concentrate on the immediate tasks of learning how to run a factory as a profitable cooperative, not how to run a failing factory. In retrospect during our talks, Ingbar looked back to that period wondering about Amir Peretz, the Histadrut secretary, and his motivations to take that move. A thought that didn't occur to her at the time of transformation was his decision to transfer the factory to the women's hands. Was it a vision or was it a cynical political gamble at the women's expense. Was his decision romantic and populist, wanting to gain some political support, and so he dared to offer a fantasy? Or perhaps was it a courageous political move? Bitterly, Ingbar smiled as if to say, "I was too naive not to understand that it was all these factors at play." This is how it works in tough political decisions.

The women were well-equipped with a large dose of passions, hopes, and beliefs. The public support and the publicity at the time of the events enhanced their mental resources, and in the first days after they got the factory in their hands, they were not alone. NGO representatives kept coming to visit and give advice, and the media still followed them and reported the transformation. The officials from the various ministries helped ease the bureaucracy, and the women had to delve into the fields of economy and business management, industrial planning, human resources predestination, trade construction, technological development, and computer programs. How could they do all these changes and learn about it all at once? How could they learn but also make decisions in the various fields that were alien to them, having very little information and professional knowledge? They thought of advisory committees that would accompany them on those first steps. The first things they were exposed to were the different contexts within which the various topics were rooted. A factory does not stand in a vacuum. It is at an intersection point where economic, financial, business, industrial, legal, and political relations are all constructed in a unique form that is all aimed to make a profit out of any final textile production. Gender plays a role of an umbrella above all of these factors. At this point, although ill gender relations influenced the situation, the women focused on the vision for their future.

Organizational culture, which could play a role model to guide them, was not something they had experienced. The women were not networked in either of the fields in which the factory intersected. They did not belong to the textile guild, as weak as it was in Israel, and they were not familiar with the way to become members in the industrial association. They didn't know of the financial options they had in the business department of their bank and how to run a business bank account. They were unaware of the legal rights for debit and credit options that businesses could enjoy when running a financial flow. Moreover, they had no idea of the rights and duties of the factory as an industrial organ or what was its legal status. All this information, which, in conditions of gradual progress, are purchased gradually, they were supposed to absorb all at once. They tried with all their might. The women moved at a drastic pace. They had to transition from a women's world, as subordinated workers who experience oppressive and cruel treatment only a couple of months before, to the male world, as the role of masters that had to run a factory. There was no standard "starting point" where they could begin. The move had to be made similar to jumping into very cold and deep water from a very high position by people who didn't know how to swim. Their experience of being exploited was the only socialization they knew in male-employer-female-employee relations. Equipped with short-term resistance experience at the strike's period and violation of old relations norms as ran in the factory the spirit was to go against the old order and disintegrate it. However, the present phase in which they found themselves was to "collect the shards" to reorganize and create new working norms, new rules, and redefine working patterns and boundaries. As new power holders, it was for them the first steps of exercising power and power relations from different directions. They knew how to organize working shifts and what the relationship with the boss should look like, which was to be collegiate and coordinating all production stages on the line.

Being on a trial-and-error track, they couldn't exercise much authority and professional confidence. It was easy for others to disobey the women, as they lacked the experience to be authoritative. They were more familiar with doubts and un-listening to their words. A general view, which is found in Donna Harraway's feminist manifesto, may have served them as "meta-narrative" and provided general context validity, which makes a significant gender difference and was absent (Harraway, 2006). The statement of "gender weight" provided the authority that stems from said context and the person who expresses it. At this point of realization, the women learned that it applies to opinions, estimations, suggestions, and decisions, and they received their value from the source of who was expressing it, specifically if they were male or female, not of some abstract objective value. They had to endeavor to gain respect and authoritative position so that what they said would be respected. The problem was very deeply entrenched in the human history of relationships and, therefore, too complicated to discover and disentangle in this already entangling case. Women's words were often taken as valueless or nonsense, whereas when men expressed them, they became "full of sense" only because they came out of a man's mouth. This true convention was already lucidly explained by the clear work of Virginia Woolf in her essay "Three Guineas" (Woolf, 1938). Women were incarcerated in madhouses for saying things that were treated as hallucinations, whereas when men said similar things, they were accepted as illuminating truths. The story "the yellow wallpaper," written by Charlotte Perkin Gilman and published in 1982, strongly illustrated this gender pattern. Therefore, the women in the factory, although introducing much women commonsense to the challenge before them, faced a very deeply rooted gender norm that was held by both men and women, which brought up doubts and distrust to the practiced transformation of becoming a woman manager and CEO overnight. The true value of what the women said was secondary to the women who said it, as Catherine Nash argued (Nash, 2010). The field of discourse remained male-dominated. The women in the factory, the Histadrut officials, the ministries, and even, in some cases, the NGOs all piled up difficulties that seemed rooted in the reason that they couldn't conform with the idea that women, specifically women workers, would be able to successfully take over the factory management. Every message concealed the idea that managers in factories "must be male." Therefore, the women leaders' tasks were not just to prove their ability to make sensible decisions but to endeavor to change entire gender perceptions and male normative patterns before they could be accepted as legitimate and authoritative CEOs. On top of challenging gender issues, they had to also stand the challenge of transforming from workers to managers. This played a crucial role in their chances to cross such a complex Rubicon. The establishment blocks, as well as the ideological and patriarchal hegemonic fortresses, did not fall. The women at the factory continued to experience obstacles despite the fact that on the surface they enjoyed much support and sympathy. The political aspect, which could open their eyes to the power relations, remained hidden to them and only really revealed itself as they took steps as they were trying to make some progress. Experienced professional managers are familiar with these problems but not these women who were so new in the field. They didn't enjoy any day of mercy. It is the kind of political knowledge that could be purchased only through personal experience, which Jean-Paul Sartre defined in his play *Dirty Hands* as the essence of the political business (first performed in 1942 in Paris).

JOINING PROFESSIONAL ASSOCIATIONS, THE GUILDS

The passage of the factory from men's hands to women's hands and from for the women workers from being laborers to becoming managers was a double phase and a crisscross weaved with the challenge of becoming a woman manager. Understanding how gender is curved and identified in the etched signs within the map of management and embedded in the indispensable experience that makes the manager familiar with the institution were boys immediately recognize as the male playground was beyond their experience. The women had to disentangle the Gordian Knots one at a time and had to learn their ways in the cobweb of power. This required time to identify actors and learn the routes where power flows and how it does so. Most of all, they had to discover alone the secrets that no one disclosed willingly, knowing that knowledge is power. The women rushed to the factory to begin to understand what those secrets were that are kept within the guild-like organizations. These guilders served as gatekeepers to protect their power within the organization.

Every professional association has its gatekeepers that are elected or appointed.

Part of their responsibility is to select the joining members according to formal professional criteria and keep those standards. The criteria regard not only to professional knowledge but also to norms, rules, and ethics. The members are educated according to patterns and terms by training according to the specific field of a profession. In a more grey area of the patterns and norms, there are power relation patterns that mark the rules of what members should or should not. These are signposts that the apprentice would learn during their education, along with the experience acquired along the way and that continues throughout membership. A good mentor would be the one who opens the gate of the guild to the apprentice by pointing out the "grey area" of the power relations. This gives the apprentice secretes of the effective tools for successful conduct inside and outside of the guild. In fact, this is the material of which the "dry" professional has their abstract knowledge "wet" by. The more the guild profession provides economic and cultural goods, the more its social and political status becomes stronger and, therefore, the gatekeepers are more fanatic to the norms of subordination. Acceptance of members becomes stricter the stronger the guild is. On this ground, the failing factory couldn't be transferred to the women workers hands without crossing the gatekeeper threshold according to guild rules. Industrialists, buyers, those in the finance and treasury departments, the labor union, and the governmental establishment who promised at the time of the strike that they would provide help and support all began to play guild games. The norms and rules that they had promised to moderate and provide longer terms of credit, promises of extended deadlines for the merchandise supply, and the like began to impel a red-tape attitude. The women had to move back and forth between being apprentices and business decision-makers. What should be the priority when the factory needed urgent reconstruction and the industrial program needed reframing? As the women guessed, the financial state was in a severe deficit, and the first merchandise orders were already on the factory management table. On top of this prioritization challenge, there were the guild difficulties that flickered foremost as a problem of filtering information, or rather keeping the secrets within the various guilds, as the women discovered every now and again. Just like in the case of the owner who literally cheated them when he demanded one million NIS for something that was worth one-quarter of that sum, at every decision the women made as managers, the information they got back was always incomplete, and they discovered that even though it could be guessed by the information providers, there was no information given out of benevolence. During that time, they couldn't know that for sure, as they followed the mentors whom they believed were benevolent indeed. In retrospective, the women recalled, in a sobering way, that they were so blind to the power relations and so naive to the vital knowledge that they couldn't imagine how hermetically closed off they were to the networks that concerned the financial world.

In my discussions with Ingbar, I preferred to focus on the gender perspective of the guild matter. I believed that was the most significant and sobering process the women went through. The gender factor was central to the entire process of learning how to become managers and part of the managers and the professional business guilds. It was the thread on which power relations depended on the various encounters the workers had. This related especially to the three leading women: Havatzelet Ingbar, Avigail Yifrah, and Larissa Vinogradov. Right after they heard the suggestion from Amir Peretz, the Histadrut secretary, to take the factory into their own hands and asked to discuss it outside his office, Ingbar recalled:

> Avigail and I went out, looked at each other, [and] we embraced, [were] confused, what shall we do? What can we do? Then I said "OK, que será, será" and went in. . . . It was the same as we behaved when we took the strike, spontaneously and decisively. We bombarded him with questions: Who is going to help us? Who is going to assist us? He promised. "you will not be alone." (second interview)

From that conversation, they understood that the assistance included escorting them in the process of delivering the factory but also assisting in the next steps of operating it. To my question of whether there were minutes taken from that meeting, the answer was yes, "but we didn't take a copy and didn't ask for one. We didn't know we should." Later on, when the factory faced promises that were not fulfilled, they wanted to look at the minutes, but they faced bureaucratic red tape. The time was pressing, and they didn't insist on the learning phase. "We wanted to make things work immediately. Insisting on unfulfilled promises may have been perceived as ingratitude, as if we [were making] trouble after they have been so kind to us," said Ingbar in the second interview. Finally, at the stage of delivering, process things were made for the women managers at their presence but not with their active participation:

> Not that we didn't try to take [any] action and insist on making the decisions . . . at least . . . demand answers, but there was this feeling that we will not understand the complexity of things and that we shouldn't waste time now.

Then Ingbar made a comment that attracted my attention, and I asked her to discuss it further. She said:

> Chetrit felt unnecessary. He didn't receive calls anymore [from the Histadrut or other authorities, HDK], no one wanted to hear his advice, and so he began to suggest to us ideas such as "You must bring a manager that will run the production line." At first, I took him seriously, not noticing that all he wanted was to make himself relevant again. I agreed, and we hired a person [named] Michael Fleishman with Chetrit sitting on the hiring committee. Very soon after, Chetrit systematically took [Fleishman's] side on questions we discussed regarding the sewing workshop's management, and [Chetrit] began to bluntly ignore my positions and decisions. (second interview)

Thirty-five women out of the sixty-seven who participated in the strike bought stocks and shared ownership of the factory. The rest continued to work as employees without shares. The stockholders now became responsible not just for the factory to run properly but also that the factory would function according to cooperative principles. That meant that the investments, the inputs, and the outputs would belong to all of the shareholders, and they would lead the factory debts and maintenance, eventually, to full recovery. The stockholders came to work in the morning, took two shifts knowing that they had to produce rapidly so that they could distribute the merchandise and pay debts, but they also had to take meetings as owners that needed to lead new policies and learn how to run an industrial business. The debts were divided into personal payment for the stocks that they bought, and collective, payment for the loans they took when purchasing the factory. They stayed after two shifts but realized that the production required them to stand behind the sewing machines two shifts before going to discussion meetings about future plans. What they heard and learned from the officials that came from the various bureaus—the governmental, the labor union, and so on—and what they found in the accounts and files about the factory situation left them with a dark cloud over their heads. The situation was more serious than they could imagine. It was clear that the debts were beyond their ability to cope with, even if they worked three shifts in a row. After a few months, ten of the stockholder employees realized that they took a risk that was beyond their ability to cope with. They returned the stocks and turned back to being just employees. This had a negative effect on the women's relations. The stockholders who remained felt discarded; the employees who hadn't bought stocks at the beginning and who did not come to the meetings had little information but heard informal news that was not so optimistic regarding the new cooperative arrangement of the factory and the chances for recovery. The feelings were mixed; loyalty to the factory differed between the stockholders, those who didn't have stock, and all the friends that showed solidarity up until then, which parted some different opinions with regard to what was best for the women. It was not anymore the women workers against the owner or manager but the women managers and the women employers versus the women employees, who felt less committed to the factory. Feelings of uncertainty and disappointment swirled in the air. They all wanted to do the right thing for their place of work and their workers friends. The dilemmas were tough; they had to choose between their jobs and solidarity with their friends; they were not the same anymore. The "good-girl syndrome" that often made them do things against their will only because they were raised with such a common gender norm of wanting to please was put to the test. These were new experiences often experienced by boys at earlier age. Ingbar, who coordinated the meetings and conducted the debates with the ex-owners and other adversaries, found herself facing her own female colleagues conversing with officials. What seemed to be issues that were easy to decide looked now unclear and with more than one option. One of the urgent issues was, in her opinion, the women's training in management and business. She gave it the highest priority on her list. She traveled on one of the first occasions to the Ministry of Industry and Commerce. The local labor secretary, Chetrit, made it a habit to join her to those trips. On that first occasion when she remained sited with the official woman who assisted her with the issues of getting more professional, Chetrit urged her to finish the meeting because "we have another meeting, and they are waiting for us already." Ingbar was surprised because she didn't know of another meeting on that day's schedule but thought she had perhaps forgotten or missed that one. When they left the office and were on their way out, Ingbar asked Chetrit about the meeting, to which he replied, half cynically, "that which doesn't help us to make money immediately we shouldn't waste time on." When she told me about that, in both interviews, she sounded defeated, as if to say "How could I be so naive and blind not to see his manipulations?" Her silence took me to the literature on political leadership. Problems of solitude when making difficult decisions and dilemmas of having to choose between good and bad alternatives are the daily burden of leaders. Ingbar told me that after discussing such issues with the board, which consisted of her colleagues, she had to learn to separate between friendship and the factory interests.

> First, I listened to myself; then I tried to discuss with the board new understandings with regard to our working relations . . . new patterns that we [needed] to develop amongst the women who didn't buy stocks . . . hence [we] were not part of the owners. Consequently, they had a different attitude to loyalty. (second interview)

Patricia Lather describes the condition in which reflexivity occurs. Intellectual experience that yields new knowledge requires space in which it can emerge and be reflected on (Lather, 1991). Shifting from the state of being a "good girl" to one of independence and freedom to express one's objection is a cognitive process that involves internal wrestling with the considerations of the cost/benefit that one has to do. This dynamic experience lies within the sediments of feminist consciousness transformation. Ingbar came with this experience from her personal life, as will be further elaborated. She seemed to intuitively understand it right after she moved to her position as the factory CEO.

In the documentary *Daroma* (Tzabari and Shlez, 2000–2001), which followed the process of transformation from the beginning right after the delivery of the factory into the women's hands, Ingbar told her personal story. She openly spoke of the domestic violence she endured during her first marriage. That was the time when she learned that she had to drop the "good-girl syndrome" and try other ways to survive the violence. In the documentary, the shift from being a "good girl" and escaping in various ways from violent marriage and to experience living on the verge of threats on their lives, the three leading figures in the factory story told their tale. All the women confessed in the documentary that they came to the factory and took on the management adventure with a similar feeling—being good girls would not be the good strategy. Apparently, it wasn't enough. However, they all reported that they moved from a zone of obedience zone as "good girls" to a zone of order disruption and walking against the stream. Each woman in her turn reported that she had recognized the lowest level of violence and left her marriage "a minute before it was too late" as Vinogradov has put it (*Daroma*, ibid.). They described how their marriage and family life became a trap in the process of isolation that reached a point of full submission to their spouses. In the case of Yifrah, she said that she was bitten when pregnant, and after she gave birth, she had to give up her child to the father after many years of legal struggle, otherwise she wouldn't get the divorce. In the last incidence in a series of violent relations, Vinogradov ran away with her daughter from Russia to Israel when her spouse came home drunk with a revolver that he put on the table. The three women describe one specific moment in which there was an intuitive cognitive shift. With no prior plans to escape until that spontaneous fatal moment for all three women, they seemed to invest all their energy in staying despite continuous years of suffering. These experiences were intuitively recognized and were memorized in the working place at the moment of their burst of resistance. Along with this experience, they had to mobilize their mental strength and shift it to the opposite direction—to resistance against the "good girl" who resided within them. The "good girl" apparently did not fade away, "she" remained the hollow inside each worker and the woman in the factory until the moment of the rebellion. In other words, being a liberated spouse did not infer that they were liberated at the workplace. Such a shift has to be on its own merit separately from the other processes of liberation. However, the fact that the women recognized this mental experience from previous cases means that they would operate with some of the skills that were purchased at the first incidence of resistance; the first instance of discovery of strength and ability to resist often surprises women who are more familiar with the reiteration of being "a good girl." This is particularly true in the cases of long years of obedience and submissiveness of poor women in the lower class. These are women who often have no choice but to conform to exploiting and humiliating conditions at heavy-duty, manual, unprofessional work that offers little in the way of wage. The entire setting brings them to what I described above as modern enslavement.

The turning point of having no power at all in her status as a worker, to the point where the power was almost exclusively in her hands, was for Ingbar a sobering moment. She understood that with power relations, there is no vacuum, it simply moves from one focus to another. The man who used to be the most powerful before the factory became a cooperative was Chetrit. In the new circumstances of delivering the factory to the hands of the women, he lost power and began to invest his efforts in preserving what little power he could. Ingbar recalled that when he suggested bringing on a new manager, she did not realize at the time that he meant to put more weight against her and be free to coordinate with the board and the other officials outside the factory, including business firms. Chetrit manipulated the women on the board as a whole, playing the game of the savant regarding labor rights and laws, which they never heard him raising before. Women's rights or feminist liberation, as Ingbar found out, were far from his interest in the new constellation in which he found himself. This insight surfaced in almost every step the cooperative made from the first instance.

"YOU, I WANT TO SEE YOU ON THE PRODUCTION LINE, NOT HERE IN THE OFFICE"

As described previously in the chapter on "being a worker," the concepts of "a worker" and being "a manager" had an operational significance regarding the women's ability to make a shift in the course of their lives. These were concepts that named them from deeply rooted social, cultural, economic, and class contexts. They were politically loaded with certain weight of value and almost graphically symbolized their relative public value and strength. The self-image of being a manager or an employee determined to a certain extent their relationship and developed authoritative abilities. Therefore, one question concerned the women's ability to go through a cognitive transformation from worker to manager and another one was to make this shift in the world surrounding them. Epistemic and ontological spheres were two arenas in which they had to make the agents' change and then bring them together. Some of this transformation depended on cognitive aspects and others concerned material aspects. Ownership, in this respect, did not relate only to receiving the money to purchase the factory but to the ownership mentality that should be built up. This required the workers to deal first with their self-image as workers, which resided within their consciousness. The political and public horizon of being a worker did not synchronize with the mental shift of becoming a manager. What was an adventure for the secretary of the Histadrut was for the women a serious mental experience that had to be done in one striking shift. Instead of assistance and support, encouragement and empathy, they faced skepticism and doubts with regard to their abilities to lead major change. This came not only from the men within the factory but also from the officials outside and, to a certain extent, from the assisting NGOs that escorted them. The fluid moment of delivery from experienced men's hands to inexperienced women's hands was a missed opportunity to change social and gender constructs. They were short-sighted actors, and the more-experienced official actors could have taken more steps of estimation before and during the process before they retreated. Perhaps it was too revolutionary for officials that were conservative and patriarchal. Perhaps if the women were from a better-off sector, upper-class women may have worked differently, assuming that women of upper-class are more self-confident. The conceptual shift was apparently too big in all dimensions: conscious, gender, social, cultural, and political. The women were expected to redefine labor conditions, business conditions, management conditions, and other aspects that were deeply rooted in the patriarchal constructs for centuries. To hold a stock of the cooperative and to still carry within the humiliating and subordinating mental state from the past was a confusing situation of simultaneous weakness and strength together, one of economic security and insecurity. The tension between subordination and liberation yielded both promising gospel and frightening threats. Unlike the legendary stories about self-made persons who are often autodidacts who grow from the bottom up to succeed, events here flowed rapidly, leaving no time to practice, digest, or learn. The media curiosity, the NGOs enthusiasm, and the interest from academic sectors and the party politicians pushed for positive information that the women in the cooperative did not yet have. The magical moment of the victory of the weak over the exploiting forces did not blossom for long. The media compared the events with heroic feminist, socialist, and Marxist worker struggles throughout history, although the women in the cooperative were far from grasping the historical idea and the terminology, including the notion of solidarity and labor ethos.

The women in the cooperative had real and substantial difficulties and were too busy to articulate abstract feminist ideas. It is common for women in similar situations to relate to such abstract ideas as alienating, especially when marked as feminist. Words such as feminism and the feminist victory of women fighter even when supported by feminist organizations tend to deny. Their reality demanded concrete and tough decisions regarding mobilizing a means of production, changing the means of production, and finding ways to substantially recover from an economic and industrial crisis the women found themselves stuck in. Ideological questions whether they were feminist could wait for other moments of reflecting. The abyss between naming and tagging, especially by the media, the experience the women went through, and the practical needs to real life where daily existential, material, bodily, and mental struggle were unbridgeable. The alienation that they felt towards the media articles and the ideological movements that approached them nullified the powers that they often incorporated to speech acts. Words were now empty, and Ingbar could call herself a manager or a worker, but this didn't make a difference to her authoritative weight.

IDENTITIES AND POWER DISPOSITIONS

Conceptions and names are expressed through words that signify identities. In this respect, subjects who are identified as belonging to certain categories are networked within power relations that are regulated by rules and norms. The power system is organized through hierarchy within networks and asymmetry that puts the subjects in competing and constant attempt to mobilize power. A power system might be dynamic, but as long as the conservative forces are dominating and on guard, it keeps its stability. For fourteen years, this was the situation in the Mitzpe Ramon factory until the women called for change through the revolt that brought change and the transfer of the factory to their hands. Purchasing the factory and transforming it into a cooperative was a call for structural change, including change of the power relations parallelogram. Changing one factory on the peripheral area of Israel was one thing, but changing the deeper roots of the power relations structure was another one. It meant the transformation of the cobwebs that tied the norms and relationships that dominated institutions, shaped the workers' consciousness and the labor culture. These women were now entering a worker's skin of manager in position as if they put on a disguise and made it real in the mode that speech acts bring to reality a fact only by stating it with words. The meaning is given by way of acting as one and reiterating the action. In a similar way to the gender speech act where stating "it's a girl/boy," as Judith Butler suggested, the same is valid in cases such as managers and workers. We can understand through this mechanism how things worked when Ingbar tried to wear the manager's disguise in a surrounding that fixes her image as a factory worker from where she couldn't release herself. It came out as if she tried to transform from one gender to another, and when she did, the stability was shaken and couldn't be accepted as "natural." It was like an attempt of coming out of the closet and claiming that she was not whom she was thought to be. The move she tried to make was not a simple move from one working position to another but instead a move that claimed a different treatment. The difference concerned old fixed and hard-to-change gender relations. This awakened a sleeping class and various gender demons. In one meeting, Ingbar recalled a dispute she had with Gil Aloni, the CEO of the labor company in the Histadrut. He lost it, and without giving a second thought, he raised his voice saying: "You, I want to see you on the production line." This for Ingbar was an indicator that no matter how deep and rapid the change she would make, the changes in the people's minds surrounding her should begin a change for even deeper conventions. Prior to the question whether the women workers could make the change was the question of whether the world around them could change to accepting them. The men with whom she worked tried ceaselessly to put her in her "right place" as a worker and a woman. Aloni's words were blunt, but others did the same in more subtle ways. It was sad for Ingbar to realize that women had finally held this perception. The problem did not lie in the open facts that she has better off with her material conditions as a manager but in her passing the virtual test of proving to be decisive or charismatic, as it is presumed automatically when a male commander is on the line. With men, they have to fail for their competence will be doubted; with women, it is the opposite; they are assumed incompetent until they prove otherwise. Ingbar, as well as her colleagues on the board, was very daring and charismatic. What they lacked was the mystification part that often is infused to charisma with power. When determining the new system of waging, some of the workers, according to the kind of work they filled in the cooperative, had to be paid for extra work as managers or board members on top of their salary from working on the production line. This was discussed when the new operating manager, Arnon Keren—a kibbutzim from a well-off kibbutz in the south—was nominated to the cooperative, at the labor secretary Chetrit's advice. The operating manager signed a hiring contract that included "regular conditions." This meant that he got car maintenance and manager benefits, including a pension and other social rights such as training funds. His bosses, the women managers, could not afford to pay themselves such a wage but they signed that contract for the operating manager. While they worked within the framework of the cooperative, the operating manager Keren was hired as an employee. The result was that he was paid the highest salary, even higher than the women managers. It was out of the question for the workers to decide differently. No one would agree to less than what the operating manager agreed, and with the financial troubles the cooperative had, they couldn't afford to take a similar salary. The situation was absurd considering the capitalist system always secured that owners and CEOs were to earn top salaries as a rule. The irony was that the CEO, and the three leading women on the board, needed cars to enable them to move from the periphery to the center and travel to meetings, among other things, while the operating manager could do his work without the car. The women were so eager to succeed that they entered voluntarily to being paid much less then Keren was with the understanding that it was temporary until they begin to see signs of financial recovery of the factory.

A few months later, the sad facts hit the women workers. Not only had the financial recovery showed no signs of happening, but also the situation worsened so that they couldn't pay Keren the promised wage. Salaries were paid partly or later than the due date. It looked similar to the previous conditions before the workers took the factory into their hands, as was during the Partouk times. The women remained working without any payment whatsoever. The project of transformation into a cooperative and the efforts to bring the factory to a healthy state of operation seemed to be away from them, unrealistic, and hard to believe that it would be possible to realize. The idea was not anymore a dream that some believed against all odds would be realized.

Oppressive systems function simultaneously with regard to each characteristic in the identity, be it gender, ethnicity, or class. These characteristics overlap, cross, and strengthen or weaken each other in ways that are not easy to elaborate when tracing through with a critical gaze. Moving from one identity as workers to another as managers, from employees to employers, threatened to disturb the stability (i.e., the prevailing patriarchal gender order). Gatekeepers woke up, introducing misogynistic comments and patriarchal manipulations wherever the women were trying to mobilize things. The patriarchal system endeavored to bring the old order back. The illusion of being liberated from the woman-worker chains did not last for long. The heavy burden that the women took upon themselves and the efforts they put into making the project work began to exhaust them. The women were first blind to the misogyny and the skepticism as they were busy trying to cope with the multiplied expectations and challenges of trying to learn fast their new jobs, coping with the financial problems, running around from one office to the other, and experiencing red tape. The feeling that maybe these are the terms of the job and they are yet to grasp the right sense of things hindered them from seeing how the business and production world worked. For the first six months, they wanted to give things time, or so they told themselves. Ingbar and her colleagues had to learn the secrets and decipher the encryptions and codes of the industrial world. It took the women time to understand that it was not only the facts that were hidden away from their eyes but also the organizational culture that they had no clue of. A gesture, or move, a face mimic, the use of a certain word instead of another—these were all part of the fabrics that they had to understand for how power systems work. It became clearer in retrospective. Every procedure, file, management meeting, and money-raising discussion had to do with power, hence with every person they encountered. It was impossible to break the shackles that trapped them within a factory worker's inferior position. The best doctor, whose skin might be darker, will always face racism for his or her skin color. The same goes for women workers: as good as the woman would perform as a manager or as any other role, the first thing that is perceived is her being a woman. Ingbar had the most to cope with in this situation:

> The more he [the boss] treated me evil, the more it made me determined to break him. Sometimes I succeed to make him move [a] little. The workers, my friends, used to say "You are the only one that can face him like that." (first interview)

Her resisting force and persistent personality showed that she was an agent who tried to move within rigid frameworks. These abilities worked as long as she stayed in her position as a worker: a woman worker. When she tried to get out of the frame, she became a threat to the system and all the actors that made it work; as she moved out of her frame and tried to change the framework itself, that which protects binary as the essential paradigm of gender division of labor: male versus female, with female being at the bottom of the hierarchy and men being at the top.

Chapter Seven

How the "Private-Public" Stereotypical System Works

The difficulties that the women workers had when transforming the factory to a cooperative and negotiating with authorities and officials—males in most cases—revealed how rigid gender division of labor was: it was a division based on the dichotomy that split male and female. This dichotomous order that split "men and women" as part of coupling-system identities according to binary construct to which other couples are arrayed as women-managers/men-managers, women-workers/men-workers, and similar. This binary order organizes cultural reality that is engendered according to coupling spheres as public and private. The spheres organize the relationship according to a hierarchy where men are above women and that respectively associates with the upper status to men. Women have made endless attempts throughout history to cross the lines and hold positions in the public sphere. These attempts were perceived as trespassing, which violates the binary order—that was held as natural—and breaks unwritten rules. Sanctions are inflicted on the violators aiming to keep social relations away from chaos. The feminist revolution of the past few decades was aimed at crossing the lines that divided the public from the private spheres and suggested reforms to the patriarchal order. They have been sanctioned when moved from the private sphere to public in the first instances. They strived to legitimize the mobility of women to the public sphere struggling for equal treatment. However, achieving equal wage and being respected equally is yet to be gained. The structures are still very much heteronormative in that the division of labor seems to follow women from the private sphere to the public. Women are still socialized to take the private sphere responsibilities with them to the workplace. They are still offered mainly caring and serving jobs when crossing the line to the public sphere. It is easier for women to get a job as nurse or a teacher's position then a one as a soldier or priest. When women "sneak in" and make it to a management or commanding or political and spiritual leadership position, they are expected to prove their abilities in which men have set the standards. If the women drag the private sphere's norms of mothering and caring from the private sphere to the public, it is considered improper. One cannot treat a soldier as a mother is supposed to treat their child. However, feminism insisted as such, and since the 1970s, women have gained some success and were able to make some new laws, mainly in the Western world, that show that the public sphere is accommodating a little bit to these changes. The rate of change is slow due to the power networks that control the gates of male gendered roles in the public sphere. Women over the last few decades of feminist struggles have endeavored Sisyphus-like projects to make changes. Time and again the feminist projects found that what works in deconstructing one system of a power network does not necessarily apply to other systems. Different apparatus has made male, patriarchal power systems differ from one another. Therefore, different apparatus make patriarchal religious power systems differ from political or militaristic power systems, and it is even more complicated when moving from a religious system in one culture to another. The rules are organically embedded within the order of things. Therefore, understanding how religious power networks work means understanding the particular religious laws from where the rules and subordinating apparatus are derived. In other words, understanding mechanisms of gender-subordinating Jewish laws does not apply to other religions gender subordination. This differentiation is valid in other fields, such as political regimes or cultures. These differences involve different languages, images, and life patterns; in short, habit resources that works for the patriarchal system and operate with particular apparatus. This sheds some light on the difficulty of disentangling the complex Gordian knot of a universal patriarchal rule of men. Women as a category that live under one culture or religion, as in the case of Havatzelet Ingbar and her friends, have taught us that if they wanted to bring a change, they had to apply their agent tools to the specific subordinating complex apparatus. In that case, the Israeli labor market apparatus that was very deeply rooted in the history, culture, and economy frameworks. The short history of feminist struggles has shown that there are backlashes that cause regression and bring back old patriarchal patterns and often hold back struggling women. That means that feminist liberation is a work that individuals must do on their own, a process that begins in the change of consciousness of single women and may be contaminating, but women must do the work one by one.

In the textile factory in Mitzpe Ramon, the celebration was too thrilling to spoil, and it took a while after things didn't work until the actors began to point out the pitfalls in the process. After a few months, however, the managers began to realize that not all the other actors believed in the vision they and the Histadrut secretary had. It seemed too revolutionary for institutions that functioned with some of the founding fathers still on the board. The happy ending of the transfer from a failing factory to a cooperative that women operated and the transformation of women workers to women managers began in the very first minutes after the ribbon was cut. The gender split occurred then, when the men who were supposed to escort the women in their challenging journey expected the women to take a male path but still remain submissive, the only path they knew. The women may have taken that path had the escorting men had the patience to learn. The journey the women began to take yielded a character of moving from the private sphere to the public. Crossing this path didn't mean that the women crossed just an imaginative line but a thick, conscious road that divided the spheres. The women found themselves in a location fo consciousness that divided the public and the private sphere. At first, it felt as if it were an in-between space, a neither private nor public sphere. In many respects, this was a sphere in which they were strangers, a sphere in which the language and the codes were not like those they were socialized for from early age. These unfamiliar surrounding required different mental resources to function according to different mechanisms from those they were used to employing at various situations in the private sphere. Where they were used to caring in the past, they had now to operate fierce sentiments that went with tough decision-making far from caring sentiments. Where they could tolerate some useful production rates now required a demand for uncompromising utility maximization to increase benefits and reach the best profits. The women managers had to learn how to differentiate between feelings of friendship and professional considerations. Mental transformation had to be practiced and trained for the different setting as an authoritative manager. Sometimes they were counter-socializing or unlearning what they had been all their lives trained to do. They stood now on the other side of the manager-worker relationship but couldn't internalize the change in one move. For the first time, the three female leaders began to discuss the problem of the solitude that leaders experience. They couldn't share with the workers some of the fears and worries they felt when they did not earn the support of the escorting men and when buyers did not come as they were hoping. Sharing these worries would have a discouraging impact on the workers.

> Between us [the three leading managers, HDK] we raised basic questions such as "What should and shouldn't we discuss with the women-employees, the stockholders, and those who didn't [own stock]. What belongs to the domains which we should teach the women-employees with regard to the new status of cooperation, and what is relevant? What shouldn't we tell the women-employees—problems that frustrated me as a person who supported transparency at work as an ideal?" These were all new questions to us, and we needed not only facts and figures but also time to practice and the mental preparation for

> interactions of an entirely new sort. Interaction that [was] now not only new but sometimes went against what we have always did. Frustration was a feeling that surfaced much in those days.

These were Ingbar's reflections two years after she had resigned from the job as the manager of the cooperative. She admitted that she didn't understand the problems at the time of the management.

REFLEXIVE THOUGHTS

Ingbar told me, twice at my request, about the moments after which Peretz, the Histadrut secretary, asked if she would consider taking on the factory and operate it as a cooperative. The first time she discussed it, it was told with enthusiasm and bright eyes. Two years later, after she had left the cooperative, her voice was flat with a tone of bitter disappointment and pain. All throughout the talk, her voice was monotone as she told me the story since I saw her last two years prior. She moved from indifference to sadness this time, with no smile on her face. The first time we spoke, she had worn a smile on her face, even when telling about the struggle that preceded the cooperative period. Our second round of meetings began when we participated in the annual conference on the Israeli society in the Sapir College located in the development town of Sderot. This conference was titled "Searching for Massoudah" (Massouda is a name usually given to women of Arab or Muslim-Jewish women, and it carries the political connotation of referring to simple, often ignorant, and poor women in the pejorative sense). I spoke with Ingbar on that conference and asked if she would agree to meet me again for a series of meetings and watch together with me the documentary *Daroma* that Julie Shlez and Doron Tavory filmed from the beginning of the process of transferring to a cooperative. I explained that I was interested in her interpretation of what was filmed and to hear her explanations and her part in the sequence of the events. To my delight, she generously agreed. We met eight times, at two hours each time. We had informal conversations and talks about parts of the documentary. All the meetings took place in her home in Mitzpe Ramon, except for the first two; one was in my office, and one was in my home, both in Beersheba, which is a one-hour drive north of Mitzpe Ramon. The purpose of meeting in Mitzpe Ramon was to spare Ingbar the traveling hassle and waste of time. I went to her place on Friday evenings and began talking while I was helping her in the kitchen as she prepared for the Shabbat meal. Ingbar was a warm-hearted host. During this series of meetings, I raised questions from a retrospective angle. I asked questions about her self-image as a worker and a manger and what her thoughts were as of what changes she expected in her relationship with her friends. When she responded to the question about the managerial experience, she had a surprised expression, then an expression that reflected a sentiment of failure. Before women make that move towards the in-between zone that divides the private and the public spheres, they go through a twofold experience: One stems from hesitance and doubts regarding their abilities to cross the gender lines. These are lines that force women to adopt masculine socialization patterns perceptions and norms. The other stems from doubts regarding their will to cross the lines and discard old patterns that served them as women, as they were taught of what it meant to be feminine and a person who was socialized for "private sphere's affairs." These experiences sit as sediment within the consciousness of women who find themselves forced to move to the public realm or to choose to run for a public position (Syrett, 1992). These are patterns that are not thought of if not required to consciously cross the line between the spheres. For long years, women hesitated and avoided taking the initiative to devote to careers because of both the fear of failure and, as it is known in psychology field, the fear to succeed (Popp and Muhs, 1982) and the frustration that put them in the impossibility of trying to be superwomen. It was not that they couldn't make it as managers but that they were expected to be what they knew they can't be: superwomen. The superwomen syndrome, however, demands a very high price: a sacrifice of the self. In this respect, the hesitant steps that Ingbar and her friends took when they decided to take the Histadrut offer were significant; they were the first steps of crossing into the in-between zone, which for them was enigmatic. The previous employment as workers at the factory did not demand radical change of the women's socialization. They were expected to obey, submit, and be the "good girls" who were familiar as they were socialized to be from their girlhood. This socialization is associated with other characteristics of being placed in the lower class and belonging to a weaker ethnic sector of society. This multi-facial periphery cohered with receipt and containment that the women were trained for as women and as responsible for the domestic realm. Their blast and strike was one turnover instance that had no other steps to follow and maintain it. Perhaps they had nothing to lose at that moment. A revolutionary spirit needed more energy than the one moment a revolt carried within its wings. The government bureaus and the other well-established institutions could afford the bet because they had nothing personal to sacrifice as opposed to the women. Those officials did not have to think of the personal risks they had to take if the women weren't able to return debts of the failed experiment of recovering the cooperative. After all, they did not sign the contracts of returning debts. The move that carried the potential of radical change in the women's lives pulled the women back to the conservation of the old order, the patriarchal dominated order that essentially doubts women's qualifications to carry on in their world. The entire move took place on the surface of the patriarchal order, in front of the media cameras, and with inaccurate communication reports that the initiative and deliverance of the management of the factory was doing. The sincere effort of the women to bring about the successful recovery of the factory, to bring about change and conclude with profitable production at the same time they were lacking so much knowledge in diverse fields, lacking the political understanding of the power games, as it seemed in retrospective to Ingbar, was impossible. She was less wondering what went wrong and more sobering of and understanding of where she should have put her management weight to try and change the grave situation. That was not knowledge that, she has realized in retrospective, was power. I think further that it concerned the hyphenation between power and knowledge.

Eventually, thirty-five women held stock in the cooperative. This was more than 50 percent of the workforce. All the women were back to work, and the recovery process was on the road. Their preliminary steps were to purchase raw material, begin to search proactively for buyers in the civil market, not just the IDF agents, prepare the merchandise orders, deal with financial bodies and banks, contact judicial services to began to learn how to work with contracts with different officials and businesspeople, and begin training for long-range economic and financial planning. This demanded considerations of labor power, professional activation, and handling of technical parts of the factory. They set up production priorities, giving the IDF and ministry of defense orders high priority, as they had already one big demand in hand. Each worker was scheduled for two shifts in a row, including the stockholders and the managers, when they could, which meant that they stayed for long hours, sometimes after coming to the factory at dawn and returning home at midnight. When they didn't travel to the center of the country, Tel Aviv, where the bureaus and business people could meet, they met for planning, budgeting, and dealing with the production issues, which was usually in the evenings and at nights. Mitzpe Ramon is very small, and their workplace was ten minutes travel distant from home; therefore, staying at the plant at night was only for the reason of being all in for work while the spouse and those who had grown-up children could take care of housekeeping. Ingbar, Avygail Yifrah, and Larissa Vonigradov began to spend long hours traveling to Tel Aviv to met with managers in the cooperation center in the Histadrut, with representatives of the industrial and commerce ministry, and with businesspeople who volunteered to escort them and advise them on their first steps in the new world of industry and business. They absorbed new knowledge in management and in the Israeli culture of management. They discovered that there existed things such as organizational culture, maximizing, human resources, and cash flow and investment scheduling. Twenty-four hours a day was too short an amount of time for what they had to fill it with. Ingbar reported that her average working hours began at six o'clock in the morning, and she came back home at eleven at night. Not very afterward, the women began to show signs of exhaustion. The women who didn't purchase stocks and had doubts from the beginning of the process regarding its success asked to alternately lessen their scheduling from two shifts in a row. For them, the change in their working place was the hope for stability and more sensitive humanistic treatment but not more than these expectations. The managers were now their colleagues and friends, not the cruel exploiting person from before. They did not imagine that they would be asked to work for free and volunteer for the sake of the factory's recovery. This was indeed the request that came not so long later, less than six months after they began the recovery process.

On our third meeting at Ingbar's place, it was already after she had resigned from the cooperative. She was making efforts to collect the pieces of her life after failing at the recovery attempt. Her disappointment was very deep, and two years was not enough time for her to get out of the crisis she experienced. What was an experiment for the officials, far away there in Tel Aviv, was for her part of a traumatic experience that is on top of the previous humiliating torturous treatment from the boss before the transfer of the factory. She had difficulties getting out of the anxiety she experienced. In the spirit of Sandra Harding (1987) regarding strong objectivity, I did not try to keep remote from Ingbar in the experiences we both had. I took the initiative on that third meeting and spoke of my own life experiences that seemed to coincide with hers. We compared personal opinions regarding similar experiences, spoke of the emotions such experiences stimulated in us, and discussed the political implications on the state of women in wider contexts, such as women in Israel, women in the Western world, and those in the third world. The topic of power relations occupied a significant part of our talks, and in the spirit of Donna Haraway's suggestion, we situated our knowledge relation to wider formal academic or political status of knowledge (Haraway, 1986). What we spoke of received its meaning from the impact it had on us rather than whether we were successful or failed in what we were doing. In this respect, it was a process of reevaluation of experiences from a personal perspective. Once, I shared with Ingbar my experience of being dismissed from my job. Following that, what came to our talk was discussion of the sentiments of shame, failure, and pain that comes with this hard experience. We lingered on the difficulty of the hard sentiment of rejection and being laid off and being an unneeded person. My personal involvement in this kind of experience and the discussion we had about it helped share the burden that the traumatic memories surfaced. Sharing this heavy burden experience also brought us to closer and allowed us to speak of other intimate topics that associated with this particular experience. The subjective aspect of our talk got looser and formal dichotomous rigidity that often dominates academic interviews was dismantled. The conversation flowed, and we could discuss steps we took out of frustration and rage and came out in more sensible states. Our next move in the analysis of the affairs was to concentrate interpreting events from a critical point of view that could emerge only after the release of the mental burden of frustration and rejection that characterizes the first instance of being dismissed. At this point, Ingbar released her rage bubbled inside her regarding the behavior of her colleagues at the cooperative. She kept it to herself until then and didn't share it with anyone. This enhanced her feeling of solitude known to leaders at the top. She told me that what surprised her was that it was not only the male officials and clerics whom she met that filled the role of gender gatekeepers but also some of her female friends as well.

FIELDS OF POWER AND PRODUCTION OF KNOWLEDGE

Conflicting interests between the actors flickered from the time the revolt started. Ingbar learned to identify the honest types of expression from those which camouflaged dishonest intentions. In the beginning, Ingbar perceived the governmental officials, the business sector, and the labor union, the Histadrut, as a triangle of forces that joined forces together to rescue the factory and the women workers. However, the more she got closer and met with particular representatives, the more she understood that some had different interests then they originally manifested. Some were found to be adversaries and didn't hide rivalries within the organizations of which she expected their assistance and support. The phenomena of competing forces and political conflicts in the public arena and within governing organizations might seem trivial, but knowing about their existence is also trivial. However, this didn't mean that seeing them and being exposed to them was not surprising time and again. It not only had to do with naivety as Ingbar stated more than once, but also with not having the privilege of growing a serious optimistic approach. This was particularly true for a person like Ingbar who learned about the public and governmental organizations from the press and media. The adversaries between the conflicting actors, such as the government and Histadrut or the private sector, designed a maze for her and she couldn't say if they were an ally or an adversary. Who is cooperating with her out of generosity, and who joined her out of rivalry with another actor? The crypts were hidden behind the deeds, and she couldn't decipher them, but one by one, due to the range that grew between words and deeds, she was learning the way. Often she received messages with double meanings, which were confusing and obscure, and it took her time to understand that it was done on a deliberate intention, and it was not so innocent

> Until I understood that things were about intrigues, maneuvers, even conspiracies, not always directed against the cooperative...Sometimes it took them one extra day to return to me with answers, only because they needed that day to

> profit a little more from the production process or the money in the bank…The idea that Dany Chetrit came up with, that I should return to the production line as a manager, should be hired from outside the sewing workshop, which I eventually accepted, turned out to be serving his interest to gain more power against my authority and stand [in] the way of my decisions. When he had difficulties to maneuver me, the manager, he began to talk with other employees out against me. These were especially with the women who didn't buy stocks. At a certain point, I realized that, over time, I came back from meeting in Tel Aviv, and he stayed in Mitzpe, the atmosphere became more hostile and cloudy against me. (second interview)

Ingbar discovered, with surprise, that the people whom she thought were her allies were subverting the project. Amir Peretz, the Histadrut secretary, had made promises to her, but his clerics and executives worked with red tape. It seemed that they had a different agenda. "The person in charge of the cooperative center may have lost some of his authority," Ingbar explained to me. This is why he wasn't anxious to help. He retained information that he was supposed to share with the women in the cooperative, but the women didn't know about that. Not knowing that, they couldn't demand the information. Looking back, Ingbar pointed out this behavior as an obstructive, if not deliberately obstructive, attitude on that clerk's part: "…our dependence on him remained the same, we could not proceed without consulting him on every step we did," she said. One of the sobering moments that Ingbar recalled was when she realized that a basic rule should be to examine everything she was told and search for hidden meaning to what she heard. That moment was exemplified by when Chetrit told Ingbar that they shouldn't waste time where they don't get money and proceeded to cut a meeting short. He simply lied about having another meeting that they were late for. On a wider point of view, Ingbar realized that Chetrit was simply interested in keeping the women uneducated and unprofessional. He did not make it an ideology, but he acted out of fear of the women who might become more educated than he was. Ingbar played with these reflections, not knowing whether they were the real reason, but when it was added up to his general approach, Ingbar was almost certain of it:

> I was astonished to realize that he did everything he could to prevent investment in our education and professionalization. In the end, I understood that he was afraid of the fact that we [would obtain] power when gaining more knowledge. (second interview)

Excluding women from fields of power where managers dominate them is not so incidental as it might seem. Usage of language in an obscure way, camouflaging intentions, and equivocal senses left the women confused. The women couldn't see the obstacles in their way to get the best advice. Lacking confidence and experience came back time and again to the assumption that they don't know enough, and so they should listen to what is said *to* them. Thus Ingbar was prevented from moving freely between the roles she had to fill as a manager, as a worker, and as a stockholder. The gender factor played a crucial role, and finally, the chance to learn more in the realm of business and production was slammed in her face. The constellation presented how effective, subtle, and sensitive the power relations are that involve gender, authority, and knowledge production. It illustrates how complicated the gender project of power network deconstruction. The first steps the women did in crossing from the private to the public sphere caught them in the middle, an in-between zone, and they remained there searching for the path that would take them on to the public sphere. The patronizing attitude of the seemingly assisting and close men in fact stood firmly in their way. What little the women were able to grasp from the meetings and conversations with professionals, such as decision-makers in the ministries and the business people who came to discuss production orders, showed the women how much more they would have to learn. They did what they could while working simultaneously and making difficult decisions on subjects they knew very little of. Often, they made the decision that was suggested to them by professionals from the NGOs without examining other options because of time pressure under which they operated. In this respect, they carried on and preserved in many senses the old patriarchal order without making progress in gaining new knowledge in the professional field of cooperative enterprise. The recovery of the factory was conditioned by making some new reforms that were hindered in the circumstances that occurred along the road.

Ingbar recalled this with sour taste and pride interchangeably:

> After Arnon Keren, the production manager, [had] left [because he did not get the salaries and the other items that the employment contract included, HDK], I took the role of management in the sewing workshop for three months. Chetrit came only to the managers meetings and asked to be updated [on] the current events [at] those meetings. I had to put much more time [into] searching for the right person in the ministries and to set my appointments with the Ministry of Defense representatives. I checked the merchandise before delivering it and made all the examinations and quality control of the products. This required that I contact the Israeli Standard Institute and negotiate for the standard marks. I learned how to do that, but had I [had received] sincere assistance from the Histadrut and the Cooperation Centre, it would have spared me precious chunks of time. (second interview).

After a few months spent trying to figure out how communication works between the different actors, Ingbar mentioned that often she felt that they played a mystifying game. They mentioned issues that indicated that there were rules that related to some old agreements that the Histadrut and the government signed and that they were held back by them. The person in the

Histadrut replied to her queries saying "Never mind, we don't have time to enter i." The women's common sense was not enough, Ingbar recalled, and it had always conjured them by hinting that they didn't have the necessary knowledge. Little pieces of misleading information and mistakes came together to make a picture that it wasn't always the women's lack of knowledge or complex systems and bureaucracy but instead deliberate deceiving advice. These mechanisms of blocking knowledge were not exclusive as far as they concerned governing and authority systems; it was the common way power systems operated as learned from Michel Foucault and as so many political cultures manifest themselves to be (Foucault, 1980, 82). The short and beautiful work of *How to Win an Election* by Quintus Tullius Cicero (2012 [64 BC]) very lucidly illustrates it. The same problem applied to the women's accessibility to legal agreements, considerations to take financial risks, commercial commitments, banking operations, discussing labor agreements, and purchasing and trying to decipher business moves. Ingbar reported that this activity put her under much stress and demanded emotional energies that involved fears and worries: "The responsibility was enormous," she said.

IDENTITY AND DISGUISE

> Imagine you speak with a businessman client on [a] one-hundred-thousand-shekels deal, on the supply terms and the deadline, in a morning that you are afraid to meet the grocer's eyes because he told you that he can't continue selling you the elementary items of bread and milk with credit as he didn't get money for the debts you [already owed] him. . . . How much chutzpah [do] you need in order to say to that textile client with whom you must do business and who earns at least twenty times your salary: "Five thousand shirts will be ready for you on X day; when will you deposit the money?"

Ingbar earned, at that time, 3,000 NIS—1,000 NIS below the average income in Israel; that is, she didn't get to reach the end of the month without credits all around, the mortgage, the grocery, school, bills, and so on.

> Imagine what a poor woman manager, who is aware of her status in the [bottom] of the social scale, when he [the buyer, HDK] is on the top? How do you think I felt when negotiating with a millionaire buyer? This alone demanded from me [a] great deal of emotional energy. (second interview)

How did she overcome these difficulties?

> [with] the hope, the belief, that we will make it against all odds. They could see that we don't know much and that sometimes we said things that made no sense, and yes, we felt ridiculous and [were] often mocked. We had this

> mindset of workers, and it was so hard to wear the disguise of the manager, to make up the authoritative jester, tone, vocabulary. For that, we needed the knowledge in the fields of textile and the familiarity with the details of the crisis, which were hidden from us in those days. We didn't know how to play the game, as if everything was OK, and that we know what we actually didn't know. . . . This I learned only after the entire drama ended and I had resigned as a consequence, among other things, of not knowing how to play this kind of fake game. (second interview)

I realized that the disguise and performance was, for Ingbar, something that no one told her about or its significance for the role she was expected to play. Neither she nor her friends knew how these roles are truly learned. Acting was not of the cultural and social inventory they were socialized to. The importance of practicing reiterated performance (of managers in this case), as Judith Butler suggested, seemed to the women to be phony and dishonest. The women didn't realize how powerful the part of performativity was in filling roles as authoritative doctors and educators and, more extensively, in heteronormative cultures in the formation of gender and professional relations. The sign that indicated their being workers or managers were the same as those that indicated gender affiliations and determined whether it is a boy or a girl, as Butler elaborated in her book *Gender Trouble* (1990).

When we discussed the issue of disguise and performance, Ingbar commented that, eventually, she realized that the world around her was that which defined for her the identity she had:

> This one is a worker and that one is a manager, no matter what agent move we tried to make. The knowledge and experience, together with the performance, made for one person the manager identity and for the other the worker identity, just as for one it is the female gender and for the other it is male. We needed a larger vector to bend off the power that could bring change in the world's relations surrounding us. (second interview)

The repeated feminist argument that claimed that women are equipped with enough knowledge in economy because they practice multitasking during their housekeeping economy was put to the test in the cooperative initiative. Housekeepers never got to go to courses on housekeeping and domestic economy, nor do they learn how to become parents. They learn intuitively, in an autodidact way, how to calculate home incomes and outcomes of house expenses without preplanning economic programs or plan for prearranged production. These presumptions were proved false for the women in the factory. The move required consciousness change that should have enabled the women to work with much larger amounts of money and expand their view of the tasks they should control. Their tasks in the factory before they took it as owners required work such as standing in front of the sewing machine, ironing board, and/or next to the bottoms machine or tags machines. It may have been complex and required organization, preparation, skills, and accommodation to maximize the supply capacity and minimize physical body distortion and pain during the days, months, and years of work. The workers' awareness was invested in these tasks that demanded different attention and organization aimed at producing the proper amount of items in the shortest time possible. There was a standard that they had set up after many years of expertise. It was a professional standard rarely rewarded or even acknowledged. What they needed now was the move to fields where these skills were essential but less significant. Management and organization techniques were now much more important and required more abstraction intellectual abilities, such as planning and estimations of future production and imagination of the impact on various fields that concerned them. How would the impact relate to human resources and to recovery chances of the cooperative? The external circle that surrounded the women—the authorities and decision-makers in the ministries along with the Histadrut—in various and conflicting interests there was not much to indicate that they knew much more regarding the best professional way to transform the failing textile factory to a successful cooperative. They showed no political or organizational prudence when they suggested to the workers to purchase the factory. The decision-makers thought the women could move resources and make financial transfer from one authority to the other and expected that the authoritative relations would remain the same. Once the women began to generate the initiative, the officials began to realize both that the women lacked critical knowledge, and also that the business relations with them must also change. In some cases, those who were the worker's authority found themselves becoming subordinated and had to submit to their orders. This inversion of the power relations was hidden until the implementation of the initiative began. Broadly, this significant experience is part of what feminist women need to go through, one by one, when trying to break through glass ceilings. When it is multiplied by moving from one subordinated position to a subordinating one, the task becomes almost impossible. In such situations, women experience primal forces that lie very deep in generations of patriarchal and class structures. The rules of the game are dictated from the depth of these orders.

In a few months, nine of the women who purchased stock returned them. Each one of the women realized that the power-relation maze and their lack of knowledge and information, such as the hidden dynamics that they could only witness, were all too much for them to cope with. Intuitively, they knew that there must be much more that they don't know and that they will not be able to grasp it all while still functioning as workers. It felt similar to the inside of the coat, the linen that no one could see from the outside but could very well feel. It was heavy and restrictive. Ingbar felt more isolated than ever. Until then, she worked two shifts in a row: one next to the machines, and the other next to the office desk when she was not traveling around. After some of the women returned the stocks, she added a few more hours of work until she was exhausted.

> [Michael] Fleishman, who was nominated as manager right after we received the factory [into] our hands, was so rude that I couldn't bear his behavior. . . . If you add to it the hostility I began to feel from my comrades and their crossing the lines to support the operation manager, the conflicts of orders between those I gave the women and those of the manager, along with Chetrit's subversion, my life became unbearable. I had to bend my principles, those for which I initially began the struggle, and this was "the straw that broke [the camel's] back." I came to the decision to resign. (second interview)

The message of the decision to all involved was that the women were unable to get rid of their image as simply female workers and that, in fact, the passage from worker to manager failed. The consciousness turnover that they have experienced did not coincide with the persistent patriarchal order that they managed to violate for a moment during the months that flowed since they began the strike. The strike should have been followed with an activity that would have maintained the momentum of change for women in the larger arena of the labor market, but it didn't. The women remained captured in that in-between zone, consciously moving between spheres, from the private to the public. The ethos applied to the private sphere and, therefore, to the women was perceived in public as a sign of weakness. In public, what prevailed was the ethos of justice, hence "of men," as we learned from Carol Gilligan (1982) in her critique of Lawrence Kolberg's moral development model (1971). This ethos is not abstract; it is lying on a political and cultural infrastructure and social apparatus that functions through socialization systems that form the male/female consciousness and determine one's affiliation to the private or the public sphere according to his or her biological sex. Therefore, when women cross the lines and enter the public sphere, they a priori stand in a disadvantaged position compared to men.

I shared with Ingbar about my insights that subjective human relations cannot be learned from objective knowledge. She responded: "Well, everything is motivated by interests and politics." I asked her for further elaboration, of which she replied that "politics" meant something dirty and contaminated with corruption, dishonesty, unfulfilled promises, hidden motivations, hypocrisy, and exploitation of the other; in short, it stood for immorality. This was not an exception from the notion of "political business," as it is often perceived from populist opinions. Nevertheless, kinship relations as they are modified within families of all cultures, as Claude Lévi-Strauss (La pensee sauvage, 1962) and Gayle Rubin (1975) suggested, are not easily applied to the public sphere. When dragging them out of the private sphere, as the women in the cooperative tried to do, they are found to be unfit for it. The women tried to adapt from the private sphere ethos to the public and failed. The language, codes, and apparatus that operated the private are difficult to apply to the public. The dichotomy is too strong, and as the women realized, it is sometimes unbridgeable. The strength of this dichotomy stems from the antagonism between what can be perceived as Machiavellian (1971[1532]), which prevails in politics in the public sphere, and *Stabat Mater* [*mother Mary's mercy*] (thirteenth century) that is expected to be prevailing in the private sphere. While crossing the spheres and lingering within the in-between space, women discover, through personal experience, things that they couldn't know before had they not lived it through. These are things that relate to the sense of liberation that cannot be purchased while subordinated and socialized to the private sphere. Experience is a crucial factor in the process of liberation. For women in the 1950s, it was in a late stage of their lives when they already had been young women that they began to be exposed to feminism. This is unlike young mothers today (the number of fathers, in this respect, grows steadily) in most cultures, which are aware of the destiny of their daughters and make serious attempts to introduce them to the public sphere habitus: a sphere that speaks different language and operates according to different codes of power interrelations. Young girls from the childhood stage of socialization grow into the public sphere and socialize early on to cope with this sphere. Although the sphere is still dominated by patriarchal order and still very much androcentric, women develop various strategies to cope with it and make changes. The women in the cooperative, however, were exposed to the first and second waves of feminism when they were already young women. Being of peripheral lower class and poor, their ability to cross the spheres while in the midst of their economic, ethnic, and politically weak situations made them walk slowly and go small distances in the in-between space towards the public sphere.

Ingbar got a taste of the liberation and the potential change from her youth. What she experienced was bivalence: men's normative behavior, which disappointed and disempowered her. Her feeling that everything emerges in power relations and everything is "corrupted with politics" represented a common view for women, which in her case was not just a populist opinion or naivety but personal experience that should have been listened to.

> The men in the sewing workshop were members of the governing political party [Mapay, later on transformed to the Labor party, HSK] and members in the union labor Histadrut. Often, I met officials that didn't have a clue [as to] what the textile branch was. They were occupied with the campaign of expending the electorate flying on the successful wings of our story. But Havatzelet [speaking of herself in third-person singular, HDK] was so blind to that. Moreover, when I understood the game, I refused to play politics; I am not a politician. (second interview)

From the first steps she made as a manager, Ingbar noticed the gender power asymmetry between the spheres' codes and values. They became dynamic obstacles. Every move she made generated motions in the direction of the hidden linen of gender tissues of forces. Almost always women reveal these hidden forces only at random, as the codes weave of forces is camouflaged within the streaming channels of the organization and are covered with layers of operational rules and formal professional patterns. The network is covered by the definitions of the goals, such as profit maximization and what is good for the factory. Often, things such as the benefit of the factory and gender discrimination cohered with each other; therefore, it is difficult to protest against the tone of the factors—the gender discrimination—without sound objection to the benefit of the collective goal of maximization of profit. Even worse, sometimes the factors that serve male gender interests consist with production efficiency ("national goals"), which are broader economic interests that seem to be hidden from particular workers' eyes. Therefore, rhetoric such as this serves the interests of subordinating forces urged with passionate drives, which is too often of men.

The cooperative functioned for a year and a half until it was finally closed. This was a year and a half of consciousness transformation of the women. They grew up in the political sense and went through a sobering process that sometimes brought them to cynicism when speaking with public figures that kept visiting the remote development town in the desert of the Negev. Their adventure of trying to recover the factory and operate it successfully may have failed, but the women experienced change that made them agents of change and helped them develop awareness to their position within the larger Israeli society as women, workers, and as residents in the peripheral area of the state; and finally, also as managers. The adventure departures from a weak position, long years of frustration and disappointment, continued with hesitance and skepticism, then exciting moments of discovery and surprise. They went on experiencing treason and confusion along with to solidarity and support in moments that were least expected. Some of them for the first time touched upon real authority and power as managers, but they also experienced dilemmas and tension when they had to make tough decisions. They managed crises and passionate emotions and interests while standing in the midst of intense and stormy events.

The term "empowerment," as it is employed in feminist discourse, surfaces a lot in sisterhood contexts. Strong and self-confident women encourage, support, and help to promote their sisters. This perception of "empowerment" connotes the idea that some women deliver power to others. What happened in the factory, and then in the cooperative, was different; the women sought power from within themselves, and the process was viewed rather as self-empowerment than empowering by outside parties. Moreover, the feminist idea of sisterhood was shaky and sometimes disappointing. Women found sources of power and trust because they were motivated to make a change in their lives and the lives of their family. They moved from the private to the public in the deepest sense of the division of labor, and they broke the rigid structure that covered so much of the political rules, power relations, and conscience. Although the women knew about other sorts of struggles, such as within their family and marriage lives, when facing local institutions and services providers such as the bank, the municipality, and school principals, they realized that gaining some experiences concerning struggles cannot be copied and applied to others. Each arena has its own rules and, therefore, chances to generate changes are bound to these specific rules. This is why the Gordian Knot of feminism is so complicated to disentangle. Each sort of oppression and subordination within each society and culture requires a specific disentangling application.

Purchasing the factory demanded very high risk, such as angry outbursts when the women discovered that they were deceived. The general warning that this was going to involve high risk was an understatement regarding the responsibility, the debts, the risks, and the hopes with which they were charged. Before taking the initiative, the women could not make the exploration they should have made, and the authorities were anxious to charge them with the idea of the cooperative too quickly, before they were ready to take it on. It took a short time for them to realize that the factory had no chance and that what they got was a dying enterprise; it was actually dying along with the entire textile branch and was, therefore, past the threshold for a chance of recovery. The Histadrut had planted, in vain, a belief that Ingbar was furious and bitter about when she retrospectively summed up the venture:

> They exploited our honest and devoted work, our goodwill, our passion to succeed, which retrospectively was full of energy that sufficed the recovery of the sewing workshop, had they been also honest with us. . . . It was like losing your innocence. . . . No one dared warn [that] "It is too big; you can't take it; do not go in." Sheer interests were the main ingredient, not benevolence on the part of Peretz [the Histadrut secretary, HDK]. (second interview)

Women discover how alliances are plotted between strong allies only when they get a closer glance at the power relations at work. Being present at meetings between business people and between politicians, they saw that these took place behind closed doors. The discovery does not come in a neutral spirit if the power relations viewed by the women who are also the subject of these relations. In long ranges of time, women accumulate not only understanding but also emotions, and sometimes these are negative emotions. Although they might hold back these emotions, it doesn't mean that they fade away. When the women became aware of this process in the factory that was when they began to feel empowerment from within. For some of them, they discovered what it took them to have a stronger urge to make a change. It is not certain that this process leads to liberation and sobering experience. Some, like in our story, might get stuck in the in-between zone. Nevertheless, this experience bears insights that do not fade away. The truth value of our story is not objective; that is, the success or failure does not lie in the fact that the cooperative became lucrative and recovered but in the distance that the women made from the beginning of their rebellious journey and the change they experienced from within their inner world, from their consciousness. Their point of view of the world, as women, spouses, mothers, workers, and many other aspects, were all influenced by the adventure they went through. For them, this was the linen layer from which the drama took place. The notions of success and failure thus become elastic and contextually dependent. Fixed values and codes become relative, and the women, particularly Ingbar, went through a dynamic change that did not cease even after resignation.

Feminist and queer literature prefers a subjective point of view from which to evolve its grounded theory over objective scientific truth. There is more to trust in subjective and personal testimony than in quantitative graphs of proximity, as Yvonna Lincoln and Egon Guba suggest (1985). The subject searches for acknowledgment to his/her truth even if scientific definitions point them out as phantasmal and deviant. The peripheral site where the story took place related to a handful of women whose lives may not allow generalizations and universalization. Nevertheless, aspects that concerned women who faced challenges left behind a rich qualitative arena with information about feminist process experiences with regard to liberation that provides us with adequate material for theoretical research. The questions of subjectivity and truth, however, remain still contractual.

This is where Foucault pointed out the need to develop new methods, which will concentrate on the construct of the subject, on subjectivity, and on intersubjective relations. This move was a U-turn departing away from scientific knowledge production and rational reflection. It was a move in the direction of learning the history of our relation to ourselves and to each other. It is impossible to reduce this field of study of the selfness to the study of "truth." The study of "truth" concerns formal ontology as a critical analysis of knowledge; therefore, it is not possible to reduce and make concise the occupation with the subject and subjectivity into scientific knowledge and rational thoughts with tools that were produced for "objective" knowledge, unless we agree to study the subject as if it is an object. The path, in which Foucault suggested to walk to bypass this pitfall, as he himself chose to walk, concentrated in the study of our selfness within a context of history and archeology of power networks. Within this context, he stressed the dichotomous pitfalls that exist between the "objective truth" and the diverse forms of the subjectivity constructs. The enlightenment philosophers, he argued, did debate the question of truth while concentrating on philosophical reflection on the formal ontology of the knowledge and, allegedly, timeless issue. However, when reviewing Immanuel Kant's short article from 1784, Foucault suggested reading it within a historical context. When doing so, the nacre on which Kant clung for the discussion on the crisis of the mind's wit of his time is uncovered. The questions that Foucault was occupied with concerned the actual reality within the French Revolution's context and the enlightenment of that era: "These two questions, 'What is the enlightenment? What is the revolution?' are two forms under which Kant positioned his own question of his actuality?" (Foucault, 1984)

Chapter Eight

Post Facts of Feminist Development

I met Havatzelet Ingbar twelve years later in 2016, having not met since I last interviewed her. Ingbar left Mitzpe Ramon and returned to Dimona, the town where she spent her childhood, half an hour from Mitzpe Ramon. She now works in medical simulation for a high-tech enterprise called Rotem Industries. For a long period after politics had shaken her life and her resignation from the cooperative Atzmaut in Miztpe Ramon, Julie Shlez, the producer of the documentary *Daroma*, suggested for Ingbar to go to Tel Aviv in search of a new path for her life. After one year of short-term jobs in different fields, such as a secretary and an assistant in various offices, Ingbar decided to go back to the south, the Negev, where she felt she belonged. At Rotem Industries, she began as a cleaning person for a while and then she asked for an interview with the manager to discuss the possibility that she gets the chance to move on to the production line. This move was one that she based on her experience as an agent. She got the chance and became a worker on the line with better social terms and salary. Ingbar is now a sober woman whose worldview is wider than the worker she used to be. She told me, not without satisfaction, that she likes her life without being in the limelight of the media and in the public. She organized her life after being a public figure on a path of stable and quite routine close to her family. When she was describing the efforts she made to return to private life, she stressed the value of privacy and the lessons that brought her to understand that. She didn't lose the value and experience she acquired when revolting. She is now directing them in more individualistic acts of negotiation and more personal interactions with the authorities. She doesn't refrain from discussing the future and asks her employers about the coming months and what are the economic insecurity options. She learned to identify the working values of devotion and diligence and substantializes them by asking for acknowledged promotion and improvement of labor conditions. After the hard time she had in the days of crisis during and after the rebellion, I remember that she almost didn't smile. Now I got to see her smiling face and a peaceful expression easily. She spoke of power boundaries, and not only hers, but also of her employers. Her vulnerability reduced and, perhaps more importantly, she sounded proud when saying that she learned to take care of herself. She could now identify inner layers of power and nuances of political interests. She knows her rights and walks more confidently towards promotion without "burning her wings." The rebellious part that she will always have in her personality is tuned now to be a mechanism of sobering and self-protection.

The time lapse since we last met enabled us to look at things with long-range perspective, reconstructing memories that filtered redundant details. Ingbar learned now how to associate her story with the larger context of women marginalization mechanisms. She is sensitive to gender relations now more than ever, and she lucidly pointed out what the gender relations flicker and how she perceived men's hegemonic positions, then and now, at the time of our last meeting. She could point out the force that stood in her way to develop resistance to the oppressive conditions in the Peppco factory.

> We didn't receive any grace days when we got into the struggle and recovery process. We were shaken between the fear of what will come out of the struggle and our uncompromising drive to put an end to the oppressive conditions. (Third interview)

Since the strike began, the women didn't have a moment alone. Sometimes against their will they were escorted by men who made attempts time and again to reinforce patriarchal norms. Having no space to be alone and discuss the problems between themselves, they were not free to develop their own views, new views which could have perhaps enable them to walk along new paths. At the same time, they walked lonely in men's yards.

During our last meeting, Ingbar could freely discuss inequality instances and moments in which she identified actions that involved wickedness.

> I will not stand humiliation and insults anymore; being fired today is not the same as it was when the kids were small. (Third interview)

Returning the stocks was not a defeat for the women, as Ingbar commented. Now she spoke in the first-person plural:

> We did not return home with empty hands. Long before humiliation comes, we make a move, we don't tolerate evil, and we also know that we didn't fail [in the factory, HDK]. Our protest taught us that obedience has limits and sometimes we rather take an action at all costs. We understand the value of being an

> agent of change and there must be necessary risk when making a shift. Change is not a matter of one event, it is a working process. (Third interview)

Each oppression apparatus has an operational context. Respectively, it has its dismantling mechanism. Ingbar's marriage was a gloomy story.

> I left him [Havatzelet Ingbar's spouse, HDK] not before I did my part. . . . I always responded, and this drove him crazy. . . . When he hit me, I hit back. Today when he looks at the mirror, he knows he once had a wife. (First interview)

Ingbar recalled that she couldn't see the resemblance of being oppressed at home and what she experienced in the days at the factory. Physical violence at home with a drunken spouse demanded a different strategy of coping from the violence that she experienced in the factory before the strike. In both cases, there was violence, she agreed, but dismantling the two types of violence required different measures. Once again, the Gordian Knot of feminism appears so that success in dismantling one type of subordination does not guarantee that the experience gained works for another type. Women must be inventive, time and again, when coping with the task of disentangling the subordinating knots on their way to liberation. To undress the workers "tight cloths" while simultaneously putting on "heavy CEO's cloths" was not simply because the worker's cloths were as a straight jacket that one couldn't open and peel off. It covered the horizon, and she couldn't see afar. Her vision was abstract, similar to a dream designed with large lines and no details. On top of it all, her first steps were of a rebel, a resistant who walked through in conservative halls of the government, the Histadrut, the industrial sectors, which were all hooped in power relations and which couldn't imagine that striking and resistant workers could make the move to their male club and be accepted as one of them. The cooperative Atzmaut was the only case of a factory where women made an attempt to rescue and save themselves from a dismissal fate. It was a bold decision and a dangerous bet.

POLITICS OF IDENTITY AND AGENTS OF CHANGE

The politics of identity developed in the 1990s. More recently, critical theories study construct elements of identity politics in contrast to more the essential approach that prevailed in the past. In our story, the identity perception that was related to the women as workers was almost essential since they had almost no way to transform to the manager's identity. It was as if the women were essentially workers that were fixed to their place in a larger heterosexual structure. The identity of being a woman worker, poor, and peripheral residents was cohesive and hard to deconstruct. In addition, the common misogynic identities often related to the women as persons that belong to the private sphere and enhanced their identity as being a mother/ spouse/housekeeper and fixed their place in the margins. The woman's place, according to this stereotypical approach, is at home next to the children and the husband, and the worker's place is next to the production line. The conservative order of things couldn't bear women's motion towards another place, such as a manager's position. This meant a violation of the order that called for the gatekeepers to take action. The idea that a women/manager would be in charge of men and give them orders, all while in the public sphere, was new and began to be seen only since the mid-1960s. The phenomena of career women and of women who take higher positions in the public and business enterprises was new and rather revolutionary. That change required consciousness transformation that did not occur simultaneously at the moment of change. It involved and still involves struggles that women conduct to gain acknowledgment as women in high-ranking positions. To break through and gain acknowledgment as needed in higher positions demands from women to be creative and develop new strategies that not only bring them to the desired position but also generates a change of dominated stereotypes of women. The contrast of the stereotype of a subordinated woman who becomes someone who holds authority requires a consciousness transformation not only on the women's part but also on the men's. This change regards identity transformation both first from the women and then the surrounding world in which they are living: the religious, cultural, social, and political settings of order and norms. When Ingbar began to walk this route, she experiences duality from the first instances. On the one hand, she was wrapped with empathy, hope, and exhortation for her moving from the marginal place as a worker to an authoritative position as a manager. On the other hand, there were forces that pushed her back and were trying to thwart her. In our conversations, Ingbar seemed to look back at herself and search for what she didn't understand about subordinating/subordinated gender and class relations. When women of the upper class, wives or daughters of industrial entrepreneurs, tried to move to management and production positions, economic space that allowed them to afford a few months or years of no income, she reflected in a loud voice that they were always enjoying family and spousal support. Within the capitalist framework, such a path was easier only for better-off women, in most cases those who were married. This idea was well-developed by Pierre Bourdieu, who termed it as habitus and extended it to the culture of being rich or the culture of being poor (Bourdieu, 1977). Therefore, richness, class legacy, and cultural resources are critical to a women's ability to make moves towards change and mobilize social transformation. The women in the cooperative worked under conditions that constantly destroyed their professional confidence instead of building it up. Their efforts to generate an agent of change proved to be a Sisyphean project. They were put back time and again to workers' status that echoed with their own self-image as textile workers in a factory but never as potential managers. All the women recognized the oppression and violent forces when they met them after the factory was transferred to their hands. As fighters and survivors, it was as if they had to accept subordinating terms imposed on them without breaking the rules. At the same time, they couldn't discard the other responsibilities for the family, as mothers, often single mothers. In this respect, the women were very strong and could mobilize the necessary mental resources as they could never before the experience they gained while rebelling. Things developed in the wrong directions of fighting negative forces, which eventually brought to failing the attempt to make the cooperative work. The energies of the women were directed to fight those negative trends rather than invest them in networking with the right bodies, forming coalitions that could strengthen them, expanding their knowledge in professional and business affairs that could critically contribute to their success. The women didn't have even the opportunity to learn their rights as women, workers, citizens, and periphery residents. They often heard about them through word of mouth, often inaccurate and too late. They were caught in a vicious circle of being workers, the women realized, which became their only identity and only when they tried to move on and become managers but not before. Ingbar still felt some embarrassment when we discussed it, as if poverty and ignorance went hand in hand with being a factory worker. This sentiment consisted with common prejudice in Israel regarding people of Muslim and Arab origin. Ingbar's origin was India. Even the workers of the ex-USSR were of southern Muslim states, which in Israel were considered less-developed than the people of Belarus. The combination of poor worker and Mizrahi was a trap rooted in the Israeli, an allegedly Western newly neoliberal state they couldn't deconstruct of its negative stereotypes of such women.

Through the method of reflection and reinterpretation, my meeting with Ingbar provided an opportunity to reinterpret and consolidate ideas that we recycled in new lights, particularly emotional lights. I interviewed Ingbar in 2016 following the unplanned meeting we had in Beersheba. She was relaxed and looked on the elapsed time of events as if she came to terms with herself. Her tones and phrases did not try to justify or look for excuses for the failed experience she had during the events. Her judgment of the events was not one of guilty feelings or disappointment of herself as she felt in the first and second interviews. Ingbar contained her emotions with more tolerance than what I remembered in the first and second instances. At the same time, the false omnipotence appearance of the manager she projected in the past was now replaced by a more balanced and calm attitude. She assumed a position where she realized that not everything was dependent on her and, therefore, the failure was not all her fault, as she had felt in the past during the early time after things didn't work in the factory. This marked Ingbar's mature, critical, and wider worldview as a person. The word "legally" came up many times in the last conversation we had and brought up other actors role and responsibility in the events' sequence. She sounded much less disappointed with herself and very much self-containing.

This dramatic chapter in the lives of the women workers at the factory in Mitzpe Ramon has two endings: the first is a happy end, and then there is a sad end. Only when looking back in reflection and critical view, the question arises: How could the story have a different end from that which was sad? The women who were involved ended up having the same breadwinning force, or even less. Nevertheless, they went through deep consciousness and ideological transformations. They were exposed to the workings of power networks, which were hidden from them before, and if it wasn't for that experience, they wouldn't even have the opportunity to see and be involved in power at work. Naked gender power relations were uncovered before their eyes. Consequently, their understanding of the inside lining of the politics surrounding them, their views of the business worlds, the industrial and bureaucratic patterns, and their working relations with friends and colleagues all changed. Talking to Ingbar, I could hear that she changed her entire view of what she thought about human nature, the public institutions, the establishment, political leaders, labor relations, and her understanding of Israeli politics. Her understanding of the division of spheres and labor became more sophisticated, and she grasped its engendered complexity. From the minute women leave home for the workplace, they cross many lines into the world that men designed and made it the world of men: professional, political, cultural, religious, and many others. At the same time, they drag with them their own socialized assets as mothers, spouses, family, and kin that are accommodated to the private realm. The adaptation burden is, therefore, doubled. The consciousness experience they went through generated disentanglement of the knots clasping their multifaceted lives. The knots loosened a little, and the women began to taste liberation. The women's obedience and self-restraints were replaced by some sense of resistance, a move which was of an irreversible nature. That is, once they burst with resistance, they learned about themselves things they were made to forget when socialized as "good little girls."

In Chapter 6 of the series *Daroma*, Avigail Yifrah explained:

> If it weren't the struggle and what came afterward, although I resigned, I wouldn't have recognized myself as I know now. I understand that I have more power than I thought I had, and I understand more in politics than I thought I did. It was like I looked on the back side of a carpet and could see the dense level and width of all its knots.

The three leaders, Ingbar, Yifrah, and Larissa Vinogradov all admitted that they have a better understanding of political speeches and are able to estimate the value of political promises. Political speech was now transparent and filtered, first and foremost, by the filter of interests intertwined with ideological views.

SELF IMAGES, TRUE REPRESENTATION, AND UTILITARIANISM

Among other consciousness transformations that the women experienced, notions such as "failure" and "success" also changed. Success is perceived as a social ideal and a normative standard in the capitalist society. It is often defined in misogynic terms strongly related to materialistic and social status achievements. It is consistent with production and wealth accumulation and with masculinity. Competition and attainment are prior to care and compassion when it concerns success. Feminist scholars contested ideals that define success according to these notions and suggested other perspectives to look at it. The case of the factory illustrates some of these suggestions. Ingbar stood in the midst of an adventure in which she led resistance and struggled against exploiting and oppressive treatment of a misogynist factory manager. She became the manager of a textile cooperative, and after less than a year, she resigned because she realized that the challenges and the problems she faced were too complicated for her to cope with by having little experience and knowledge. The resources she was granted made the obstacle enormous. She concluded that she should resign. Her resignation and her first self-perception as a CEO who fails to stand up to the mission on the recovery of the factory were measured by narrow notions of success. However, later on, after long reflexive conversations, I heard different thoughts regarding Ingbar's sentiments and self-image as a CEO. She deconstructed the entire experience relating to the first stages of the rebellion as a full success. The resistance experience she carried with her since the strike stayed with her even fifteen years later, when she spoke again of the adventure. For her, it was priceless to learn how things work behind the political curtains and how power relations are networked on professional platforms such as business, media, and labor relations. Corridors and restrooms are the real locations of making major decisions, she reckoned: "It was like Golda's kitchenette..." which is a reference to an Israeli political and cultural proverb based on Golda Meir's pattern of decision-making. "How couldn't I see [Shetrit's] maneuvers?" she repeatedly mentioned with astonishment. However, in the third interview, she said, "My blindness and innocence [have] disappeared now. Instead, I sometimes feel obnoxious regarding the hypocrisy and phoniness." From now on, Ingbar was able to separate between the "coat and its lining" of what appeared in front of her eyes and what the motivation that stood behind it really was. Success and failure became more elastic, and complex notions and her feelings of failure were moderated. As mentioned, she did evaluate the first parts of the struggle as a success, and her self-esteem respectively improved. She learned along years of gender discipline of being "a good girl" how to silence within her voices of resistance against evil and injustice, at home and in the factory. Barbara Ehrenreich called them "poisoning positivity" (Ehrenreich, 2009, 13). Ingbar took full responsibility for failures and hardly related to external obstacles around her as part of the circumstances. In the hard years at the factory, what mattered was the quantity, the proper amount of shirts, or trousers that could secure the minimum wage for the day. Once the strike began and the rage burst out, Ingbar recalled that she felt it was a turning point. Restraints over what she thought or wanted to see removed and her self-discipline loosened, she expressed herself easily, and all of a sudden, she had words that she never used before. Calling the factory "cruel" and "exploitative" and highlighting the success part of the struggle against all odds were acts that Ingbar expressed with a new sense of freedom detached from what seems to be once her oxygen pump. The story she told in the last interview was free of the need to be coherent and faithful to all the other actors except herself. This was a new pattern that indicated her revision of the set of values. The fixed image of work seemed to be disentangled, and the linear story was now more complex and full of various contradictions, reflecting the real life she experienced. It was more of a Rashomon effect in which every individual had his or her own version of the event and they were all different. Ingbar was now faithful to her version more than all the others.

Chapter Nine

Vicki Knafo

Radical Rebellion of a Single Mother

This chapter begins where the previous ended, when the women in the factory crossed the line that divides the private and the public spheres. It is the location where they were blocked and did not have the chance to proceed and learn the information that emerged from the lessons of being the agents and to operate on the ground. The women in the factory did not receive the mercy period from the public and official authorities they needed on their way to become managers. They were caught at an "in-between" space, the space that divide the private from the public, the socialization space that women practice in different ways and times than men practice. While men are socialized to accommodate to the public sphere from a very early age and they develop as persons to become familiar to it, women are socialized and become familiar to the private. Therefore, when trying to cross the lines that are designed according to certain rules—mostly patriarchal ones—they not only are expected to discard their private sphere rules and norms but also purchase the rules that prevail in the public sphere. Crossing the line to the public sphere, which is controlled by patriarchal norms adjusted to men, immediately put the women in a severe and unfit situation where their consciousness and normative socialization had to transform. Such a transformation requires time and patience. When on top of it, the women in the factory case had to transform from workers to managers and acquire skills of business professionals, doing so from a starting point of resistance, and the challenges they faced became too complicated and difficult to disentangle. The women had to experience liberation of the consciousness simultaneously with the processes of learning how to make independent decisions. The nature of this process involved the passage from oppression to liberation. This is a process that women from the 1950s to the 1970s experienced personally and became familiar with following the first steps of the feminist revolution in the Western world. It was a social and gender revolution, but it still had to be taken individually, woman by woman.

In this chapter, I will further analyze personal experience that one woman, Vicki Knafo, went through while crossing the "in-between space" of practicing resistance and attempting to change the state's economic policy towards single mothers in Israel. It was an experience that etched a page in the collective memory of Israeli society. Violating the binary principles of changing the terms of the living conditions of women begins with identifying the binary paradigm—the understanding that patterns of reflection and thinking structures rely on differentiation of values and of positioning them one against the other in opposition. These differentiations don't always make sense but necessarily relate to each other. On the one hand, black-and-white oppositions or day and night are bridged through grey and evening, respectfully. These are the logical bridging moments of these oppositions. On the other hand, the differentiation between man and woman is not logically essential. De Beauvoir made this observation in the second volume of her monumental book *The Second Sex*. Moreover, the differentiation and passage from one sex to the other, as Judith Butler argued, is not unambiguous. Between the allegedly clear two sexes, feminine and masculine, there exists an in-between space that does not receive enough attention in gender and sexuality studies. Queer studies made first steps towards an understanding and inquisition of this secretive space, uncovering a whole range of in-between possibilities that the androcentric world endeavored to repress. This range thickens the seemingly thin line that divides the male/female symmetrical dichotomy. The arbitrary nature of this dichotomy reveals when one gender, say the male, tries to crossover to the private realm which women are socialized for. They are socially perceived as alien to the sphere on which they encroach; and vice versa, women who cross the lines, from the private to the public sphere, are perceived as alien to the public sphere.

The public sphere does not change much to fit a woman's relocation. They find themselves struggling to make changes and be acknowledge as "newcomers" who are socialized to be women. Women, on the other hand, try to adapt to the rules of the public sphere often by adopting male norms, such as male socialization codes and behavior. They try to overcome their duties, which they consciously dragged from the private sphere, such as the family care and children rearing, to the public, instead of insisting on the public and private division of labor to remain unchanged. Therefore, the women had to developed impossible syndromes, such as "the super woman" and "second shift" to try to stand up to the dictates of both spheres and function well in the public sphere while standing up to the responsibilities of housekeeping and family care. The difficulties that resulted from these syndromes prevented many women from daring the option of crossing the sphere lines, and only upper-class women in the Western world dared take the initiative in the first stages from the 1950s to the 1980s. Nevertheless, upper-class women, even when affording assistance in home keeping and family care, still had to face the public spheres obstacles when conservative patriarchal gatekeepers tried to stand in their way out to the public sphere. These were demonstrated through birth and body control, as well as wage inequality and power abuse in the workplace. The first crucial steps for women were of consciousness transformation: a transformation that can be compared in some respects to a transgender transformation. First, they had to violate the rigid sexual differentiation that decreed the rules that women cannot do this or that task. They were exposed to sanctions that disobedient individuals experience when trying to move beyond the boundaries that limit them. One of the first syndromes was the "good-girl syndrome" of the obedient girl or woman. Just to condemn a woman as active and independent meant that women went beyond the lines they were allowed to cross. Betty Friedan, in her article "The Problem That Has No Name," revealed the anxiety and oppression women in the 1950s and the 1960s went through. Young, capable women lived through ordeals in their attempt to go against their active and creative nature to conform to the binary gender order. It took a while until women found courage to redefine the heteronormative, dichotomous order of misogyny. This very old term was buried for generations until women began their first steps of liberation in the twentieth century.

The story of Knafo illustrates one personal case of how this journey is taken from the first step to motivate an attempt to make a change through violation of the omnipotent, androcentric order. Following the illustration of the case, I will analyze the aspects that were presented previously in abstract theoretical lines. I will discuss the woman's dynamic motion from the polar that sanctifies the binary androcentric order towards stimulating resistance urges, which violates the order committed from within the heterosexual degrading trap where women are caged. In the case before us in the Vicki Knafo affair, the story is of a woman who is a single mother, a situation completely different from dual-parent motherhood that the scholarships hardly focus on. It is usually told along with the poverty of women and mentioned by the facts of being a poor woman. Therefore, it misses the uniqueness of what it means to be a single mother as opposed to a dual-parent mother. The following affair unfolds as radical feminists who struggle for the acknowledgment of the single mothers' rights. The single mothers' conditions, as the Knafo story illustrates, reveals heavy burden of parenthood that usually is incumbent on two parents, most often of different sexes, but is instead imposed on one parent. As this affair unfolded in the public eye, the burden was usually not just doubled because the family consists of only one parent and one wage of a lonely person's responsibility, but it is multiplied as the single parent, in most cases, is a woman who must maneuver between the public space, which is already difficult for women to cope with. Such a woman begins with gender economic disadvantages and lag after upper-middle-class, docile women and men; then, it is usually relates to cases who are on the margins of the society because they belong to poor sectors, such as racial, religious, or ethnic minorities. "Coming out of the private sphere" is an action similar to the action of "coming out of the closet" for homosexuals. It means that the subject experiences hesitance, fears, and anxiety when violating the gender socialization rules they were trained and expected to submit to from early life. This is a process that the individual is taking on with much loneliness. When a single mother crosses the sphere lines, she is found in a foreign land, not knowing the codes or language. She is in a migration-like move within an in-between zone.

The term "in-between" is discussed here in various contexts in which women find themselves when attempting to transfer from one realm to the other and still feel for long chunks of time "neither there nor here." Scholars such as Gayatri Chakravorty Spivak, bell hooks, Luce Irigaray, Chela Sandoval, and Gloria Anzaldúa (Spivak, 1988; Irigaray, 1974; Sandoval, 2000; Anzaldúa, 1987) pointed out existential experiences of women who intersect the passage through the spheres. This is a continuous, existential experience in an in-between space that resembles a "twilight zone." It is fuzzy and confusing with many implications on their future lives and on their chances to gain from the process of getting out to the public sphere. While being in the in-between zone, the women experience the need to pave the way out to the public sphere on their own. This is the very process of becoming a feminist. It is a process that stimulates wonder and identification but also rejection and abjection. In the Knafo case, she became intersected with another axel—the ethnic, Mizrahi axel. It was a debatable and contesting issue that made her attempt to resist the destiny of the single mothers in Israel even more challenging. I will analyze the case in the light of two scholars who laid theoretical ground to multifaceted oppression cases. The cases are often viewed as intersected oppression, and I will refer to bell hooks' (1984) and Chela Sandoval's (2000) operational theories.

"THE IN-BETWEEN ZONE" AND THE POLITY

The coupling of "female/private" and "male/public" appear in political theory as ideals of the right order. Hannah Arendt in her book *The Human Condition* (1958) wrote of her discussion of the idea of "*vita activa*" on the culture of coupling. Coupling emerged during the ancient Greek era as deeply rooted in Western civilization. It works as binary paradigm, and the active life takes place in the public sphere. The paradigm demonstrates order in the human condition that is initially chaotic and horrifying, as Mary Douglas well described (2004). The culture, especially the political culture, enters the chaotic experience through a splitting function that creates couplings in an attempt to institutionalize and organize chaotic disorder. The term *vita activa* in its initial sense means differentiation and creating splits that help distinguish human life and actions of intervention. Arendt identified this action as the political ideal that develops in the public sphere. Arendt classified the levels of the human action in three categories: labor, work, and action. The first refers to material and physical activity of human values as the elementary. It is the kind of work that the human species does to provide basic existential needs. The next level, work, requires professional skills. It grants the doer with creative satisfaction beyond the provision of the basic needs. The third level, the highest, is action. This one contains the other two levels and also includes the action viewed as the polity. The human reason abilities are involved in this level of doing, and it brings human uniqueness to expression. At the same time, human action brings to order the relations of humankind not only to things but also to other human beings. Political and social orders are institutionalized in the level of doing. The three levels of doing have far-reaching ethical implications from where Arendt extrapolated the claims regarding moral commitments in social condition. The doing levels unfold on both spheres while the private is functioning as infrastructure for the public sphere. The private sphere contains reproduction, family, and parental functions. At top of it, the ultra-structure is constructed, the political and cultural functions. In other words, the household and the family, along with the state and the market, simultaneously change to fit each other and maintain the order from falling back into chaos. In this respect, the private and the public spheres are first and essential coupling on which order is based and on which the binary paradigm of reasoning is constructed. According to this paradigm, family and the state are part of an inseparable coupling, and from this one, the other coupling, such as production/reproduction and male/female, stems. The more sub-splits and couplings are produced as a consequence of the human action, the more the order remotes from chaos. Therefore, whenever an attempt is made to violate the couplings, there will always be gatekeepers in charge that will try to preserve the order of things. Within multilayer and complex stratification, individuals operate to preserve and to change the order within which they live. *Vita activa,* therefore, involves creation and maintenance of political order and is soaked in political, economic, religious, and cultural arrangements and regulations intertwining within and supporting each other, which includes engendering regulations. In this respect codes, norms, laws, sanctions, and patterns are constantly cultivated and coordinate the changes that pop up ceaselessly.

NETWORKS AND CONNECTIONS

The binary structure of the human order is held by multi-splittings amongst which class splittings uphold dichotomies according to parameters based on property, religion, race, and culture. The coupling that preserves fixed correlation between gender and spheres coupling dichotomies is the class splitting. Until not long ago, women status was a function of dependence on men. In the heart of this structure, the family is placed and fostered as an ideal that responds to a dual-parental heteronormative standard that exclusively prevails, leaving no other optional forms of family. The legal framework gives form to standards as the only right form and bores other forms but places them as deviations. In spite of the feminist revolution and the efforts women do to make changes in family ideals, the dual-parental, heteronormative model remains exclusive. The head of the family and the breadwinner is still dominated by patriarchal norms, which is that men dominate the economic labor market and the political power positions and women are the main parent that keeps the household and performs child-rearing tasks. This family model, however, is kept as part of the general political order where the state is the larger format of keeping away from primordial chaos. The heteronormative order, in this respect, is politically kept by marriage contracts that are limited to heterosexual couples. The legal status until not long ago was strict with regard to unisexual marriage, and only at the start of the twenty-first century did the struggle for such a model of marriage and family begin. The family cell is the basic brick of the heteronormative state that keeps away from chaos the division of labor and the separation between the spheres. Changing this rigid format involves a political struggle against conservative gatekeepers. Single-parent families that result from personal circumstances—widowed or divorces—were until not long ago the only options of single parenthood and were perceived as resulting from unfortunate personal circumstances. Only in the twentieth century did the option of divorce and single-parent families by choice begin to surface in the public discourse. This is due to feminist struggles against the religious authorities, which in this case were the common political force that was in charge of arranging marriages and divorce contracts. Economic and property factors play crucial roles in the organization of the family model. Property accumulation and preservation in most societies is subordinated to inheritance legal system aiming at the preservation and production means to remain within the family (Engels, 1940, v), the same as kinship and marriage arrangements that are aimed to preserve male sexual domination over female and their sexuality (Rubin, 1997). Within this framework of the political, family, and economic order, the family also functions as the first and essential socialization force. Engendering and consciousness formation are of the main roles that the family is in charge of. The basic format of binary order is male/female divisions of labor with the sphere formations and coupling being implemented at an early age individually. An individual's dependence on the nuclear family at his/her early age secures the range of their choices in later stages of life. Deviations meet social and legal sanctions but still are kept at the margins, and violations are sanctioned. In this respect, the substantial value of the family for the state order can be underestimated, although it is possible to point out cultural differences between societies and generations and differences between historical eras and religious systems. These arrangements dominate comprehensive existential human orders and rely on conservatively solid apparatus. In this respect, religions, cultures, and states are all instrumental means for order maintenance. Widowhood, divorce, bachelorettedom, and parenthoods that don't rely on dual-parenthood or a heterosexual parenthood are deviated cases that still universally signify the exceptional. Socialization forces—along with social sanctions from all forms, including religious, cultural, gender, familial, political, and legal—are so powerful that they effectively deter "deviation" and reduce the attempts to violate the conservative heteronormative order. The moral status within the format of the conservative order is one of the most effective sanctions. Within the religions, it is often the "will of God to punish the individual," and in cultural and ethnic context, deviations are signified as foolish or fatalistic. In a political context, it is viewed as inefficient, useless, and a failure to do the right thing. The surrounding community forces the individual to retract his or her way by any means available. The common point of all these contexts is that the responsibility is, eventually, put on the individual's shoulders rather than the collective within which his or her life.

The Knafo affair that began as an individual and innocent journey of one woman who wanted to protest against a governmental economic decision bundled together all the mentioned possible "deviations," here exposing herself to multiple condemnations of the "righteous" heteronormative dual-parental society. She was twice divorced, economically poor, and a single mother of three who functioned as the breadwinner and head of the family and who worked at three jobs to raise her children alone. When she came out of the public sphere, she appeared to be a person who refused the fatalistic role of a victim whose life circumstances brought her to the situation where she was poor and alone. A political decision made by the treasury minister, Benyamin Netanyahu, to cut single mothers' allowances raised her up and motivated her to dispute what she saw as a wrong policy. She had no idea that she was contesting, at the time of the dispute, a deep, heteronormative, conservative order apparatus, as the follow-up circumstances revealed. Eventually, Knafo's contestation argued the exclusivity of the heteronormative order along with its legitimacy altogether. She had exposed its fragility and brought the political state apparatus to be put to work even though the challenge seemed to stem from a single, marginalized, poor mother that did not appear to be a serious threat to the politicians. In response, she was condemned as a failing mother and being a spouse twice over. She was represented as a person who couldn't preserve a dual-parent family cell and save her marriage (from an article published under the title "Hudna," 2003). Knafo didn't know she was violating the deep-rooted patriarchal order. She had made a somewhat naive move when she was unaware of the rules of the public game as she crossed heteronormative boundaries, as a woman and a single mother who wasn't aware of the guilt she should have felt, as the other righteous people espoused. Her struggle was a struggle of an individual who was living on the social margins in a peripheral town in the desert; it didn't cross her mind that her individual act of protest would drag enormous public condemnation on one side and enthusiastic support on the other. After all, being a single, poor mother was not a unique personal situation, and there were hundreds of thousands of such women in the country. What garnered the support of the public support was again—as in the Peppco factory case—the enormous rage that burst out that led to wide and public burning protest. In this instance, the long-term public frustration was lit by one move of the fiery rage from a struggling single mother. The wider public support magnified her right to a measure that stood up to the economic national policy decision that was extended far beyond a problem that concerns just one person. The personal protest penetrated liminal lines and met socialization issues that concerned embodied, feminine, motherhood, and sexual aspects of being a woman in a heteronormative society and state. Knafo's case of a single mother's crossing of boundaries violated family and state binary and coupling standards.

Chapter Ten

The Journey from Mitzpe Ramon to Jerusalem

On the morning of July 2, 2003, Vicki Knafo left her home in Mitzpe Ramon and began a march of 200 kilometers. Her destination was the minister of the treasury in the government borough. A few days before, she declared during an education television transmission that she intended to meet the minister of the treasury no matter what so she could tell him, personally, that his decision to retrogress her to the poverty threshold, along with many other single mothers, was wrong. She stated in that TV interview that she would even walk to Jerusalem if necessary. She and other women, a majority of them single mothers, gathered in Mitzpe Ramon in at the Histadrut—the local labor union office. The Histadrut promised to help with the public transportation expenses to Jerusalem but seemed to have difficulties in raising the funds, Knafo decided that even if she would have to walk all the way to Jerusalem, she was determined to meet the minister.

> I went to the bank, saw that they had cut 1,200 NIS, which was half of what I used to bring home from work and [as a] single mother's allowance. . . . My account was in negative balance, which meant that the bank [would] cut interest fees for that. I figured that there [was] a war going on. . . . The Histadrut tried to organize buses for the morning of July 2, 2003, but came up with no messages as to when we were supposed to receive the answer whether they had the financial means for that. I said: "We don't have time for games, I walk to Jerusalem." I was bragging, I didn't really mean it, but once I said it, I wasn't able to retract [it], so I told everybody that I have had to show that I am serious about talking with Bibi [the nickname for the treasury minister, Benjamin Netanyahu, HDK]. If he was so smart to promise to fix the state economy, let him show me how he was going to pay the settlements and the state's debts

> out of the single mother allowance cuts. Let him begin by one household, my household. (Orientals and Peace, 2005)

The sound of spontaneous refusal was clear. It was a voice that she restrained for long. She felt for a long time that the state was supporting the settlers at the expense of the marginal groups that lived on the peripheral areas within the green-line boundaries of Israel. The economic imbalance was always on the lower deciles expenses. The minimum wage during those years stood at 3,600 NIS; the allowances were one-third of that, and Knafo was working two jobs where her income didn't reach the minimum wage. She lived through these conditions for many years, and she declared, "It's time that Bibi will hear about it."

Having no proper shoes, no medical escort, no guiding plan or maps, and not knowing the specific track, she began her journey. She described the events many times during a conference of women of Mizrahi origin that gathered in Mitzpe Ramon in 2005. This journey, she already realized in 2005, had changed her life and registered one more page in the history of social protest in Israel. Knafo was in her forties, divorced, and was raising her three kids on her own. She began walking in July, which is one of the harshest and hottest months of the year. She walked on the asphalt road where busses swiftly passed her. Not knowing the route, the busses road was her guide markers that indicated she was on the right track. During the first days, she went a few kilometers until she reached Bedouin villages beside the road. A few of the children curiously escorted her for a small distance, and when the evening came, more adult Bedouins came along and took her to their tents and gave her food and water. She went on walking, then came to a few nearby kibbutzim who heard about her journey and kibbutzniks came and took her in for the night. She went on the next morning, and once she passed near Beersheba, the "Negev desert capital," almost 84 kilometers for her journey's start, the rumor of her journey had spread all over the country. A few people came to escort her along parts of the road, and then the media began to arrive when she was halfway to the capital of Jerusalem. She recalled:

> On the way, the entire state began [saying] . . . Joan of Arc . . . I thought of nothing but how to arrive to Jerusalem. . . . My message was to meet with the minister of the treasury and to explain to him what was it for her to be a working single mother whose two jobs were not sufficient [to] provide for her to bring food to put on the kids table. (The Mizrahi feminist conference, 2005)

She was determined. Social justice organizations heard about it and sent escorting delegates to the locations where she arrived on her journey, aiming to join her protest march. Famous and well-established NGOs, such as "Shati," the "New Israel Fund," "My sister," the Mizrahi feminist organization, and "Yadid," yet another social justice organization, all had sent volunteering representatives to join her journey. These were organizations that were operated by small numbers of employees and CEOs, basically counting on volunteers, particularly on raging individuals against the established evils and bureaucracy. In other words, these organizations depended on the needy activist population, and Knafo came as a ripe fruit to their hands in the "silly season" when the population that most needed them was overrun by the cruel economic policy. In the last quarter of the road to Jerusalem, Knafo was already being escorted by dozens of NGO volunteers and activists and by the media. On her fifth day, she made her last kilometers to Jerusalem, heading to the treasury ministry. With all the media and people escorting her, she was certain that the minister wouldn't refuse to meet her. Wrapped with the Israeli flag that she got from one of the cheering escorts and fully covered by the media, she was received by the Jerusalemite public as a champion in a race. Knafo, who was driven by her impulsive act with no plan, was met with a surge of empathic solidarity of a national rate. Astonished at the potent reaction, she had no proper words to respond to the questions regarding her protest intentions and goals. Knafo had no plans apart from the intention to meet the minister of the treasury and speak to him from the bottom of her single mother's heart. However, this was not her individual show anymore. It was for the wide public for whom she spontaneously expressed rage against economic distress that went well beyond a single mother's anxiety. The public's rage was growing as the poverty rate was expanding steadily over the last few years. The class gaps deepened, and the rich became richer but fewer. The state's GNP and GDP were prospering without indicating the improvement at the household level. Knafo, the anonymous single mother, became a famous figure overnight, and she began to realize that she was expected to lead not only the struggle of single mothers but also an entire wrecked and downtrodden population that was on the verge of famine in a Western country that was economically solid. In the shock of the bustle, she made a "conscience U-turn" and came back to her senses. She was careful to introduce her self-image as a sturdy woman who was not disabled, hungry, or unfortunate. She was proud to state that she worked two jobs and refused to receive the national allowances that the unemployed received as welfare assistance. She introduced herself as a devoted mother who raised her kids but who couldn't carry on doing it independently under the neo-liberal and allegedly free but wild economy that continued for more than the last twenty years. This has caused her evil. Her spontaneous march and determination "to speak with the minister of the treasury," as she has repeatedly said, reflected a position that there was no hostility towards the minister of the treasury. It was simply that he "may not understand something, and I am going to explain it to him. After all, he doesn't know how the poor live, and someone ought to open his eyes." As tough as Netanyahu maybe was, Knafo believed in her ability to convince him that she was right and that there was justice that had to be shown by someone who was really hit by the cuts. She was certain that the minister would realize that he lacked knowledge on the impact of his decision on single mothers. Where did she take this civil chutzpah from? What made her feel that she was equal to the minister and not inferior to him, and why did she assume that they are not standing on opposite sides of the social justice fence? These were questions that I posed to her at the time of the events and that I will discuss further herein. Knafo's statements regarding these questions echoed deep faith in social rights and equality. She didn't have a rich vocabulary to express these faiths but she was certain that this is what she fought for. The public in Israel, which was still hoping to see justice in a state they believed was democratic, gathered behind her and was carried on top of the protest momentum and continuous disappointment from the disintegrating welfare state.

THE EROSION OF THE WELFARE STATE, ONCE AGAIN

In the prolonging process of privatization after the legislation of 1979 under the rule of Prime Minister Menachem Begin, the welfare state came down to yet a deeper bottom. Salaries were cut down, employees were fired in large numbers from governmental and public firms that were part of the national resources, and public debates concerning the economic policy that the state should implement spited too many larger groups in the labor market. Low-tech employees were busy surviving and took little part in the public debates that concerned them the most. In the next two decades, until the turn of the millennium, a large number of strikes and public companies and enterprises went through crises. As was presented previously with regard to the struggle of Havatzelet Ingbar and her worker friends, the Histadrut began the process of privatization from a powerful starting point as part of the triangle of the government, the private sector, and the Histadrut, the labor union. The Histadrut, led by thirteen strong unions that controlled the national infrastructure that included water, electricity, communication, air, transformation, and so on, secured the larger unions and neglected the interests of the smaller labor companies. It was easy to cut down the budget when it concerned welfare issues of the weak. During the 2003 economic crisis, they were the single mothers. In 1992, legislation dealing with single mothers promoted two laws (Grinberg, 1993), but due to the cuts, the treasury minister decided to abort them by cutting down assistance to housing, kindergarten, and mothers of small children. The legislation of 1992 was aimed at coping with the problem of single mothers that became acute following the ex-USSR migration to Israel. The number of single mothers increased significantly due to the migration from Russia after the fall of the USSR in 1989, and the number of single mothers and children who lived below the poverty line was scandalous. This, together with the crippling of the wages erosion, brought Knafo to desperation. Single mothers of Russian origin joined Knafo in small numbers. These were mainly women of the southern states of the ex-USSR, indicating the class division that prevailed in the integration abilities of the Russian population that flowed to Israel in the 1990s and continued the class division between Russians that came from the Muslim states of the ex-USSR and those who migrated from Belarus. This division combined social and ethnic marks and added to the traditional ethnic split between Mizrahim and Ashkenazim that dominated the Israeli social and cultural relations since the first years of the state. The small number of supporting women from Russia indicated the social relations in Israel and the political culture of the immigrants from Russia. The Russian immigrants were not familiar with the culture of protests as it prevails in a democracies freedom of gathering and expression, and they didn't experience much in their country of origin. On the other hand, their history of dissidence since Stalin onwards through to the fall of the USSR is glorious. However, Knafo practiced her freedom to protest, unlike the Russian single mothers who carried totalitarian regime experience and were still reserved about using the right to protest. Knafo's protest was not expected to be the typical agent citizen and, in many respects, it surprised the public and the politicians as she represented the most vulnerable and subordinated social sector in Israel. Nevertheless, the protest itself was part of the Israeli democratic social justice practices. As in the case of Ingbar, here too Knafo's protest had awakened the gender gatekeepers.

THE PROTEST CAMP IN THE ROSE GARDEN

When Knafo arrived in Jerusalem, she went to the governmental borough and stood right in front of the ministry of the treasury. Cheered on by the overwhelming public empathy, she was certain that the minister of the treasury, Netanyahu, wouldn't ignore her dramatic march of protest and the publication it got and he would immediately come down to show respect to her call for justice. However, he disappointed her and remained locked in his office. That evening, someone brought Knafo a camping tent, and she crossed the street to the Rose Garden that was located in front of the treasury office very close to Knesset Hall, the Central Bank, the Hall of Justice, and the other ministries. This garden occasionally served demonstrations by protest groups against various government policies. She spent the night there with a few supporters with the hope that perhaps the treasury minister had important things to do and he would find a few minutes for her the next day. However, that didn't happen either. For Knafo, this was the first lesson in real politics and the first democratic slogan to disintegrate, the slogan of freedom of gathering that brought no effective fruits from its wings. The world of politics as one that is full of contradictions began to unfold in front of her eyes. The differences between what she thought was the political and the public affairs world and what she was now experiencing revealed before her for the first time as she has never been involved in public activity. During the night, she began to reflect on the intensive experience she had over the last few days, and she questioned her understandings of politics. The basic perception that political leaders are responsible and trustful people and are very busy and care about the public began to sound naive. The belief that the minister of the treasury did not receive her immediately because he was probably very busy was now changing to sobering thoughts that he must probably have other intentions with regard to her protest. If the minister could ignore her, it was because she was just Vicki Knafo; this could be grasped, but how could he ignore the commotion that emerged around her by the public in the cry against the evil of unjust policy. That surprised her as she was certain that the minister of the treasury might have been ignorant to the lives of the poor, but it can't be that he was cynical, so she thought and began to think of the strength politicians need in order to stand up to this kind of the public pressure. The moral that grew within Knafo was that even one person's plea shouldn't be ignored, although she experienced bureaucratic red tape on the officials part. However, the minister is not a clerk, she was thinking.

When Knafo came out to the public, she was found to be very sharp and clever, full of charisma and quick perseverance. She began to grasp that the minister was perhaps too busy, but also that he abstained from meeting her as a tactic. This added to her rage of humiliation, and she drew strength from that and from the empathy of the public. She decided that she would maneuver the public momentum and stick to her demand to meet the minister of the treasury, "Bibi," as she referred to him, no matter what. Later on, she told me that the minister's avoidance insulted not only her but the entire public and, therefore, she decided to struggle for that meeting for the public sake as well. This marked her becoming conscious of the public role she began to fill. For the minister of the treasury, it was fine to protest as long as it does not violate the public order and the basic structure of the state operations, but Knafo didn't realize that yet. Her spirit was firm, and she demonstrated this in front of the entire ministries in the governmental city as people began to arrive and expanded the camp in the Rose Garden. At the end of the second day, the media published the news and more tents began to appear around Knafo's. The single mother who was a private person two days before had now become a leader of the marginalized people. Her tent became a headquarters where other social leaders came to pay a visit. By the end of the week, the Rose Garden was filled with hundreds of visitors and dozens of tents of single mothers. A sort of "hide park" was developing and voicing the public's advice on how to make the minister come out to meet her. As it often occurs during public events, the sequence of events does not always run according to someone's plan and the actors involved pulled them in various directions. Knafo found herself leading agendas that she wasn't planning to lead or had even heard of. Women whose children were taken by the authorities, homeless families who didn't stand up to their mortgage payments, divorced fathers who couldn't see their children because they didn't stand up to the alimony payments—these were only a few of the groups that gathered around Knafo. She understood very little of those issues and had to make quick decisions as to how she was going to cope with the challenges that brought her eventually to stand at the head of thousands of people. Her intuition told her that leading, although she became a public persona, all these groups would obscure her clear call for the single mothers. She was not a woman of higher education, and her clear voice of the evil, when she spoke it up, was in simple language but was as lucid as crystal. Her words sounded populist, and the more sophisticated and well-off classes dismissed her with no interest in what she had to say the more they pushed her farther from her goal. After a week, when the minister wouldn't show up, the public kept arriving and supporting her cause. After some critics in the media were brought to her attention, Knafo was confused: Was she right to do what she did? Was it right to do it in the way she did? Who did she think she was other than "the last of all the single mothers in the periphery of Israel?" Why would anyone show interest in her fate? These emotions she recognized from her experience at moments of desperation reflecting on her self-confidence that the minister of the treasury would resist her call, her hopes seemed false. These moments resembled those of not knowing what to do when her kid's father (of two marriages) crossed the lines and became violent. She practiced in the past collecting pieces all together and stood up against violence. The feelings were not different, she recalled, but soon she was going to discover that the strategies of struggle must be accommodated to public affairs and be different. As opposed to concrete power relations within the family, which involved physical violence, here in the public affairs of opposition to the minister of the treasury, the violence was mental, insulting, humiliating, as it was operated in the "marketplace" before the public eyes. The rules of the game in the political "playground" were yet to be learned. In those first critical days, Knafo had reconsidered more than once to pack up everything and go back home. However, "I have already committed myself; I am not going to retreat." In the meantime, in the Rose Garden, things took off. Talkbacks in the social networks criticized Knafo for her using the national flag to demonstrate because, it was argued, this gave the minister a mark that she would not go all the way and she would remain faithful to the national commitments (i.e., the state's policy). Others criticized her as a mother and as a person. As a mother: "She wasted money on hairdressing and cigarettes and nails, building instead of saving that money to put food on her children's table. . . . When she gets to 3,000 NIS . . . [only, the expenses should be saved for basic needs, HDK]" then again, "What she spends in a month is the amount of the mortgage of a young couple. . . . If she doesn't have enough, let us collect some charity and help her pay her cell phone expenses [cell phone, in 2003, was an item that not everyone could afford, HDK]" (Hahudna, 2003).

More than two hundred women and a few dozen men, who were all single parents, surrounded her with their children and also set up tents. The officials complained about the noise the public made, and they called the police, saying "We can't work like this." The police sent more forces to keep the public order. Knafo and the other camping supporters were invited by Jerusalemite residents to take showers in their homes, and others began to bring food and baby food to the compound. The teenage daughter and the eight-year-old son of Knafo were brought to her from Mitzpe Ramon to Jerusalem and joined her in the camp. Now it was clear that there was no way to retreat, and the struggle should take a firm stand and move on with more demonstrating steps. However, Knafo didn't have a plan. The only item on her agenda was "I stand here until Bibi comes down to talk to me."

July and August in Israel are the summer vacation months from school and many parents take holidays to spend time with the children. The camp began to look similar to a children's camp. Moreover, the supporters began to bring toys and volunteers organized educational activities for the children. Knafo embraced all this support and began to seem to enjoy all the commotion. There were talks and debates regarding the topic of what she should do next to make the treasury minister come down. The officials that came every morning to the office in the governmental borough, hundreds of them, crossed the camping tents and had supporting smiles, although they were expected to be loyal to their position and keep their mouths shut. This kind of protest was ideal for the authorities as it made them look tolerant and democratic without having to pay much for that. There was only the waiting game that pressured the treasury minister to come down and the "silly season," which for the media and the reporters was now filled by that affair. The catch in the demonstrations in democratic regimes came to exhaustion here: the public practiced freedom of speech and gathering while the government could carry out its policies at the expense of the lower-class dociles who gained some attention by the wider middle-class public. At moments, it felt like it was a protest that was planned for "public rage release" and all actors were satisfied. It was too polite without having many people heading the strategic organization, and the voices that were raised expressed frustration against the government and its exploiting policy within the public order. Knafo grasped it with her senses and was searching for ways to bring herself out of the confusion so that she could make another move, a move that would leave the treasury minister no other choice but to meet her.

Advice from all directions came to her: the NGOs, the mothers, the volunteers. The media teased: "Aren't you go to do something? Isn't it insulting that he doesn't come down to talk to you?" Knafo began to decipher hidden contradicting messages that concealed manipulations and contradictory information when the treasury ministry spokesperson came down to tell her the minister would tell her if and when he would be able to meet with her. At first, it cheered her up, but then the days went by, and during the second week of waiting, Knafo thought, "I don't believe he is lying." In the meantime, she gave interviews and the TV screen seemed to like her. She was found to be determined and charismatic, and she spoke fluently, convincingly, and with passion.

> Up until now, I have kept all my promises, and I will keep them on. If necessary, I will go on [a] hunger strike and won't retreat until the minister of treasury will agree to invite me to a meeting.

Again, what she spoke was faster than her mind, and she released that statement before she was certain she was going to do that. Once again, she had to stand up to a promise she didn't mean to make in the first place.

Her fresh public persona appealed as she spoke out of intuition and spontaneity at a world that ran different rules of the game, where communication is rational, calculated, and, in many respects, artificial or even hypocritical. For women crossing the threshold from the private sphere to that of a public sphere meant that they have to cross an extra distance in the sense of learning the rules of the political and public game and understanding the public sphere's norms of behavior. These are norms that sometimes contradict those of the private and drew other ethical lines, in the Machiavellian sense. Much pressure was put on her to begin action, specifically political action. Some of the single parents were very explicit and called for more effective action that should include violence, such as burning tires. Knafo adopted two principles in this respect: First, she made it strictly clear that she didn't want any violence involved in the protest, neither physical nor verbal. "Shouting and raising one's voice, yes; swearing and cursing, no," she said loudly through the megaphones.

> You may repeat the same complaint all day long when gathering in front of the ministry office gates. Repeat your rage against the cuts of the mother's allowance, but don't use violence.

In spite of the pressure, she clearly drew the protest campaign of nonviolence boundaries. The other principle was to draw once more the boundaries of the campaign around the agenda of the single mother's cry only.

Keeping exclusive to the single mother's protest, not mixing it with other evil social agendas, caused splits and controversy in the camp, and in two weeks, the solidarity around her showed some cracks. The number of supporters lessened, and other groups gathered separately to forward their own agenda. Struggles within the demonstrators emerged, and Knafo was accused of missing the chance to bring changes to the many. However, Knafo insisted that no violence would be used and to keep it exclusive to single mother's struggles. Nevertheless, regarding the public debate, the debates were stormy and passionate and became an effective show of democracy in action. Goals and strategies were discussed, and new ideas were suggested as to how to take an effective action to change policies that concerned the lower-class interests. The ball was now kicked to the treasury minister's court.

LABELING THE STRUGGLE'S BOUNDARIES

The controversies around the best strategy to make the treasury minister come down to meet with Knafo were brought to her tent people who were experienced in street demonstrations and popular famous leaders. Ayala Sabag, a leader of the Katammonim, from a lower-class neighborhood in Jerusalem, tried intensively to bring Knafo to agree to use violence (*Beit Halahmi*, 2003). She even made some attempts at tire fires and found herself in confrontation with Knafo. She left Knafo's camp and moved to organize her own camp. Knafo found herself coping with issues that popular leaders must face but never occurred to her before: How was she to navigate the struggle and keep the public support on her side? How was she to keep the powerful momentum while having no mature political and social justice agenda? How would she politicize her own personal problem, and what exactly did she want to say to the minister beyond complaining about the cuts? Now it was not only she, but it was an entire group whose social category stood at the intersection of being poor, women mothers who were deep with continuous deprivation. This was a critical point of time in the social justice debate for the public, and Knafo had to make a tough decision and reconsider whether to concentrate on the limited issue of the struggle of single mothers or take it further and widen the lines of support by opening the agenda to other issues that would concern larger parts of the society. The risk was that had she widened the lines to mothers that lost their children to foster families by the welfare authorities and to the homeless and housing problems, among other issues, her main concern as a single mother who lost her allowances—for which had been the entire struggle—would dissolve into larger abstract social justice agendas. This would play the role of popular protest but become obscure and difficult for her to focus when meeting the minister of the treasury. Her senses told her she couldn't carry a larger agenda; it was beyond her competence as a person who feels the injustice of all these issues. Knafo chose to stick to her personal cause to the protests and disappointments of the supporting groups. The implications of this decision had a crucial effect on the future of the struggle. The Rose Garden now had a few camps that carried different slogans and different social groups. However, the agendas of all of them together, one couldn't be mistaking, was the exploitation and oppression of much of the deprived, poor population of society. The public debate moved to secondary critique, which condemned Knafo for her wrapping herself with the national flag and presenting a right-wing political position: a position that consisted with the minister of the treasury's political party and lessened the resistance power of her action, so they argued.

The left-winger NGOs didn't hide their disappointment and critique from Knafo. These NGOs traditionally tended to hold liberal or socialist opinions. Their understanding of civil rights and social justice didn't stem from strong nationalistic political positions, which in Israel was always affiliated with the Israeli-Palestinian conflict. This issue always interrupted the debates. The paradox was that the activists came mostly from middle-upper-class bourgeois families who lived in the big cities at the heart of the country, in Tel Aviv, Jerusalem, and the rich suburbs near them. These differences made it difficult for them to understand where Knafo came from, not only geographically—from the margins—but also ethnically and culturally, since she was from the Mizrahi ethnic sector whose default vote was against the traditional labor party rather than in support of the national party. The majority went on to support religious, traditional parties that offered a combination of tradition and national sentiments of longing for Zion. The majority of the NGOs activists were of Ashkenazi, non-observant Jewish origin; Knafo was of Hispanic-Moroccan origin. The activists wanted so much to embrace her, but these differences made it difficult for them as she didn't compromise or give herself to any of the groups. Her faith in her way as traditional and national was hard for the left-winger supporters to digest. The activists called with righteousness to make traditional social justice movements and strategies, proactive strategies by organizations such as Shatil and Ydid—often operated by Israelis of Anglo-Saxon origin. They were affiliated with Jewish liberal donators in the United States, supporters of the political, left-central wing in Israel. Knafo's inclination to the right was for them difficult to fathom; her loyalty to national values was a dividing line between them. Therefore, they did help and supported her but with a reservation that echoed a patronizing attitude on their part. For Knafo unlike for them, the state wasn't a hostile entity, though she did raise her criticism against the settlements, but not because she objected the occupation but because the resources allocated to them was at the expense of the peripheral and marginal groups. Her focus remained the minister of the treasury, the man and the politician. She had no hate towards the political institutions, nor did she hate the police forces or officials that came down to talk to her. Social order and the rule of law were elementary to her, and as a citizen, she believed she should keep it no matter what. This behavior was what the social right NGOs understood as a paradox as the right-wingers in their eyes were always those who violated human rights, the Palestinian human rights, and for them, a nationalist person such as Knafo, who at the same time believed in the rule of law, was inconceivable. In this respect, Knafo was a confusing and counter-stereotypical figure for the left-wingers who strived for a figure to support. They interpreted it as if she simply didn't understand the rules of the game of which she was the heroine and refused to give her the credit that she knew what she was doing and saying. In her case, the mob's stereotype that merges poverty with stupidity and shallowness proved to work. Many confused her poverty with her allegedly being stupid. Otherwise, they believed, she would have understood how the minister is extorting the poor. However, Knafo continued insisting on meeting the minister and didn't lose faith in thinking that she would convince him no matter what his political opinions were.

Other undiscussed paradoxes prevailed in the events; activists mostly came from liberal bourgeoisie ranks of the society, ranks that in fact enjoyed the globalization capitalist economic policy of the right-wing political party of the minister of the treasury. The social structure in Israel since the 1977 political turnover revealed this paradox, which was disguised for years by seemingly socialist political rule. After the Mapay Party, the labor party lost power, and the real estate assets that they dominated through public institutions and national infrastructures, along more than thirty years of government, remained in their hands for many years after they lost power. Only the privatization process could change it, as Menachem Begin, the right-wing prime minister, believed, by transferring the control over these assets to the hands of free entrepreneurs. The paradox, however, remained in place; the people that were close to power and the rulers already formed the upper-class ranks in society and allegedly represented left-center political wings. What held their position as allegedly left was their political position regarding the Israeli-Palestinian issue. They supported negotiations and showed more flexibility in the major issues of the conflict. Therefore, as far as it concerned the economy, they were more right-wing and conservative whereas in the conflict they held more flexible positions toward the Palestinian, which in Israel is labeled as left wing. This picture was clear to Knfo, although she had a limited vocabulary to express more subtle views that she had. She was also sensitive to the ethnic split of Mizrahim-Ashkenazim. However, she made it clear that what she was interested in was to meet with the minister tête-à-tête, confident and determined that no political opinions would move her from her initial intention. Once he invites her, Knafo believed she would find the human points through which she was certain she could communicate with him.

BETWEEN POLITICAL STRUGGLE AND PUBLIC BUSINESS

Guided by her intuitive democratic senses, with the belief that the public order must be kept, and with her self-determination that she could and would make the minister of the treasury reconsider his harsh policy towards single mothers, Knafo stuck to her own route and moved along the struggle from one day to the next. On her way, she began to grasp the sense of the political power relations and discovered the passions and aspirations that operated those who were attracted to political and public affairs. Before she started the journey, Knafo didn't have a clue of what politics was about. Her idea of what politics was came from TV broadcasts and false perceptions from the talk of manipulative politicians. How sophisticated were the seemingly simple talks in front of the camera she couldn't grasp. Now she realized what double-meaning expressions were, such as simultaneous support and flattery that had nothing practical behind and expressions such as "the minister really understands what you go through, and he will come to meet you soon," as his spokespersons told her more than once. The political grammar began to fascinate her as she couldn't say they were lying but realized they spoke no truth either. She tried to distinguish between opportunistic moves of supporters and real advisors who were honest (Mizrahi conference, 2005). She surprised herself when discovering that she was able to fearlessly communicate with officials, which for her, when she was in Mitzpe Ramon, were anonymous faces "there in the ministries in Jerusalem." It was one thing to imagine that she was able to do that and another experience to realize that she could work it out. It was a source of strength and an increase in self-esteem. She practiced conversations and negotiations with media reporters, TV journalists, and the official representatives that came to speak with her on a daily basis. It resembled a training course in practical politics, of behavior in the public sphere. She was asked about issues that she never really thought of before: the settlements, the military conduct in the occupied territories, the reforms in the educational system—in short, issues that politicians and decision-makers are often chased for. This was how a politician or a public figure feels like when asked about public affairs, she thought. She experienced for the first time how politicians felt when demanded to relate to issues that they were not always familiar enough with. She began to read in the newspapers what she was saying to the reporters and learned about the gaps between what she said and what they wrote; she learned for the first time the workings of the political context. She looked at the public figure she became through the journalists' eyes. Knafo didn't recognize the reflection she saw in the papers' articles. Some thought she was pretty, others untrimmed. Her private life, too, began to be discussed in the newspapers. It was all new to her. As far as she was a fresh figure to the public, she learned about her new public persona. Intimate details from her private and family life were put before the public eye, and the thirst for tabloids rolled in. Who was this single mother who didn't fit the public sphere image and knew nothing about how to walk through it? This was a question that lit the public curiosity and sent paparazzi to discover her personal story. These detailed, beyond the dry facts of the struggle of a single mother now demanding to enter the exact amount of income, how exactly she spent it, the occupations details, and her daily schedule with the children. They wanted to know about her marriage, divorce, family life, ex-husbands, the children's ages, and other intimate details, such as her difficulties in raising the kids and their relation towards her current activity. Other reports went further, asking about her self-image as a woman, her body, and her sexuality. Details regarding a drug addiction of her oldest child and the anorexic problems of her second child began to leak out. The public response was of the sort of "nodding with their head, ahahah," as if the stones fell into place and the enigma was finally cracked. This, in a stereotypical way, "explained" to a certain extent why she was poor and failed to raise her family in the right way and why she was dependent on allowances. The talk-backists celebrated on the reason behind that non-conformist woman. The conservative opinion that was expressed following the tabloids came out was that she should be returned to her rightful place and position as a poor, single woman who should be taught a lesson as to how to raise her children and know her place. Her struggle against the allowance cuts seemed to be less justified now, and her image moved to more of a parasite who sucks public money. Conservative fear of a woman who made too much commotion grew stronger. Her personal life as a failure removed her from the image of the heroine of a struggling single mother to that of a dangerous woman whom decent people should be aware of not crossing her path (Hahudna, 2003). Some saw her as an irresponsible mother and "…if I were she, I wouldn't spend my money on nail polish and [a] cell phone. Where does she take the money from?" (Hahudna, 2003). Overnight the conservative voices turned her into a Lilith from whom they should be wary of. In larger and more remote circles, some of the political organizations wanted her to join them and support activists for the Israeli-Palestinian conflict and resolution, assuming that with her charisma she would be able to carry away masses. However, she was at a point where her life as a public persona was not hers before she understood she must protect herself from it. "I started my journey because I had no choice," she said to the media. "There was nothing more I could do in order to put bread on my children's table" (Hudna, ibid.). From that point on, she was not in control of the events that took her away, having no time to reflect on what was happening and understand where to go from there, what the public empathy meant for her, and what was the public response—both the empathy and the cruel thirst for tabloids. She wasn't familiar or equipped with the skills of surviving in the public sphere.

THE STRUGGLE'S CLIMAX AND FIRST MOMENTS OF DECAY

The summer holiday of the children from school was coming to its end. The minister of the treasury stuck to his attrition strategy before considering meeting her. Knafo's message from the newspapers pages called: "Just give me back my 1,300 NIS, that's all I ask" (*Haaretz*, 2003). The meeting was planned and prepared for to the last details. She came to the meeting escorted by experts in economy and social justice activists who wrote working papers and lists of the demands that single women require in order to be able to live a decent life. All the parties agreed that the media cameras would be present to document the meeting. The minister of the treasury promised her at the end of the meeting that the needs of the single mothers would be carefully reviewed with the agreement that they indeed need conditions of relief. After a short while, the media published some changes that gave them a discount on the housing expenses of single mothers, kindergarten payments, and leaving the workplace one hour earlier. Knafo felt that she didn't leave empty-handed ("Single mother," 2012). The summer came to its end, and the mothers had to return home and prepare for the children to return to school. In September 2003, the camping tents were folded up, and this chapter in Knafo's protest came to its ending by making one more page in the collective memory of the history of social protest in Israel. Ten weeks of protest by single mothers made Knafo an icon, which awakened the public discourse regarding the disintegrating welfare state. The debate continued around the question of whether Knafo's struggle ended with success or failure. Knafo went back home and back to the private persona she had before, of a resident of Mitzpe Ramon who lost one of her jobs having unstable income, but things were not quite the same as they were. Her life, consciousness, and understanding of the public and the private spheres changed, leaving deep scratches in her memory and being. Since then, the media kept communicating with her and asked what she thought of this or that public or social issue. Andy Warhol's promise of "fifteen minutes of fame" ended, so it seemed. In the next few months, Knafo's economic status deteriorated, and she asked the media when they contacted her to publish her plea for public assistance in finding a new job.

Chapter Eleven

Back to the Body, Sexuality, and to Femininity

Vicki Knafo felt no need any longer to protect her privacy after her detailed, intimate life story was published during the period of demonstrations. In desperation, she was ready to open more of her private life to get assistance in finding a job. The media, a diverse field where different actors play with different interests, brought opportunists that identified Knafo's desperation and came with abusive proposals, which involved reference to her sexuality, her body, and femininity. Advertising companies and private businesses wanted to use her short-term celebrity status and what she represented. She cooperated, allowing the use of her pictures and quotes of her interviews in return for a little money from royalties. Knowing very little about royalty rights, she thought it was a beginning of a new occupation in the field of advertising. She didn't see the difference of business publicity and the previous political publicity, both were the same: two parts of the public sphere, but they operated according to different norms, which Knafo knew very little about and soon fell into the trap of cynical opportunists. One year later in September 2004, pictures of Knafo, nude, appeared on a pornographic website called Parppar 1 (Butterfly 1). The cruel abuse of her distress and her lack of knowledge of how to negotiate such things brought her to agree to publish pictures of her body in the nude along with social protest slogans etched on her breasts and bottom. Obviously, the pornographic website owners were interested in the nudity rather than in the social justice statement, but they knew what buttons to push to make Knafo agree to the terms of publication. Once again, her naivety, along with her economic distress, was abused. She was paid 3,000 NIS and was interviewed following the publication of the pictures. She explained about her despair and deep disappointment for people in general:

> I gave them [the decision-makers, HDK] what they didn't want to hear; they had to see it written on my body, on my skin . . . The establishment have fucked me. . . . I became a dead human being walking. I have nothing to lose, and I thought that what was left for me is to commit suicide. (Meiron-Shaked, 2004)

The porn website didn't miss the chance, and she, on the other hand, was able to make the connection between the global economic policy and her concrete, substantial hunger as she felt it in her body. Her hopeless situation as a mother of hungry children was embodied, and the abuse of the website felt just as the abuse of the economic policymakers. She said she didn't feel the difference between the abuse of the policy from the ministry of the treasury and that of the pornographic website: both exploited her tragic situation. The abstract words of the ministry of the treasury were no less harmful than the injury inflicted by the porn website. She explained that the pictures on the website were a last resort in her attempts to shake the public and the decision-makers since they remained deaf to her pleas. The effect was quite the opposite. As she was condemned in the last weeks of the protest as a neglecting mother, so did the website pornographic pictures add to this issue. The slogans on her naked body indeed caught the public attention but brought harsh reactions against her from conservative, righteous sectors. The pictures were not perceived as part of her social protest, as she wanted them to; instead, they were perceived as a subversion of the public order. Once again, the conservative gatekeepers awakened and made her realize that she had crossed the unseen sacred lines, the lines that the decadent bourgeois gatekeepers hypocritically etched for the separation of abuse in politics and abuse in pornography. There was a short public debate around this event, which gave voice especially to the puritan righteousness that is often heard against prostitution.

Decision-makers who design economic policies or decide to make budgets' cuts almost always do not meet or talk to the subjects on whom their decisions apply. The marginalized bear the dreadful consequences and the implications of the decisions after having no say before or after the decisions are taken. It is very rare that decision-makers get to see the face and the bodies of those to whom the decisions are made at the time of the decision. In this case, Knafo exposed her face and body, her femininity and sexuality, on whom the economic cuts were inflicted. She presented and illustrated the implications of the budget cuts making her body speak up. It was a unique demonstration that reified the despairing implications of the policy cuts. She was right to assume that the wider public, not just those who were on the margins, wouldn't remain indifferent to the pornographic demonstration. It generated larger debate regarding the women who work as prostitutes and those who work in the pornographic industry in order to make their living.

What the public prefers not to deal with in everyday life was now forced to be seen and discussed. What was difficult and surfaced in the public debate was the explicit mixture of sex and politics in an unusual and intertwined way. This was not as a tabloid discussing a politician's mistress or other common scandals. This time the mixture of politics and sexuality involved an act of protest. In this respect, it was confusing, and the public reacted as if it was another scandal, not grasping again the charismatic and nonconforming attitude that guided Knafo. There were also other reactions—of mercy for the "poor single mother" who works for her children: "Look how low she got." Most reactions were that sexuality shouldn't be used for political protest. Once her body and sexuality, her femininity and pornography, entered the stage, the public couldn't bear that. She became promiscuous and condemned, not anymore the "saint suffering victim," the "stabat mater" that separates the saint from the prostitute. For Knafo, just like for Havatzelet Ingbar, this was a sobering lesson that she was standing right at the economic bottom, painful and having nothing left to lose. The opposite reaction from that which she experienced when she first began her journey taught her a lesson about hidden lines that she wasn't aware of, and there were codes that she didn't know how to decipher ("A Protest in Nude," 2004). One code she did decipher, however, the rule of the power of the media and the mixed interests that pull many entangled strings behind the publications. She tried to play in this yard knowing very little of the codes, and for a while, she seemed to succeed.

A few months later, Knafo was invited to participate in a TV reality program in a campaign that advertised beauty and body care products, plastic surgery and gyms. This gave her an opportunity to present her version of why she had agreed to use her body and sexuality for the purpose of protest. She left the impression that everything she did was out of choice and that her life was under control no matter how radical her actions were.

A year later in September 2005, it was published that a tragedy occurred to Knafo: her oldest son, Nathaniel, who was arrested for suspicion of a crime that concerned drugs, committed suicide while in detention. This tragedy put in some proportions the public debate around her when revealing with what she was coping with in her private life. This was the last time was in the public eye before she returned to anonymity for another six years, until the next social justice protest occurred. In 2012, Knafo was interviewed regarding the summer protest of 2011. By now it was clear that if there were no security issues, the public would come out with some protest against the economic policy. This time it was the high rent rates and the overpricing of essential items of food. A protest brought thousands out to the streets for the same reasons Knafo initially began her own protest: the economic policy of the same minister, who now had become the Prime Minister, Benyamin Netanyahu (Sharoni, 2011). This protest was called "the cottage protest," which was made against the expensive price of basic foods such as cottage cheese. It began with the youth population that protested against high rent prices and the cost of living. The specific characteristic of this protests was that it was not only the poor who came out to the streets but the middle class and well-educated young generation, which couldn't stand up to the cost of living. Israel was not the only place where the protest and demonstrations of youngsters took place. Occupy Wall Street was happening in the United States, and similar demonstrations were occurring in Europe. This time there was a unique and common ground with the Middle East where youngsters in Egypt, Libya, Jordan, and other Middle-East countries faced riots for similar reasons. Globalization became a full sense of events that embraced East and West. Knafo, however, reacted cynically, saying that the protests made her laugh because the people didn't yet know that nothing would come of their protest. It is like "the dogs are barking and the convoy is passing on," as the Hebrew proverb says. She seemed to be staying within a liminal area, almost political, almost public, but not quite. Once again, a woman remains trapped in between the public and the private spheres as many before her who tried to break through to the public sphere but does not always make it because of the firm separation line between the spheres. We usually center successful stories of women who make it all the way from the private to the public and neglect the majority of the cases of women who either fall and remain trapped within the in-between zone or simply refrain from making attempts and stick to the traditional socialization path of staying at home and taking care of the family (i.e., staying in the private sphere). Although we see many women in the labor market make numerous successful attempts, women still "take" the home and the children to their workplace and intertwine them within their careers (Slaughter, 2012).

THE ABSORBING ABILITIES OF THE ENDOCENTRIC ORDER

Knafo's journey shed light on theoretical questions such as: What is the nature of that twilight space in which women walk when they want to make a change in their lives? What does it mean to "walk" in the "in-between zone"? Why do they often find themselves trapped within this twilight zone? How can they identify and decipher the codes and obstacles that stand in their way to make a successful and complete journey from private to public? What is the apparatus that enables the system to absorb protests and dismiss them even in democratic regimes so that women are discouraged to take action?

The Dialectics of Gender from Discipline to Subversion

Friedrich Engels and Hannah Arendt identified the rigid schemes of the social order and pointed out the forces that conserve them. They followed the classic path of thought and criticized traditional perceptions that make the "good state" and the "good family." Arendt didn't stand on the problem of women exclusion when discussing the ideal modern state in her book, *The Human Condition.* She acknowledged that the spheres are necessary for the political order and the division of labor. She has also ignored the hierarchical nature of the spheres order: the public sphere is prior to the private in the division of power and labor. Therefore, the coupling or private/women and public/men preserved male superiority and the rule of patriarchy when transferred from the traditional order to the modern state without reform. Engels had before suggested that the family must be dismantled if the state was to be abolished and equality achieved. He stood with the family as the cornerstone of the state and the instrument that perpetuates the means of exploitation of the proletariat. Engels, to be said, wasn't interested in women's fate per se. Both Engels and Arendt were interested in the broader human condition and the ideal political order that should fit within it. These philosophers, and others before them such as Jean-Jacques Rousseau, John Stuart Mill, and G. W. F. Hegel, held the order that organize around binary principles regardless of the subordination of women that derives from it. Gender scholars identified that coupling paradigm and the spheres binary and directed their critical suggestions to the hearts of the problem in which change should be made to bring about equal gender relations (Pateman, 1988). Feminist movements and gender scholars identified the rigidity of the division of spheres (Walby, 1994) and pointed out its extensions in multiple arenas, as in religion, politics and culture, in economy, military and law, in family, marriage, and kinship, in sexuality, and in the body and the soul. The feminist work focused and still does on the subordination of women in all its forms, first and for most their subordination to reproduction with its ties to the biological factor that motivates women's potential of giving birth. This natural ability of women subordinates them and leads to their exclusion, inequality, and oppression. Some women see the change through the contestation of oppression by rebelling against the subordination to the trait of reproduction.

The public critique against Knafo, as presented above, in this respect is consistent with the fear of the conservative forces. The belief that the coupling order is an apparatus that should be protected from dismantling attempts and reproduction should be secured; moreover, production and reproduction are coupling that maintained order to the benefit of traditional engendered order that must also be protected. Although one can imagine the decomposition of the coupling male/production as women took part in the industrial world since its beginning, the coupling female/reproduction is still impossible to dismantle. The result is that women end up taking part in both production and reproduction while men participate in production in greater parts. Technology may bring about the possibilities that will increase both women's participation in more equal ways in the production process while men will be able to enjoy technological possibilities of reproduction. However, even if it will be possible, the challenge that needs to be faced lies in cultural, historical, and normative roots, since they are so deeply planted and reiterated till they seem to be natural and essential to the human existence and part of the biological nature of the human. The cultural history that was constructed around this binary order and the fact that the order is intertwined within all the social constructs that were crystallized and survived for thousand years, requires a fierce and persistent struggle to crack it. In this respect, it is rooted in social orders for as long as slavery had been and required similar persistence and resistance. As with struggles against slavery, every small step demands energy from the enslaved, and as with slavery, struggles do not spread around and immediately bring enslaved followers to join the resistance.

A woman's struggle for liberation also does not bring followers, although it is obvious that subordination must be abolished. The most difficult thing is the reactions that the conservative gatekeepers invent to maintain their domination. This proves that maintenance is not a one-time task but a constant and viable activity. Women do not cease subverting the order, and feminist experiences show that women are sanctioned for trying to violate the conservative patriarchal order (Dahan-Kalev, 2013). Therefore, subversive attempts on women's part and re-disciplining on the patriarchal conservative forces' parts interact dynamically in a dialect manner that does not stay in place but develops and moves all the time, receiving new rhizome-like forms of gender subversion and subordination. In the Western culture, the subordination expended to large collectives and organized protests only since the end of the nineteenth century. Gender scholars concentrated on exposure of the disciplining women forces that used and abused their sexuality, body, femininity, reproductivity, and motherhood. These scholars endeavored to show how subtle the disciplining apparatus was in using means directed to these precise virtues of women as human females. Cultural ethos praised and idealized the submissive woman and the woman who devotes herself to the home and the family. These were glorified and bundled with reproduction and national values. The woman symbolized the nation and became one with collective ideals of the state and the people. This apparatus served as a "lining regime," which no one could see its hidden function as the scaffold on which the political order was constructed. This structure is not unique to totalitarian regime as it might seem, but democracies, monarchies, and aristocracies hold it as well. Feminist scholars had, therefore, invested those efforts in exposure of the oppressive roots that envelops all sorts of regime and political orders.

They have shown that the lining is always patriarchal and phallic in its essence. Suffice it to refer to Robert Filmer's (1949 [1680]) philosophy of the genealogy of the political order. He justified patriarchy as descending from the creation of Adam, the first father. Although this might sound religious and archaic, the issue is that conservative patriarchal gatekeepers still hold such perceptions around the globe, East and West worlds being religious and secular. Feminists continued to protest and point their goals to the phallic elements of the order by exposing its unnatural, arbitrary constructs. They challenged the idea that man is privileged because he is superior. They stood on problems of exclusion and prejudiced tokenism of women as morally backward and inept for the public sphere roles. Hegel warned not to put the helmet of government in the hands of women for it endangered the state (Hegel, 2008). Feminist scholar's developed subversive studies next to the struggles of the feminist movements and registered so far quite a few achievements, such as opening public arenas for women and mobilizing them from the private to the public expanded them along with rights for equal opportunities for women. What began with high feminist hopes for emancipation in the 1950s brought women out of home to the public arena. It began in Western liberal regimes and continued along radical paths, and then post-colonial feminism emerged from the margins by activists of a lower class and of subordinated ethnic, radicalized, and religious groups within modern democratic societies. Feminism in the non-Western world followed this trend about a decade later.

The distribution of the struggles since the beginning of the twentieth century was modified and accommodated to specific realities from which they emerged. Feminism was directed to specific problems under which women were subordinated: radicalized, religious persecuting, or ethnic discrimination, often putting women in intersectional oppressions. Feminist activists from the third world and the marginalized women in the West developed various strategies that aimed to cope with multiracial oppression through intersectional feminism. It is well-illustrated in the case of Muslim women in Europe who struggle for the right to wear the hijab. The women submit to a Muslim law that is dictated to them by men. Their lives in Europe, which are essentially Western lives, also experience discrimination and inferiorization in the hosting countries, though they are allegedly liberal and patrons of equal rights for women. In this respect, the women are trapped between the hammer and the anvil as they are discriminated for as immigrants of a Muslim and Arab minority on top of their being discriminated as women, both within their ethnic community and as second-class citizens. Feminist activists of these communities politicized the traditional norm of wearing the hijab and sometimes use it as a protest act against their hosting country that discriminates against them. They made it a political choice on the women's part by expressing their protest against the discriminating Western order, bending, for a while, their position for the hijab altogether. Their loyalty to the tradition and culture as well as to Muslim law is in this respect politicized too. This example shows how feminist struggle is always contextualized, and the strategy of the struggle must accommodate to the circumstances to be effective. The development of feminism is expected to invent subtle means to cope with the sophisticated, oppressive apparatus.

The push that feminist movements and scholars gave the struggle of women stimulated various reactions amongst the wider public and non-activist women. A backlash came from various social categories that dismissed the achievements of women's liberation as a false vision. They pointed at the "second-shift" syndrome along with the "glass ceiling," the "queen bee," and the "superwoman" syndromes as developments that enhance the subordination of women rather than liberating them (Dahan-Kalev, 2001). The new arrangements that seem to emancipate women and give them equal rights are proved to be syndromes that double the burden on women in the gender division of labor. On top of it, they pointed out new problems that caused many of the women to discard feminism as a no-less subordinating woman. The unfulfilled promise of sisterhood put women of color and women of lower classes in double oppression, not only to men in their communities and to men in general but also to women of upper class. This disappointment was so bitter that those of the disappointed women who didn't discard the battlefield attacked back the upper-class feminist women (Dahan-Kalev and Marzel, 2012). The general lesson that was learned from this experience was that women, as human beings might be very active as feminists but the larger social mistreatments are rooted in habits and norms that they didn't do much to cope with and get rid of. In the 1980s and onward, it was easy to see that women in career and higher economic class and political positions exploited lower-class women whom they hired for household and childcare. In other words, the private sphere remained the responsibility of women, both those who left it for a career in the public sphere and those who were hired to replace them in the private sphere and were subjugated to their exploitation. The male spouses, until the beginning of the twenty-first century, remained exempted altogether from private sphere responsibilities. Very slowly this process changed when individual couples where women with awareness of a more equal division of domestic tasks began to change the situation on a personal basis. That is, again, transformation depends on the practice by the individual.

One major obstacle was the family-state bond that secured the patriarchal order. Until the end of days of unequal wages that enable men to earn about 30 percent more than women and conscious responsibility of women to maintain the private sphere continue to play a significant role in a families' economic consideration and bring couples to prefer that, man will continue to be the breadwinner while woman stays at home or settle for the second breadwinning job after her spouse. This, of course, sharpened the serious situation in which single mothers find themselves when trying to be the main breadwinner and serve as both parents at the same time. The state, in the case of Israel, does not go all the way to take an equal political plan for single mothers. They enjoy some mitigation, but these still leave them under the poverty line. These arrangements lie on sediments of patriarchal order maintenance by the gatekeepers of the order. The reproduction obligation is the nuclear from where it grows (Pateman, 1988), an obligation that women don't really contest with reference to free choice. Feminists argue that the most difficult thing for them is to discover the betrayal of sisterhood on the part of upper-class women, which, in the end, ironically serves the backlash position. In other words, women may have received permission to mobilize from private to public but only on the condition that they continue to fill the reproduction and family-life duties (Dahan-Kalev, 2012).

When looking at the larger picture of the feminist struggle, it is clear that the double-burden responsibilities on women, the heavy-duty tasks, and the new backlash syndromes that flourish under the feminist struggle all play into the hands of the patriarchal gatekeepers. They are even presented as feminist achievements, leaving on the side of the road many women who failed in this race to seemingly struggle for liberation and equality of all women. Perhaps the single mothers are the category that pays the highest price in this venture. The class gaps between better-off women and worse-off women, along with gender gaps between men and women, are thus fastened while a seemingly changing reality is occurring. In this state of affairs, Knafo was the people's enemy, being a single mother and of a lower class. The initiative to change her life was a challenge to the deepest patriarchal norms that needed to be protected. The power relations proportions were of a "David and Goliath" proportion, putting her in a ridiculous light simultaneously with the first reaction that made many stand up side-by-side with her against the economic policy that was blind to its gender and consequences for single mothers. She did touch the nerve of the "justice and moral of the weak," but she only did so for a short while. The "justice and moral of the weak" doesn't go well with human and feminine permissiveness, the conservative idea of the "justice and moral of the weak" goes all the way to expect a martyr, a victim that stands up to the righteousness standard. Mundane conduct contradicts this image, let alone a woman who doesn't conform to the wife and mother allocated to her by the patriarchal order. Knafo, therefore, lost much of the public support because she violated the moral expectations that were standard within the patriarchal society that still prevailed after the feminist revolution that changed women's lives in the 1950s around the world. Knafo's attempt to be herself and not to conform to the traditional couplings of victimization and feminine submissiveness was too difficult for the patriarchal, conservative forces in the public to accept. She crossed all lines: the private-sphere lines; the lower-class and marginalized place; the simple person who demanded to speak with the ministry of the treasury; above all the traditional channels of communication between a citizen and a higher-ranking official; the common sexual lines of permissiveness; and the motherhood ideals of sacrifice. Reading the talkbacks to her steps and decisions demonstrates how conservative the public around her was towards her attempts to reinvent herself and move away from the traditional lines women conform to. Women didn't enter high-rank positions and powerful jobs. Until our days, there were no women who held the title of chief of staff in a militaristic position, or the Pope, the chief rabbi, or the Imam's authority. Women began by entering the production lines in factories and education and health services positions; these were fields of occupations that earned the term "pink collar" jobs because of it. In Israel, where the two arenas of militarism and religion are so significant and hold immense power over the state, the chances that women would step into those authoritative positions seemed to be an illusion. Nevertheless, women contested the convention and, little by little, saw some success every now and then in the legislative realm or political norms.

THE WEAKNESSES OF SOCIAL JUSTICE MOVEMENTS

Women experience slippery walls to climb in modern states and in factories in the third-world countries where globalization and rampant capitalism both prevail. Every attempt they make to improve their living conditions often results in one step forward but two steps back, as the Israeli feminist scholar Dafna Izraeli put it as early as in the 1970s. On this ground, Knafo's demand to speak with no less then the minister of the treasury was almost absurd. There are two mechanisms embedded in the state that makes such attempts look so ridiculous. One is the comprador states' mechanism, and the other is the social justice NGOs. In the case of the compradors state case, a colonial power and allegedly enlightened capitalist ruler mobilize cooperation on the middle class and the intelligentsia sections of the colonized countries. Therefore, they breed the loyalty of the middle-class forces in return for protection and benefits. They become the apparatus of the colonizers and operate the state's institutions for the colonizers. As Jan Drahokoupil argues, this is what makes the comprador states survive and exploit the local, lower-class population (Drahokoupil, 2008). Production and local economy function to the service of the comprador state as a large firm in which the messengers of the colonizer are local forces that operate the apparatus to control their people. Today, this situation goes further to prevail not only in colonized countries but also in countries that host mass immigration of labor since the end of

World War II. Israel is an immigration country, and similar to many others, as Gayatri Spivak says: "On the other side the international division of labor, a subject of exploitation [of] woman can't recognize the text of women's exploitation and speak it, even when the not-representing intellectual evacuate for her the space to talk, it is ridiculous. The women than suffers multiplied discrimination" (Spivak, 1988). This was exactly Knafo's situation when she first stepped out to her struggle. She immediately earned about public empathy. Social justice NGOs maintained for her the public stage and stood behind her, ready to give advice and let her talk her words without mediating expert activists. The idea was to protect her from opportunistic politicians and communication advertisers. NGOs, such as Ahoti (My sister), Shatil (plant), and Yadid (companion), stood with her. These were NGOs that lived on contributions from the United States and Europe of grants for proactive Jewish foundations. Knafo discovered that spontaneous rebellion and resistant passion were not enough for the deconstruction of the robust and complex engendered capitalist spheres. She started her journey as an elementary-educated woman with limited abilities and expressed her thoughts and explained why she did what she did. She was at a zero point of the language, as Roland Barth defined it. Her bubbling emotions were mobilized by the evil she felt was done to her. She took action, almost with no word and no structured language. Ideological formulated ideas were strange to her. She spoke the truth, which was yet to be dramatized for the political theater, as Louise Althusser suggested when discussing the idea of interpellation.

NGOs that act as proactive for social justice and community rights tend to take control over initiatives of the sort similar to Knafo's resistance. Being more experienced and professional, this qualified them to better express evils caused by the state's social policy. These NGOs flourished, especially with the decline of the welfare state, and many became the arm of the third sector after the governmental and the business sectors. The trouble with these organizations is that they lack the passion and the rage that bring victims of evil to rebellion. They are operated by a limited number of workers that act as proactive in the community but lean on community frustration and anger from local volunteers. This results in a paradoxical effect where the NGOs serve as shock observers of the rage and spontaneous forces that urge the subjects injured by injustice to step out into the streets. The energies that motivated Knafo were the rage and frustration of the situation in which she was caught. No mediators stood between her and the public sphere. This is what initiated her to take her radical move, a move that might have dissolved if she were surrounded by NGO professional activists who must be loyal to remote donors who pay their salaries. What she had to contribute to the cry of the wretched was an act that was unique and didn't dissolve in the political structure theater and that allocated to each actor his or her own preplanned role. Knafo simply did not belong to the cast and didn't know the rules of the game. As an outsider, she didn't assimilate or imitate the common patterns and couldn't even recognize herself as an outsider. In the *Methodology of the Oppressed,* Chela Sandoval highlights the importance of remaining separate from the "usual discourse of justice" if change is to be mobilized. The deviation of the resisting forces from the usual path of the social justice political business is indispensable for mobilization of change. This is at the heart of social agency, and there, Sandoval argues, lies the starting point of resistance, refusing to dissolve within the general discourse even if it is a discourse of resistance that comes from inventive and creative passion. It is not motivated by the subject's will to join the mob but from a liminal threshold that steps out of previous ordinary, subordinating behavior yet not joining other resisting subjects. Knafo stayed in this liminal space, contrasting herself to others around her. These others were the governmental and nongovernmental forces that participated in the political show. With her spontaneous protest, she remained genuine and difficult to miss within the public bustle. In *Methodology,* Sandoval suggests that this is the source from which the oppressed can inverse the direction of their previous subordination and target it against the oppressing forces. Knafo, for this matter, managed to escape the regular political language that, as Sandoval suggests, turns off the protest fire that burns for short instances. The irony in such a struggle is that as soon as the NGOs join the genuine act of resistance of a rebellion, the chance to carry on and maintain the protest fire is turned off. In opposition to the NGOs, Knafo needed time and space where she could develop her own language of protest, to find/invent her own strategic acts and words exactly as she did in the first place when she invented the idea of marching two hundred kilometers to meet with the treasury minister. In this respect, the NGOs that joined her and tried to help functioned as comprador force; that is, they mediated between the subordinating forces of the state the capitalist donors and the resisting actor that stood up against them. In reformulating Knafo's words so that they would "make sense" to the "public and actors' ear," they sterilized her spontaneous urge and its refreshing taste of the rebellion. They made her potent cry sound more rational and sensible in a way that it consisted of the regular social critical discourse that prevailed for years since the decline of the welfare state. This was a discourse that the patriarchal political business professionals could understand and knew how to deal with, unlike Knafo's action that moved on the line of genuine and was difficult to understand without making efforts to decode "the noise" that she brought to the marketplace.

The potential feminist mark that she brought with her also got lost in the translation of Knafo's message by the NGO's to the public and the actors. Hélène Cixous and Julia Kristeva discussed this in-between stand as one that confronts male written language. They argue that when women write or speak themselves, they immediately stand up against the patriarchal order. The language that tried to mediate Knafo's peculiarity, her wild cry, which demanded to make an effort to decipher it and interpret its meaning, was not "translated" by the NGO's speakers who transferred her uniqueness to familiar but depersonalized sounds. When the NGOs translated her rage to something more familiar that can be better understood, it was received as merely one more protest comparable to what was known before to be the problem of single mothers. It moved from the unfamiliar Cixous's "laughter of the Medusa" and was chalked by normalizing forces that cohered with the traditional and familiar demonstrations. These were demonstrations that in democracies are protected by the right of gathering and protest but also so common and structured that they lost their fierce resistance power. To these common protests that state became used and had the right apparatuses to cope with them, not much impact is attached. In translating Knafo's act to the familiar political discourse, the surplus value of the energetic protest was lost, and its passion and pain and suffering were rationalized and, eventually, extinguished. It was like taking the spirit from the breathing body and leaving it as a corpse. The common language used slogans such as "the evil to single mothers," the "welfare services functions," "social injustice," and, in the case of Israel, "unequal burden of military service," "money to the needy, not to the settlers," and many more. The NGOs drained Knafo's force of resistant action to channels of order preservation, the principles of the public sphere operation, and the binary boundaries protection. Knafo did her best to stand up to the standards of the "proper mother," the "proper woman," and the "proper single mother" and the NGOs that stood behind her used clichés to justify their support as long as she didn't deviate from these images that coincided with their agendas. They wanted to present her not as the particular case of being what she was—Knafo, the woman being—but reduced to the single mother representative of so many other oppressed single mothers, who are lower class and marginalized. Knafo wasn't one of many single mothers. She was the person that stepped out of her small development town in the desert and who contested the patriarchal order. The exclusivity of the journey and of the person who took it dissolved once the NGOs incorporated it to their larger agenda instead of highlighting her uniqueness. What remained of that burst of resistance was the case of a woman who broke her chains but still wasn't set free.

The common thing for women who break through to set themselves free remained that they must do it on their own and one by one. Knafo did it on her own all right, but as soon as she found herself in the public sphere, she realized that the bustle around her had deafened the public from listening carefully to the nuanced message she had to say; the lesson of breaking through in the many respects of consciousness, femininity, body, sexuality, motherhood, and many more were all lost in the public noise that surrounded her. The discovery that this is the nature of the public sphere and that the mob has other ways to hear sounds made it clear that the political and the public language were yet another thing that women learn when they cross the lines between the private and the public spheres. Politicians learn this language when they are advised to be superficial and popularize their phrases for the largest common ground of the attention of their audience. This is how public orators learn that slogans should be short and sharp but also hollow. Eventually, this fell to stereotypes. Knafo needed time to understand all that, but it was time that she didn't have. However, once the words were listed, they became political actions in the sense that they were not a dialogue between two but a monologue that received its sense from the promise, a political promise. The term *parler*, which in French is "to talk," sits at the heart of the idea of the parliament. Talking in circumstances of struggle or resistance may conceal silences that have endured long before the burst of a resistance. It is, therefore, important to understand the silence that existed prior to the act of rebellion for it to embed the potential energy that accumulates before the moment of the burst. The force of the political action is within the prior moments of that silence. Knafo's journey could become the mobilization force of change for the many marginalized people who felt solidarity on the first day of the journey. The intervention of the other forces—the media under the democratic rules of the game; the ministries and authorities responding to the journey along all the three months of the camping in the Rose Garden; the support of the NGO opportunists, and many other factors—played the role of ventilating the public rage along with Knafo's rage, and it lost the potential energy of real upheaval that could lead to deeper change in the situation of single mothers, to a change of the patriarchal operation towards single mothers. Knafo went through an emancipatory process and her worldview of the political game and rules of the public sphere changed. Her self-image and feminist consciousness opened, but she still had to understand the sense of standing on the liminal space and grasp its nature.

DISCOVERING THE LIMINAL SPACE

Along their struggles, women keep discovering, time and again, each in her turn, how vital is the line that separates the spheres and how powerful its renovating nature is. While wandering between the spheres, women discover that this is a personal journey of crossing the lines within their consciousness as women. Socialized as women from their childhood, they realize that they should sometimes go against their own self, each one in her turn, and no one can spare this process for the other. Women discover that they first have to find solutions to responsibilities to which they were socialized, such as the household and family and the childcare, with all that stems from maintenance in the private sphere. Emancipation for a woman means that she has to figure out how to settle the responsibilities to which she was socialized for in order to step out of the private to the public and still function in both spheres adequately. The obligation has first to be met as part of the emancipation process. Women spend time and energy in exchanging personal information as to how they have solved this challenge. Each one must invent her own solutions and accommodate to her specific personal circumstances the proper means. They must find solutions to the stereotypical social constructs that form the expectations that they must marry, bear children, have families, all in an exclusively heterosexual format. These are the huge challenges that they must each face. All of these are formative categories that are given to women a priori, and if they don't want to proceed in these trajectories, they face the need to reconsider the options and be prepared of the price to pay if they deviate from them. For this reason, they linger before they begin to cross the lines of the spheres and learn about the obstacles and prices they might have to pay on that way. The line that divides the spheres is found to be not just a thin thread but a large space, a sort of wilderness that the woman who crosses it walks alone and may lose her way because it has no signs and no clear paths. It is a space that is neither private nor public, a liminal threshold that is bi-directional that they were socialized for is useless on this road. There lies the root which was hidden from the women's eyes when socialized. A woman who crosses the road discovers the roots of socializing constructs to be heteronormative family constructs. The problems of disentangling the complex socializing gender forces are intertwined with other power networks: religious, ethnic, racial, sometimes militaristic, cultural, and political. They get down to the last details of the personal, the specific set of socialization of the particular woman who makes an attempt to emancipate herself. This is what forces each woman to find her right way to get away from the socialization chains. In that way, women learn that socialization is operated on a personal level; it is adjusted to the particular woman within the particular culture and particular community. Therefore, it is up to her to find the "right key" to get away from the "particularly socialized as a woman cage." Particular obstacles—religion, politics, culture—socialize women to certain beliefs, values, and norms, but it is also the individual personality, individual family story, and specific life circumstances that must be faced that have women take the path towards feminist liberation. The circles that embrace the women are tied to each other with power relation cobwebs. Therefore, pioneer women who dare to contest heteronormative order are women who pave the way for others, and by doing that, they make a personal sacrifice. They "lean on the barbed fence" so that other women can "step on them when crossing the barbed lines." They serve as role models, although they can't spare the personal journey that the followers must also do. The work each one must do is to personally deconstruct the private sphere burden. This is the essence of the experience of liberation feminism. Theoretically, the responsibility of reproduction and the biological virtue remains the only natural trait that women continue to bear. It is up to them whether to deconstruct the patriarchal moral obligations and take responsibility to reconstruct their own. Many women died before they took this journey; it is the feminist ideology that mobilizes women to begin the journey or to abstain from it. A personal crisis is very often the trigger that pushes women to take the first step, as our Knafo case showed.

THE AGENDA OF SINGLE MOTHERS

When she left Mitzpe Ramon, Knafo was certain that it was a personal journey. She was not the only poor, single mother, but she was aware of the fact that other women before her took actions and worked collectively to bring change in their lives. This journey, which simultaneously took place in the consciousness, departs from obedience to resistance. This part is personal in that it is separated from solidarity; it is not moving from one to the other but sprouts and emerges from personal initiative. In this respect, it needs no external support. There exists tension between the action that involves or requires solidarity, but the idea that women must mobilize their consciousness from the subordination phase to the liberation must come from their own will. The latter is individual, functions in isolation, and dares to take the first steps from the private to the public. Women can support each other, but in the end, it is a mental and psychological process that starts from within the subjective women. This explains the frustration of feminist activists who express disappointment from "the women who can't see the oppressive truth that lies within the patriarchal order and continues to submit to the subordinating rules of male hegemony." Knafo had begun the process before she stepped out to take her journey; she was isolated long before, and with her back to the wall, she had to struggle as a single mother. She did not belong to any feminist movement before. Her idea of liberation began when she felt that "enough is enough," and she went out to give herself a voice. The irony was that when she stood ready in the public eye and was surrounded by NGOs and empathic activists, she was belittled again and put in the "right proportion" of the small woman, of the single mother versus the "giant" minister of the treasury. Her struggle, however, was unique and couldn't be reduced or merged with another agenda of feminist mothers. Before she was escorted with the NGOs, who reduced her struggle to make it similar to other struggles and, thus, made it more familiar to the public, her struggle was Knafo's struggle, the unprecedented struggle of a single mother, the single breadwinner, a woman who lived on the margins of the society, in the geographical periphery of Israel, who lived below the poverty line—she was the one and only Knafo. Once she was escorted by the NGOs, it left the struggle with a very small number of women who could correspond to this category; moreover, it demanded a very subtle agenda that would correspond only to the particular group. In the almost one hundred years of feminist struggle worldwide and a few decades of feminist struggle in Israel, the unique voice of a mother was not heard without being reduced to other feminist agendas, let alone that of single mothers.

The particular problems of single mothers dissolved into larger feminist ideologies of subgroups of mothers, families, spouses, working women, and so on. Nevertheless, their being the heads of their families and the main breadwinners did not consist with the feminist agendas of married women, women who lived in heterosexual families where women are often the second breadwinners, or mothers who often fill the role of two parents, unlike mothers within two-parent families. They suffer from inequality not only in relation to men but also to women who are not single mothers. Knafo's struggle helped to elaborate these differences and surfaced the fact that single mothers are not just mothers but also women in themselves whose unique situation deserves separate attention from women who mother in dual-parent households. In the case of the LGBT, we could see that they have separated themselves from other feminists and created both, theoretically and politically, their own field of studies and battles. This did not occur in the case of single mothers. It is a question that has yet to be addressed. In other words, single mothers live as human and as female, as feminine and as parents, in a unique way that is not reducible to the larger categories but still is not studied enough. Thus their claim for equality does not stem from the larger feminist agenda, and it requires separate reference to the topics of their problems. Furthermore, women as single mothers sometimes have interests that stand opposite to those of married women who live in couples. They are not "a team" in the family cell as parents; neither are they one out of two breadwinners, and when facing the public authorities, they are coping alone without the intimate support that women who live in couples can enjoy. This format multiplies the burden of single mothers not in two but in triple and more power trajectories. Single mothers are not just single but live in personal loneliness. With difficult familial issues, couples have the privilege to consult about and even share, discuss, and take or reject each other's advice; this does not exist for single mothers. They might wander around talking with themselves, but in the end, the responsibility of making a decision is only theirs. Knafo's affair brought the issues of single mothers, with all their complexities, to the public discourse. Moreover, her struggle sharpened the hidden conflicts that exist between married women living as couples and single women. For example, the idea that the heteronormative family is that which is constructed as a nuclear family of a couple but that the number of such formats is lessening for reasons of increasing divorce rate and of nonmarried women who strive for motherhood as singles, that is not out of misfortune in marriage circumstances or widowing. In this respect, Knafo succeeded in registering a significant page in the collective feminist and social justice book of resistance memory, titled "The Single Mothers" issue. The restraining apparatus that normally operates electively and adjusts to specific "order of woman violator," in the Knafo case, came from righteous women who wanted to protect the conservative family order and the submissive woman model, thus supporting the patriarchal gatekeepers. The sanctions that "tame" shrew women are adjusted to specific culture as we can learn from the way Arab women sanctioned for adultery as opposed to a Jewish ultra-orthodox woman for the same violation of the patriarchal order. Preservation of the public patriarchal order is the ultimate goal of gender socialization in the division of spheres and division of labor. The techniques of preserving the order may differ, but the goals are the same. Thus, in the case of Knafo, in her first instance of resistance, she did confuse the gatekeepers as she took an unfamiliar step to violate the patriarchal and political order. This may have demanded the gatekeepers to encode her genuine action. However, the NGOs made it easier for the establishment when they reformulated her struggle in familiar terms of a poor, single, marginalized mother. In other words, when women take an action in a genuine way, they may go through creative experiences and transformations of consciousness as women, but this doesn't imply that the establishment has a genuine response. Unfortunately, Knafo's struggle was perceived as a failure in the end but she certainly experienced subversive action and learned a personal lesson of public affairs as they are "cooked in the political kitchen" as she had never experienced before. For her, it was an opportunity to grow up in the political sense, which was rather sobering. She diverted from the "good-mother" format by challenging victimization and modest-woman patterns. More generally, her case illustrated the impossibility of fulfilling the "ideal-mother" model in the case of the single mothers who struggle to survive. On that dramatic moment of the cry "no more," she protested against the impossibility of the situational life conditions of single mothers, who are expected to conform to a bi-parent family format. She left the game yard making big noise against it.

Chapter Twelve

The Journey in the Twilight Zone

CONSCIOUSNESS JOURNEY

In the previous chapters, I focused on evaluating the capacity for social agency and the consciousness impact on it. I suggested that "success" and "failure" must be reformulated in the light of power relation in which women are involved when targeting change of social conditions and using resistance and rebellious strategies. I suggested that even if the agency action is followed by a change in the personal awareness to her living conditions, the fact that the action fails to achieve the stated goals, it can't be considered a failure in all respects. A new evaluation is required to assess the multiple aspects that rebellious actions involve in order to determine more subtly its success and failure elements. Both being and doing and being and thinking are separate vectors that determine whether something was a success or a failure. The resistance of Vicki Knafo was first and for most a resistance and refusal experience that occurred within her consciousness. She had deviated from the path of obedience and subordination that she used to function through all the time before that. The forces she put in the act of refusal had to be redirected. According to her socialization convictions, it meant no less than apostasy of the basic order that reflects from the binary paradigm: male/female, private/public, man/woman. The journey that was allegedly spontaneous burst out of an upheaval that broke through the paradigm in which most women are trapped: the binary paradigm. The paradigm that is responsible for coupling and constantly splitting the consistency of the private/public spheres split, the first of all splits. The burst of such redirection occurs first in the mind as a reflection, and then reflects in operation, in doing and thinking, in the existential conditions of the agent. Knafo remained a single mother and a stranger in the public sphere in which she didn't earn recognition as a politician or a woman leader. She wasn't even recognized as a social rights activist. She was objectified in this respect, as she remained the object of evil committed on single mothers. Her stormy experience and the changes she went through remained in her inner world. In the public sphere, where she turned into an icon, reified the symbolizing of the issue of single mothers. Her active subjectivity was not allowed to manifest herself, and she had to settle with the public image that was attributed to her. She earned the public respect for her standing firm for her family as a mother, but at the same time, she was condemned for failing in her marriage and her miscalculating the domestic management. She walked in a twilight zone that was new to her, a liminal and unknown thin ground that belonged to neither spheres. Being blinded in a zone where she wasn't anymore the "women who knew her place" as it was in the private sphere, nor in the public sphere where the rules of the game were those that patriarchal codes dictated, she had no choice but to listen to the voices inside herself. This time, they were rebellious voices. She needed time for reflection and for planning her next steps. In conservative societies where rules are rigid and there is no room for change, submission is automatic and each subject knows her place and if there is consciousness transformation, it is hardly manifested in public. Moreover, the gatekeepers are standing by to block unwanted subversive actions, let alone not recognize claims that may grow changing implications. Only on the margins where patriarchal gatekeepers aren't as alert can women succeed in making minor changes. More significant changes in motherhood roles or marriage relation had almost no reform chances. Therefore, the twilight zone—the zone that lies in between the spheres is that in which women who make attempts to bring changes—is the space where women can take their time to meditate and plan their next steps of consciousness transformation. Knafo was in this third sphere in the consciousness sense; all the time she spent when in the Rose Garden in Jerusalem. The gender rules of the game were now lit in a new light and painted in different colors: all the old convictions of motherhood, marriage, and being the single breadwinner in the family, and so on. "Women's time," "mother's devotion," "employee loyalty," "divorced women status," and many more notions went through engendering processes in her mind, a process of revaluation of these functions and their significance. Her self-respect for her being a woman-parent, a woman-employee, or a woman-divorcee was changing and differently estimated. Clearer voices from within her echoed the outside appreciation she heard in the first days of her rebellion from the public sphere. It sensed right to be in the twilight zone and reconsidered the old perceptions with changing, more self-estimating ones. True, she was facing deliberations and doubts, emotional crises and aggressive impulses, inner conflicts, confusions, and frustrations, all much more than she had before. This was intensification that characterizes consciousness transformation. A resistance journey is not a resistance journey without this emotional turbulence. The feeling of losing the way is imminent to the experience and generates fears and uncertainty. The old compass that had brought the subject to the same move in the same direction disintegrated, and a new compass with different polarities must replace it. This time, feminist polarity must be discovered to be inconsistent with the old patriarchal one. The deconstruction of the patriarch compass is very slow, but once the deconstruction begins and the subject walks loosening her way, full of doubts and confusions, she is on a search for a new path that sometimes is found in one strike, as Knafo had experienced, or in slower rhythm, as Havatzelet Ingbar experienced. It seems that nothing could stop Knafo when she was determined to start her journey. It was a journey that changed her life. Since then, her perception of reality was clearly of injustice and distortion, as she said many times, which she didn't see before. The task since that point was to pave new ways to craft new strategies and be creative about them. This is a part of the feminization process: each woman, in her own time and ability, designs her personal feminist agenda and walks along step-by-step. Feminist scholars must analysis to study these personal experiences to decipher the endless variations of liberation agendas as each woman has her own ignition point and personal reasons to begin their journey. Feminist scholars hold the convention that feminists strive for peace while combats and war are alien to it. I contest this perception as feminist history shows that there are no feminist achievements that we could point out as an achievement that was not gained without a struggle. The journey is always on a battlefield, as Knafo's experience showed.

A JOURNEY TO THE UNKNOWN

As mentioned above, a woman's journey from private to public is personal, made by individual women full of quests, loneliness, and uncertainty. Leaving a "blessed" and familiar routine, although it is discriminating against women on the gender aspects, is still comfortable and, therefore, preferable to the unknown. Scholars such as Gayatri Spivak and bell hooks marked this journey and other similar journeys as an un-learning process. Where the departure is from the world of the subordinated to the liberated, the struggle involves shaking up the subject's world from within. The hidden dark continent of femininity, as Sigmund Freud referred to it, is brought to the public sphere and contributes to new insights and original formations of the constructs of the public spheres, such as institutions, public affairs, policy formations, and the like. However, all that begins with a journey of resistance that women can't avoid from taking at the start, inverting the direction of subordination into rejection. Models that were constructed for the private sphere and functioned according to codes that were adjusted to it were sources for designation of feminist model construction in the public sphere. The scholars Carol Gilligan (1982), Jean Bethke Elshtain (1981), and Nancy Chodorow (1978) in their works implied that emotional management in the public sphere could take a clue or two from the empathy and the compassion that prevail in relations of mother-child, intimate married couples, and family, all taking place in what is considered the private sphere (Syrett and Hogg, 1992). However, it is difficult to imagine these forms in public institutions such as the military company or battalion, in the religious hierarchical establishment, or the high ranks of state officials. These are institutions that remained immune and impenetrable to such intersubjective formats. Women indeed crossed the lines from the private to the public and often had to adjust themselves to the public spheres codes rather than bring their own private spheres codes to it. On the other hand, men hardly switched their sphere of action for materialistic reasons, power control and prestige. The women who crossed the lines all the way to the public sphere did not receive any assistance for their old responsibilities of childcare and the family and domestic maintenance. They had to invent, again, on a personal level their own solutions to the tasks at home, and they still stood up to the position requirements they began to hold in the public sphere. In addition, their image as sexual objects extended, and the women suffered increasing harassment in the new sphere that had entered into their workplace, educational and political institutions, and so on. Women became discriminated against in the public sphere in new variations, finding it difficult to be promoted and equally access competing carrier workplaces. In other words, these were not liberating conditions for the women feminist who wanted to make a change in their lives. The women persistence bore among other options the option of women adjusting to male power relations. The "male-ish woman" was constructed as a stereotype next to the other feminist patterns to make a difference. Legislation and political activism persistently surfaced motherhood issues, second-shift problems, and equality demands in various domains. Every woman's achievement paved the way for others but didn't spare the journey to the followers who came after her. The paradox was that the problems that women faced doubled and acquired for them the title of superwomen. The women learned to maneuver between both spheres in hostile fields that responded with ingratitude. If women don't fill their motherhood or family tasks properly, they are condemned, even if they excel in their career. The problem extended from the time that women stepped into the public sphere en masse, not just upper-class, well-off women or one heroine exceptions.

The in-between or twilight zone, as elaborated previously, is a consciousness site that exists in the imagination of women, whether they are aware of it or not. Women become aware of it when searching for inventive solutions to the double burden that they face when beginning to cross the spheres. When Knafo began her journey, the question of childcare and the breadwinning were the burning issues that she had to find a solution for. However, the fact that she had to face the deep, patriarchal socialization rules stood before her and didn't allow her to move forward before she made a decision whether she crosses the lines. Luce Irigaray described this discovery journey as a journey in which women begin to doubt the truth of the binary idealism. Women begin to understand that what they see are images, like in Plato's Cave. This binary idealism holds them tight with an inability to turn their heads and see the sunlight (Irigaray, 1985). "The active life" that organize the human condition and hold as ideals stand in the eyes of feminists who experience consciousness transformation as objects that must be criticized. Irigaray's writings reformulate the Cave Allegory. She discusses the moment of liberation from the chains before the subject gets to see the sunlight. The liberation process is occurring in the space between the original sitting position and the exit from the cave. Irigaray suggests that these moments are moments of rebirth that happen in an in-between space, neither inside nor outside of the cave. In this moment, women mobilize all the powers they can get within them to cut off the chains. These are the refusal powers that bring women to rebel against gender-subordinating life conditions. This moment of refusal is the moment of "turning their back to the fire in the cave" and seeing strong beams of sunlight. The first instance is experienced as a blinding moment. The binary order has to either be reproved or discarded; the heterosexual family, marriage, sexuality, motherhood, and all the institutions to which they were socialized are reconsidered, erased or discarded. This is a process in the person's mind that overwhelms her with a waterfall-like demand for intensive reflections that should be met with crucial decisions on the path in which the liberating person must walk. She can also be lost, as a shedding skin process leaves old life perceptions away and moves to new paths of life. Irigaray took the Cave Allegory one step further and simulated it to a birth moment, the moment of slipping out of the womb through the cervix when the eyes are still blinded to the world's light. It is a fluid moment of navigating between new and old normative orders of two spheres of the world. With lack of experience in being free, confused, and uncertain in the consciousness state when in-between, the new compass of a free woman must be constructed and adjusted to herself only by her. This is an experience of self-invention and reinterpreting existential meaning and reconstruction of the new identity beyond those to which the liberating women were first socialized under the patriarchal world. The patriarchal world may not adjust itself to the liberating woman and leave no space to practice new experiences of being liberated and free. However, one crucial thing clarifies what seems to be natural in the context of the patriarchal order for it was forcefully reiterated, which is now revealed to be culturally constructed, artificial, and arbitrary, with different nuances of adjustments according to various ethnic, religious, racial, and other contextual differences. This is where women find the need to invent new languages and words that express completely new feelings, thoughts, and actions that come from new insights and they push them to begin to practice. It feels similar to a disillusion from an old faith—the patriarchal faith and reorganization of a metaphysical world and a new journey in which women begin to recognize their inner world with new perceptions.

Gloria Anzaldúa stood on these experiences from a Chicana feminist perspective, who were often single mothers, very poor, and literally living on the geopolitical border between Mexico and the United States. Like Knafo, these women live precarious lives, which are unstable, and have no political status "neither here nor there." Living for long periods in this situation, Anzaldúa found out that the women developed patterns of living a "hybrid life": norms and patterns of a mixture of the life they lived before, in Mexico, and the life they imagine they want to have in the United States but still don't have, like a free zone. Fluidity and uncertainty dominate their daily existence, and at the same time, they constantly invent new techniques of adaptation to unfamiliar conditions. They learn how to hide themselves and their children from the guards that chase them on both sides of the border and learn how to cope with the constant fear that they will be captured, imprisoned, and separated from their children. All for the hope that they will get to cross the border and get a chance to offer new life options to their children. These dangerous living conditions from the unknown future and the condemned past are of the main animating forces of the resistance action. The life reflexes that women who live on borders experience define liminal life in its substantial essence; it is life on the edge that requires a dynamic balance and takes from both sides of the border. Eventually, these are lives that can't be reduced to either form of life, either Mexican or American. The women who live on the border develop these life practices within their consciousness and their mental life, their intersubjective relationships, and eventually, develop original gender identities. "Active life" in this respect means an irreducible life that begins with and preserves resistance and continues with fluid and creative activity (Anzaldúa, 1987). Mentally, it can be drowned from the understanding that aggressive forces of living that reside in human impulses are now directed to the creation of free living conditions rather than the past submissive living conditions. The "good wife," the "good mother," and the "faithful woman" are evacuated from their old content at this point of walking in the twilight zone and release occupied spaces to be filled with new life actions.

The studies of Chela Sandoval and bell hooks continued this lineup of resistance of women who stay in the twilight zone. Their works helped to understand the deep mental processes in which weakened and subordinated women develop resistance practices. Each of these researchers pointed out how women identify oppression traps that chain them and elaborated on the possible awakening of the refusal consciousness of women who live radicalized on the margins of society. Sandoval and hooks introduced models of crossing the twilight zone and eventual liberation. They stress the significance of critical mass compilation as a force that can subvert the domination of the patriarchal order by elaborating on political practices. hooks relates to processes of unlearning of radicalized subjects who internalized inferiority only for being black, and Sandoval turned to the methodology of oppressed people. All these experiences are taking place in the twilight zone.

HOOKS, SANDOVAL, AND KNAFO: REFUSAL, RESISTANCE, AND EMANCIPATION

The idea of subversion and walking in the opposite direction against the disciplining direction of the patriarchal path was already suggested by Michel Foucault (1976) and even earlier in a different context by Walter Benjamin in his theses on the philosophy of history (Benjamin, 1940). One of this idea's insights relates to the fact that marginal groups are tightened to hegemony in a way that cannot be unchained. The subordinated and the subordinator can only exist as long as the oppressive technologies are maintained in a binary format. The binary order is all present and subordinates the subject in every aspect of life; therefore, she can't act from within it without using the subordinator's tools. The dilemma then becomes whether the subordinated should apply the master's technologies and direct them against the hegemony or maybe there is a way to subvert it otherwise. Both hooks and Sandoval suggest taking the same disciplining paths of subordination but proceed in the opposite direction. This approach differs from Audre Lorde's suggestion that it is impossible to win the master with his own tools. I will discuss hooks' and Sandoval's liberating ideas hereby through their conceptual contributions, "unlearning" by hooks and "methodology of the oppressed" by Sandoval.

UNLEARNING

Hooks, an African-American thinker, has put on the feminist agenda in the United States the issue of the struggle of the black woman against the double oppression of being a woman and of being black. Three gatekeepers maintain this double oppression: white men, black men, and white women. Each category employs different oppressive technologies that determine the nature of the relationship with black women. A white woman's relation with a black woman is different from the relationship of a white man with a black woman. It gets down to power relations and the relative power each category has in their hands in relation to each of the other categories. hooks suggested to see these types of oppression within socializing contexts and trace the multigenerational technologies that implant them within different social, economic, and patriarchal dimensions, which are all emerged within interracial relationships.

The socialization of oppression of black women diversify according to the intercategorical constructs so that black women are subordinated by white men in a different way from their being subordinated by white women or black men. The cultural socializing contents are subtly adjusted to the particular type of relationship. hook's contribution to the understanding of this oppressive technology matrix regards two faces of oppression: gender and racial. hooks continues, which Angela Davis's breakthrough project (1983) also shows, by adding the polarization issue of the bifacial oppression. That is, the problem both scholars discussed is taken further by taking out of the victims' yard and relocating it in the racializing and sexualizing forces yard. This move had a redundant effect on liberal and radical white feminists and revealed their limits and accommodation to white, middle-class women only (i.e., the feminism that emerged by and for women in the United States middle class in the 1950s and the 1960s). hooks' analysis exposed how women categories often are prone to racializing the weakened neighboring groups and this is what explain why women sometimes betray their sisterhood commitments. The same, she argued, was true to black men that are prone to oppress black women, as they are the closest weakened category. The crucial stage in this analysis is that in which hooks elaborates embedding modes of oppression technologies amongst black women by themselves and, consequently, their subordination to male hegemony messages—black and white. These uncover the roots of the notion of what it meant to be "the black good mother," "the ideal of the black good woman," which is different from the white-women or white-mother stereotype, including constructs that pertain to a black woman's body, sexuality, femininity, and the like. In her book *Feminist Theory: From Margin to Centre* (1984), hooks suggested to reconsider those notions from the marginalized point of view and search for premordial psychological constructs that mirror in an opposite reflection of the interracial and intersex relations. This is, of course, a suggestion to make a mental exercise that might help change racist and sexist perceptions, both on the part of the racist and the sexist, and on the part of the radicalized and sexualized consciousness. This idea resembles Irigary's, who suggested that we should look at gender reality as speculum in camera obscura, where objects are reflected smaller and upside down. For setting free of the trap, hooks proposed to employ a strategy that she called "unlearning": a process that deconstructs the assimilated submission to the oppression. By taking an inner journey and searching for early-age internalized obedience to commands that became automatic submission and accepting oppression, the subject begins a process of peeling what she has internalized.

The unlearning process is done as a process of dropping down educational subordinating forces (hooks, 1984, 55–56). The journey is taken in an opposite direction of education as absorbed and internalized at an early age. hooks suggests searching for correlation patterns between education to commitments to obey and points of acceptance with ideals such as "the good mother," the "good wife," and so on. These correlations, which allegedly seem to be accepted out of free choice, will reveal when looking from an opposite point of view—from margins to center—as silencing the voice of women and black women. These sites are where women lose their free will and subordinate to disciplining order that is present all over the life dimensions, leaving no evacuated space. The complicated tangles between the desires and needs of black women and their obedient conduct lie in discourse and practice that constructs those images of the "good wife" and "good mother." They work as if it is chosen out of free will. It seems as if women command themselves to be enslaved. This is a mirroring move of a subject that introspects and examines the assimilated slave within her. This is an action of an agent that pushes towards the urge to refuse and resolve the inner conflict by an act of resistance. When a woman begins the journey of resistance, she practically walks in the opposite direction, the direction of unlearning, a manifestation of disobedience. Layer after layer of socialization marks are peeled down, the "good wife," "the good woman," the good mother," and other experiences of subordination. While doing unlearning processes, the women go through deep reflections about who they are when they are called mothers, wives, nurses, or secretaries. Their bodies are involved in these reflections as well as their souls: their sexuality, their femininity, and their desires and repression. This is a feministization process that may involve fast transformation but sometimes it involves regression and pauses, as we could see in the cases of Ingbar and Knafo.

Women who begin the process may not finish it, given their living circumstances. Althusser referred to this feeling of helplessness as a sign of the hegemony ideological success that works with technological means (i.e., the state's apparatus). The force of these apparatus lies in the fact that the state doesn't have to put a policeman to guard every citizen. Every obedient subject immediately turns his head to respond to the call "Hey, you there." The process of unlearning is thus meant that it is a process of disentangling knots that connect personal obedience and ideals of what was determined by the hegemony as the proper order; in feminist terms, this refers to the patriarchal order of things. Voices of guilt might be heard regarding the evasion of responsibility by the citizen or the mother, but these are emotional remnants of past socialization constructs of being that good woman, wife, or mother. In more conservative societies, it is assorted by religious emotions, rewarding and punishment fears, but should be perceived as part of old socialization that was so effectively internalized with pedagogic, psychological, and medical technologies, as Michel Foucault has put it (Foucault, 1984). In the case of black people, this is by the white ethos, the women, the patriarchal ethos, the religious authorities, and again the male religious spiritual leaders. The subordinating technology in which Knafo functioned and strongly rebelled against echoed within her consciousness with great effort to unlearn the subordinating socialization forces. Her dilemma was that she was trapped between the need to "behave" as a "good mother" and "good worker" ethos, which she was socialized for, and to unlearn them to move on to a liberating consciousness phase. The turning point was, in her case, the moment that she realized that the ethos won't bring remedy to her problems. Obedience and subordination won't bring her children food or better living conditions. It was not a political agenda when she started the journey; she didn't mean to be a female "Robin Hood" or "Joan of Arc," as they called her. She didn't think she represented any deprived group, such as women or Mizrahim. Yes, she was aware of the ethnic split and the feminist political agendas and wanted to surface issues of racialization and discrimination against women.

However, these were not her first concerns when she began her journey. She didn't even make use of them when she realized that they might be beneficial to bring them up when speaking out loud of injustices done to single mothers. Her discourse was and remained very concrete and very faithful to her beliefs as a mother/woman/feminine/single/working woman, and the decision to cut off the allowances to single mothers was the trigger that caused her resistance. This, she was able to motivate and relate to, when she spoke in public and to the minister of the treasury about the economic policy. She stretched a straight line between her personal situation and the implications of the broader economic policy of cuts, an action that took the implication of the abstract decision-maker to very personal and concrete ground. She simultaneously was experiencing a peeling experience, entering an unlearning phase. From the words she spoke, it was possible to hear her explain and analyze the bad consequences of the new economic policy. She argued that the money that goes to the settlement in the occupied territories was at the expense of the peripheral populations in the southern desert of Israel. This critique sounded stronger than any other in the left-wing movements, although she never claimed to be a left-winger. On the contrary, she was a middle-right winger, as she has explained: "I am a Zionist, and I love my country," she argued. Presenting more sophisticated political positions gave poor, single mothers words and leadership that they never had since neoliberal and globalization invaded their lives. Knafo walked in the twilight zone going through the unlearning process where she could make sense of the "noises" she always thought of political business and never understood the grammar of it. She could substantially process them in real political time. hooks stresses that unlearning is not a political strategy that calls for the replacement of the oppressor through the adoption of its oppressing strategies, similar to Audre Lorde (1984), who coined the understanding that mastering tools of the master won't bring about salvation. hooks calls upon the oppressed to resist and learn how to criticize the disciplining discourse. This is an action that should be learned on a personal, subjective, and autonomous basis, part of a liberation journey that copes with racism and gender discrimination in which black women are trapped. Unlearning is similar to devoting crabgrass that is creeping all over, in this case all over the life spheres: psychological, cognitive, body, creeping everywhere. hooks ideas consist with the analysis of racism by Frantz Fanon (1963) as a disease that touches the subconscious and contaminates the will of the subject and conscience without being aware of it. Disputing racialization is turned against the conventions regarding the universal character of the human nature. The assumption that the human being has the potential of making moral decisions and find within himself the capabilities to do the right thing should also assume that the human being is capable of recognizing a mistaken choice. The human being is according to that, a learning being, and can elaborate and see what is wrong in patriarchal socialization not only what is the right thing to do.

The luring and unraveling is an autonomous action that is taken within power relation trajectories. They consist of what Foucault has suggested regarding the subversion of power, that it should be taking the opposite direction of obedience and subordination in the form of taking antiestablishment direction rather than subordination to rules of law that oppress weakened social categories. Knafo did just that; she walked against the current and to a certain extent she succeeded: she doubted, in an agnostic sense, the truthfulness of what she believed until then it meant to be a good mother, a good wife, or a good citizen. Moreover, she took the path and stood on the line, leading and playing a pioneering role for many other single mothers. As an agent and an opinionated woman, she was embraced by NGOs who were thirsty for a genuine voice that she made a sound. They wanted to touch her and to be close to her. The budgets and the workers who did their social justice proactive projects had no sense without women such as Knafo. In the late twentieth century, most of the NGOs and social justice organizations fell in deep political sleep and lost the fresh activism of the mid-1990s. The fundraising and the contributions that flourished around the peace process of Oslo talks died with the political murder of Yitzhak Rabin and were replaced by the neo-liberalism and globalization trends, as detailed in the previous chapters. By the time the Jewish contributions were donated and supported NGOs, the lower-class women organization hardly enjoyed donations because the maintenance of the NGOs became too expensive. Knafo and women like her hardly felt the support. Her discourse was with the state, with the parliament representatives, and with democratic institutions. Therefore, wrapping herself with the Israeli flag symbolized both her loyalty to the state but also her claim that it is her state just as much as the minister of the treasury's. Her contestation was not a disloyalty expression to the state but a contestation to a particular economic policy inflicted on the single mothers. This subtlety was not clear to NGOs and left-wingers as they condemned her as if she was approving settlement policy in the occupied territories the moment she wrapped herself with the flag. The activists had a hard time grasping this tension and saw it as a contradiction that needed to be resolved. However, Knafo as a person who lived through so many contradictions was more sophisticated in this respect. Condemning the minister of the treasury with regard to the policy for single mothers didn't mean that she condemned the entire economic policy, nor did it mean that she condemned the political policy, but as it often happens, the public discourse dismissed these nuances and stuck to the superficial and misleading picture. Her ability to do these separations indicated her abilities to grasp with her senses more subtle and sophisticated political perceptions that inspired of her being a person with no more than an elementary education. Expecting her to demonstrate clear leftist views similar to those of opposition of the minister of the treasury was an insensitive expectation on the part of the NGOs, which often make the ground for patronization and underestimation of their "clients." She was neither feminist nor leftist in the ideological sense of belonging to political movements, but this didn't mean that she wasn't a feminist or socially conscious. Situated at the twilight zone, she still didn't have the language, the unlearning of new language to formulate her new insights, but at the same time, she refused to fall into the arms of the NGOs that wanted so much to embrace her. This precaution on her part did not made her popular, and the organizations couldn't see in her more than a lower-class, simple woman whom they wanted to render a feminist, a "Joan of Arc," an icon. However, she insisted on remaining who she was, a rebellious woman very focused on her agenda, as narrow as that agenda was—an agenda based on the lower-class single mother.

hooks has directed her unlearning method of liberation towards black women, but this method is valid for all oppressed groups who struggle against enslavement socialization that hegemony inflicts on them from an early age and secures its continuous control over them. The practice of unlearning is adequate for every man and woman who is captured in the chaining hands of subordinating order that employs oppressive technologies. In this respect, hooks' solution goes beyond poor black women liberation. Her model becomes a universal model for anyone who wants to resist her subordinators. Knafo, a woman of Middle-Eastern origin, a woman from the periphery, from the margins, from the southern desert of Israel, stood on an intersectional point of oppression. The unlearning process that she had to operate on her multidimensional oppression was very complex and required a sort of Gordian Knot solution (i.e., disentangling the complex knots by cutting through rather than untie the strings one by one). Unlearning, however, was for her a very complicated project as it implied untying the knots one by one. During her journey, Knafo identified the knots between oppression and subordination and could point out the factors that brought her to personal economic depression while the state she was living in was prospering. She marched her journey in the opposite direction and crossed the lines of the order in which she was captured. The images of the good mother, the good citizen, and the good woman were hard to crack, but she finally did so when she came to the verge of starvation. Until then, she remained in the twilight zone. Her journey was an irreversible consciousness waking journey. It mirrored her practices in the public sphere, which for her were the first instances of experiencing public affairs. Eight years later, in the protest that was known as the Cottage Protest, Knafo was interviewed giving an analysis that indicated how she understood political business and had nothing to do with personal loyalty. She even sounded cynical. It is hard to exaggerate the value of transformation of the consciousness and reflection that conditions the agent's act of resistance. Gender scholars expanded on that and focused on its significance for the task of deconstructing the multidimensional oppression that imprisons marginalized groups and keeps them at the bottom of the social order. Sandoval went further to develop a paradigm, which helped to ignite a process of change—that critical moment that requires much more energy than keeping resistance working. She called it "the methodology of the oppressed."

THE METHODOLOGY OF THE OPPRESSED

The discourse on struggle strategies was formulated in the context of the analysis of the Hispanic women's conditions in the Southwest United States: women migrants who were not white but not black either. They literally live in the twilight zone, on the borders between the United States and Mexico, and they make up a marginal group of women: socially, politically, and geographically. They struggle for survival, mostly as single mothers, living the same culture the women to whom Gloria Anzaldúa has referred to when writing of Chicana women. As a theoretician who first studied and lived among the Hispanic women in this area and as a Hispanic woman herself, she had developed complete, assembled practices for subversion and resistance actions. It begins with learning a theory of control and oppression technologies, continues with a methodological process of oppositional consciousness construction, and ends with a personal and collective emancipatory act that transforms consciousness awareness. The larger forms of oppression reflected from globalization and late capitalism both within the Western world but also in the colonized countries of the past, Sandoval elaborated the hoops that hold neoliberal values that are coined within modernity and the Western culture and showed the roots of the progressive technologies in operation. She pointed them out showing that Western modernity goes hand in hand with exploitation and bears faint fruits of cheap labor, especially of third-world women from both their comprador countries but also when they are in hosting Western countries, such as the women migrants from Mexico in the United States. In the book *The Methodology of the Oppressed* (2000), Sandoval developed an operative agenda that helped identify and deconstruct oppression hoops. The process that she described correlated many of the elements Knafo applied in her struggle. Like Foucault and hooks, Sandoval focused on the significance site of consciousness construction for the understanding of autonomous action. She argued that consciousness has no vacuum space; it is occupied with oppression codes that are acquired along the disciplining process that never ceases to be cultivated. The codes signify what "good" and "bad" conducts are. Autonomous consciousness, therefore, always involves an oppositional action. Sandoval focused on the significance of developing resistance forces as a learned practice of protest activism against perceptions that are rooted in the political, historical, linguistic, and mental fields, which together construct a cultural discourse and operates as a steamroller of knowledge that deepens and generates consciousness transformation. This is a personal body of knowledge and experience that is constructed by the subject and relates to broader cultural discourse and maintains the affiliation of the individual to the collective peer group. The individual's desire to belong to a larger group encourages her to also invest in devotion to loyalty and obedience to the group.

With oppressed people, loyalty is overdetermined and exceeds the personal will and personal interest. Free will is dissolved, and the larger discourse elides the personal will. The individual's power of will is determined by disciplining discourse and merges with the will of the larger group, appearing autonomous. The individual can either cooperate with the hegemony or abstain. Abstaining in itself becomes an act of resistance. Sandoval discussed the assimilation aspect of the oppression apparatus and elaborated seven types of subordinating technologies that operate as Janus face where the observer sees only one of the two faces of the relationship between the subordinator and the subordinated. The scholars that referred to this process, each from her/his perspectives, used different formulation to describe the formation of this type of power relation: Foucault related to the oppressor and the oppressed as relations of sovereign-subject; hooks used the terminology relations of racializing-racialized; and Sandoval defined this relationship as subordinator-subordinating or oppressing-oppressed. Although these notions don't fully correlate, they are all overlapping and center on the hyphen that constructs these relationships. In all these relationships, there exists more than an obedience option on the subordinated subject part that she, by and large, skips because she sees only one face of Janus and doesn't see the other side, that which the subordinator sees. Although the illusion that both see the same reality, similar to the illusion that occurs in Plato's Cave where the chained subjects are certain they see the only reality possible and the fire for them is the only existing source of light. Sandoval defined these oppression technologies "poses" or "postures" of consciousness (Sandoval, 2000, 118). These poses feed the passion to belong and be accepted by the collective. The discourse is the feeding means that constructs a subordinating-subordinated relationship. One of the oppression technologies that Sandoval elaborated was the inoculation. The hegemony applies this technology to appear as a peace-seeker, as an evil fighter, and as a power that progresses towards more just society. The practices of seemingly social reforms operate to protect all the people, including the hegemony from social injustice, although injustice originated from the hegemony in the first place. In this way, the hegemony inoculates itself from acting against the curse of the injustice that keeps feeding the prevailing public order that serves the hegemony. The effect is that although there might be seen that there is action taken against social injustice, the hegemony would take an action that is meant to abolish it by taking one or two cases of injustice and act against it, but the roots of inequality remain sedimented in the prevailing order. The cases often are prominent figures that highlight the operation, such as a very poor black woman who was offended by the system and begins by admitting the system's mistake, then mobilizes the person, and uses her as a token of its liberal policy and sensitivity to the weak sectors of society. The cause of the evil is not abolished, however, but helps a few of those who suffer from the evil population become the inoculation against the accusation that the hegemony doesn't act to abolish the injustice but only to make believe in their efforts to do that. Often, the most obedient are those whom the hegemony identified and targeted to be well-groomed. The subordinated, on their part, identify this attention as an opportunity to relieve some of the subordination burden and the chance for equality.

On the hegemony part, what they see is a chance to secure peace and ease down potential resistance and unrest, making sure to explain that such reforms take time and the subordinated should be patient while in the meantime the tokenism apparatus is working on individuals leaving the majority of the subordinated in the same oppressed situation. Moreover, the act of political speech is applied so that hope for change appears in instances of politically correct expressions—which is yet another subordinating apparatus. The effect of these technologies helps to blare the class, race, or gender division and stimulate some hope amongst the subordinated that there is a change going on. For example, the nomination of a black woman to a very high post, such as the state's secretary or chief of the World Bank illustrates the case in which each of the parties from two sides of the Janus faces understands this move in different terms. A servant working in their master's house may expose the servant to the norms that prevail in this house, and she might watch the mode of the operation of power relations. This observation is made from an alimental arena from where she won't have access to the source of power. Sandoval argues that the blame for the subordinated fate is rolled on to their responsibility. From the point of view of the subordinator, the servant is seen as lazy; she is the one that is inept to do something with her life, she is not proactive, and so on. These are not simple prejudices on the part of the subordinator, but part of the apparatus according to which the technologies help the subordinator to control the power relations and construct an appearance of mending the wrong and that the wrong is taken care of. The selected marginal reforms also serve the hegemony to bleach its conscience and present that in the apparatus of public relations. The surface of the subordinating-subordinated relationship seems to be in motion while deep roots of these relationships remain stable. The binary division of spheres, races, classes, religious, and ethnic groups is preserved. It restrains the will to take action on the subordinated part and yet leave some space for moderate protest. In the three months campaign that Knafo spent in the Rose garden with camping tents camping, such an act seems to demonstrate this apparatus in action.

Another pose that demonstrates the oppression discourse was an ironic identification of the oppressors with the oppressed allegedly expressing a common fate: rhetoric employed by the oppressor to echo the same voices against exploitation or depriving work conditions (Sandoval, 2000, 118–27). For example, rhetoric such as "You complain of hard work?! What should we say? Don't we work as hard?! Who doesn't work hard?" This discourse helps the exploiter trivialize the exclusivity of the subordinated hard situation and, therefore, nullifies the justification for the complaint. The exploited subject's voice loses its power as a unique voice and gets lost within the voices of others. These oppression conditions work as apparatus that de-root the practices of oppressive complaints and implant instead silence within the oppressed consciousness. To generate motion towards emancipatory practices, Sandoval suggests that subjects must reach deep layers of the unconscious where they were implanted. Again, similar to hooks and Foucault, Sandoval couldn't exaggerate the significance of the language that communicates the oppressor-oppressed relationship. Sandoval leaned on Roland Barth when analyzing deep, cognitive layers that are rooted in the subconscious. She assumed that after internalizing the oppressive discourse, its consumption and replication are innocently operated by the oppressed, and only losing this innocence by learning the methods of opposing these practices and getting sober of the subordinators practices would enable the subject to begin an emancipatory process (Sandoval, 2000, 126). A discursive practice that stands as a subordinating apparatus relates to national unity. National unity should be guarded if the public good is to be achieved. Through national interest, the lines between the oppressed and the oppressors are obscured, and solidarity is called upon for the benefit of all. This apparatus applies in the case of Knafo using her own loyalty when she wrapped herself with the national flag. National loyalty did not contradict her being oppressed by those who were also loyal to the same nation and flag. This oppression technology is especially powerful and difficult to be deconstructed. After all, contesting national loyalty would backfire the subversive action in generating betrayal fears of the opposed. The "zero degree of writing," which Roland Barth suggested as a cognitive state that doesn't use metaphors for discourse, Sandoval argues that it is possible to develop a differential oppositional discourse that deviates from the common inclination to follow collectives. This is again the mark of the path that couldn't be mistaken for which Knafo chose when she began her journey. "No more" was the differential position choice she took. It was first and for most a personal subjective choice. Knafo constructed an experiential effect within her consciousness then searched for a way to communicate it with the world surrounding her. The idea of consciousness differential, according to Sandoval, operates as a device that helps escape from the binary trap that keeps feeding the circle of subordinating-subordinated loop. Sandoval even points out the Chicana discourse highlighting the "*la consciencia de la mestiza*" (Sandoval, 2000, 148). There are different moral perceptions that must be awakened so that the subordinated takes their first liberating move. Sandoval discussed the Chicana culture and consciousness the same way hooks discussed the moments that unlearning starts—the moments of inverting the inversion of the direction of learning. Both Sandoval and hooks refer to these moments as a function of the desire to set free the oppositional or resisting forces. Sandoval adds that these are moments of the reunification of the *mestiza* subject with her deeply rooted myths: children who were born to European and Indian parents in Latin America. These moments explain the oppositional *de la consciencia de la mestiza*. This action is autonomous and occurs in a zero cognitive point, a point that isn't fed from hegemony resources. It is differential in the sense of opposition that occurs at a dramatic moment of decision to stop keeping silent, submit, and begin to protest. This is exactly when Knafo, in my opinion, felt that the only thing she could do was to begin her journey, both the march to Jerusalem and the consciousness transformation. This is the "differend" that Jacques Derrida coined as an exit out of the binary closure (i.e., neither affirming not negating but stepping out to a third path, a liminal way that does not submit to binary laws). This is where the twilight zone was cognitively possible to be grasped. While stepping out of the subordinating sphere but not yet in free of subordination sphere, women experience liberation processes but not freedom. The eyes are blinded by the sunlight right when "the subject stepped out of Plato's Cave"; she hardly can "see" the endless possibilities that the freedom offers. This is a methodological phase in which she learns, compares, searches the similar and the different, and observes and experiences, just like an exploring child. The passage experience of women to the public sphere is completely different from a man's experience in the same sphere.

Unlike men, women were socialized to the private sphere and stepping out to the public at a later phase, which men didn't experience, the phase of socialization for the private sphere, is a completely different experience. The moment of the unique action when the subject uses her subordinated voice as a transition point to play on a check board where existence has no bottom is the moment where Derrida encourages her to find the "differend" and to stay within the difficulty, especially in Western realities of life. In this reality, he argues, metaphysics serves as a normative behavior: thought and talk (Sandoval, 2000, 148–50). This deviation is an award action of shifting from the comfortable affiliation with the collective and discarding the familiar conducts that a subject has in favor of searching for new ways in unknown zones walking on one's own. This shifting is taken on a first-order change layer that turns the "check board" from binary to bottomless, opening to third and fourth and perhaps fifth order splits. This change occurs out of the pose moment and avoidance from submitting to the usual order of the binary spheres. It occurs in the interval between the future's individual consciousness and the past ties with the collective. It is the separation moment from the seeming freedom of the subordinated, the past perception of interpellation with the hegemony ideology of the state. This is the promise of freedom but not yet freedom. This is the site where women take the first steps on their journey to the feminist experience of liberation and the first steps of subjects of subordinated class and race who make their first attempts to practice oppositional consciousness. The first steps are happening in the psyche, Althusser suggested (1984); they are taken at the writing zero degree, before the language is literally formulated, a degree where love and passion are not yet literate but already make the resource of the autonomous action (Sandoval, 2000, 140–41). The significance of pre-linguistic space, which is very difficult to be allocated, is in this instance at work. This is the subjective operation that occurs in liminal space, the space that overlaps the twilight zone of consciousness. Knafo walked on this path, having no one escorting her and having no one to prepare her; she rushed soaring to the sunlight rays as Icarus, not aware of the political business hit that eventually burned her feeble wings. She needed more time to learn the political business; as a subaltern in the playground of the subordinating, she had first to learn the methods of political power operation. Knafo began her jumping point from too high a level, and when she began to drop down, she had no refraining steers. The fall was painful. To find her way out of the subordinating loop, the subject needs a personal liberation methodology, a methodology that

Sandoval called "the methodology of the oppressed." This methodology has a few stages that involve learning the oppression technologies and developing an ability to detect the differential potential within oneself in order to be set free in a third way; for women, it concerns multiracial gender oppression detection. Oppressed people who generate change within their lives do so through learning moves; they identify and decipher epicenters of oppression power with these methods. Operating the methods involves inner struggles within the consciousness of the subjects, not only struggles with the world around them, and they are necessary for progress to the next stage of empowerment. It is what Sandoval identified as autonomous action. In summary, like hooks, Sandoval does not restrict her news to Chicana women only, but she instead believes they are relevant to any subordinated subject who is oppressed. The methodology she offers is like Foucault's idea; it involves learning and understanding how power operates within human relations, what are the methods, and who is interested in camouflaging them. The aim is setting free the oppressed, first by working from within, from the subject's introspective and identification of the internalized subordinator's views of norms and social values. The goal of the oppressed is to first squawk the hidden technologies of oppression and make subjects aware of the disciplines that breed the oppressor-oppressed relations. An oppressed subject cooperates with this relationship thanks to ethic socialization that is acquired early in her life through power technologies. Squawking and becoming aware of this order of things is the start of a process of dropping oppression forces that were internalized and paused to develop modes of being aware to liberation poses.

Chapter Thirteen

Theoretical Conclusions

The term "discipline" has two meanings: One has to do with rules of behavior that come with conditions of reward and punishment; and the other relates to fields of studies and knowledge production with particular rules, methods, and subjects typical to the field. Both senses of the word contain definitions of right and wrong, and they come with rules of acceptance and rejections. According to Michel Foucault, both these senses of the term "discipline" and "disciplining" work to normalize the subject not only in madhouses or detention locations, but also, especially, in education institutions and, in the modern era, capitalist institutions, hospitals, production loci, and so on (Foucault, 1995, 184). The vital control of population is aimed to secure prospective production. This was a draconic rule in the factory in Mitzpe Ramon and became a major obstacle that the women faced during the recovery phase. It was not just operation rules of production but also a mechanism that secured that the right order would prevail. Thus moving one person from the station of production to the position of the manager was identified immediately as a violation of the right order.

The well-functioning of the system with its rules of disciplining the workers came to operation immediately when the system identified a potential violation. The apparatus worked so well that when things became difficult, even the women at the cooperative contributed to rendering the old order back to work. In a short while after the cooperative began the recovery process, the women supported the idea that the three women managers should also go back to the production line. In other words, they were part of the patriarchal gatekeepers. "It was strange to see me sitting in the CEO's chair; even I felt strange the first time," said Havatzelet Ingbar. Yet, she shifted from the "norm" that was imposed on her and violated the "peaceful order of things that served the others but not us," as she said. However, there were conflicting interests of those who supported the old order and wanted to take no risks and those who were in the midst of personal turnover and wanted to motivate a revolution that would follow the successful rebellion they began in the factory. This is where the astonishing secret is rooted. The enormous difficulty that women experience every time they try to impel a process of change they face the solid old structures that even when they come to power they realize that they are forced to adopt. This difficulty stands in the way of women' solidarity and sisterhood. The feminist spirit is blowing in the opposite direction to that of the old conservative order, and the patriarchal apparatus is always there to push back any attempt of agency.

The apparatus of control is comprehensive, and it is weaved within the patriarchal power network so that even the minor attempts of the poor women from Mitzpe Ramon awakened the gatekeepers. This might be the explanation why women most often prefer the "defeated" way a priori, giving up gender agency and accepting obedience and subordination, even self-restraint, as we could see at the beginning of this account. This brings up the idea that women don't function within the patriarchal system out of false consciousness but out of the understanding and calculations that conforming with the terms is more beneficial then objecting them, as long as their power is insufficient for the critical point of enough power to generate change. The power the women in the factory were authorized with proved to be insufficient for the change they wanted to make. For the deep foundations of the patriarchal order, the power the women needed was more than a one-time exception that couldn't provide enough weight against the long patriarchal domination. To destroy misogynic norms of management and construct new patterns that could contain women's experience as managers, as short as they were, the women in the cooperative needed much more power than they had all along that experiment. The feminist literature discusses issues such as styles of women managers and of being leaders versus men. The feminist ideology is interested in the personal experience of women who gain authority and hold leadership positions.

My interaction with Ingbar focused on these aspects from which we thought new knowledge and understanding of the field of action could be produced. We searched for points of intersection where she thought that there was a shift from the old rigid rules. We searched for "true knowledge" of the story every time we went over parts of the events. "True knowledge" regarding the events in which a human being is involved depends on multiple parameters and specific conditions in which the account is reported. It is almost impossible to comprehend the entire knowledge even when the events are reported more than once. The status of the truth of the account is eventually determined out of personal intuition and cross versions. This is due to the fact that the information emerged within power relations that cannot be separated from the facts. The metaphor of a lining that makes the infrastructure on which the facts are placed is more complicated in the sense that the infrastructure contains feelings, moods, and consciousness states, which change from one point of time of reporting the account to the other. The relationship between the actors are significant, and at the moment of amassing the information, there exists many fragile moments that become part of asymmetry of the relationship between the informant and the knowledge producer, the scholar—in this case, Ingbar and myself. Sandra Harding, Donna Haraway, Susan Bordo, and others, whose ideas were discussed in Chapter 1 regarding the question of the feminist point of view while producing knowledge, stress the continuous violation of the tri-fold balance of what is correct knowledge, what true knowledge is, and who has control over the knowledge. The present research produced knowledge through intersubjective critical dialogue that resulted from ontological events reported from the ground of reality, which is out of the academic world. As this is a particular case, it contains unique experience that can't be reduced to generalizations by saying that the lesson of what was discussed here is applicable to all women. Telling the story of one individual woman stems from the traditional positivist approach of knowledge production that requires submission to objectivity and quantitative codes of production. The analysis, however, focused on the politics that enveloped the story of passing a factory from private ownership to a women's cooperative, particularly women who until the moment of passage were the production employees in the factory and then became its owners. The affair involved not only the owner and workers but also the state authorities, the labor unions, and the media. Consequently, the public was opinionated and followed the events with much interest but did do with enormously diverse perspectives. This case is unique in that it occurred in the heart of a global capitalist economy in which the idea of cooperation was perceived more or less as an idea that belongs to the past. When I collected the data and began to analyze it, I had some presumptions that guided me, of which one was that the cooperative idea had already experienced some failure in various places in the world. This in itself wasn't innocent in the search of the storyline, and it re-emerged in front of me and guided me. I was interested in revealing some of the questions that should have been asked when the events took place in real time but ultimately weren't. It was clear to the actors involved in the affair that the women had no experience in management but believed that the skills could be purchased as they were going through the process. How could the actors in charge, those who made the crucial decisions, believe in the possibility that while operating the factory as a cooperative, women could also acquire the knowledge in so many diverse fields, such as the textile market in Israel and the world, or how to purchase raw material, or find the best deals without having previous experience in marketing and pricing? What knowledge did the women have in order to formulate the right questions regarding pricing, sales promotion, and funding, along with the modes of payment and allocation of the best places to find the proper materials, fabrics, bottoms, and sewing threads? It was one thing to market uniforms to official organizations such as the military and another thing entirely to enter the free market. The women bought, escorted by the national labor union leadership, a failing factory that was on the verge of bankruptcy. The labor union knew the problems of the business collapse when concerting a production line relates first to its material condition. In the case of the factory, the very elementary conditions of the sewing machines, the chairs next to them, and the basic equipment such as the scissors, measurement tools, and the like could indicate that they should have considered that the case was almost lost. The labor union did not escort the process in this respect. The women faced those problems all alone. They knew they must allocate new buyers, negotiate with them, and prepare working contracts, timetables, payment commitments, and divisions of labor. In these aspects, the women were left all alone. All these issues couldn't be successfully implemented without experience and professional escort. Eventually, except for a few NGO's that volunteered to give advice but normally worked as non-profit organizations, the women walked alone along the business paths, knowing very little about them. In light of all the obstacles, the idea of passing the factory to the women's hands and loaning them one million NIS, the conclusion was nothing but a populist and cynical decision on the Histadrut secretary's part. After all, he must have known something about bad the situation present in the textile branch. Assuming that he and the other government officials in charge knew all this, it is possible that they had even made a vicious decision, a decision that they went into with their eyes opened to knowing it eventually wouldn't come to a successful end, but they abstained from sharing this probable assumption with the workers at the factory. These reflections bring to mind cruel ideas of deliberately directing the naive women workers into a trap. Unfortunately, there is no other conclusion to this study. The officials abused public resources and deceived not only the women but also the public and the people's resources. The implications for feminist insights are no less significant.

FEMINIST INSIGHTS

Feminist insights relate among other things to inverted perceptions or redefinitions of concepts such as successes and failures when they concern women. The "other sex" or the "second sex," as De Beauvoir has defined it, redefine an entire world that makes the concepts of "other sex" and the "second sex" possible to understand what they mean. Women existed before, but the notions didn't. This is especially true when women begin the journey of resisting and refusing to accept the order of things according to androcentric doctrines. When the women workers began their rebellious journey, they didn't carry any toolbox or blueprint as to how the patriarchal order is to be transformed. They started with spontaneous rebellion and with the violation of heteronormative rules. They didn't even know that what they were doing was to shake the deepest gender relations roots. Notions such as "agency," "change," "rebel," or "misogyny" did not occur to them when they did the moves of resistance and strike. In that godforsaken town and in a factory, the women of Mitzpe Ramon walked in-between gender spheres in the attempt to change their entire life prospects. In the research, I focused especially on the tensions and gaps that subsist between heteronormative forces that serve as gatekeepers and the rifts through which women try to sneak out to the public sphere. As I observed, the women couldn't begin any such attempt without breaking through by resistance and opposition. Breaking the gender chains had to begin by rebellious acts or at least a self-conscious rebellion. They didn't title it a revolt or a feminist resistance, but they became aware of the feminist aspects when the public and the media reflected it out to them by naming their action "a revolt." For a very long time, they were aware they were being politically, socially, and economically marginal but not marginalized. This wasn't what brought them to rebel. Their act of resistance did not result from an ideology and wasn't structured within an agenda and apparatus. They simply moved from the phase of fixed obedience to a phase of resistance and tried to destroy the dam that blocked them as women from flowing en masse from obedience to resistance. This was the conceptual location where this research took place and searched for understanding the motivating forces that generated seemingly passive and obedient women to make the critical move of resistance. Before the actor resistance, we could see that the women were obedient as a tactic rather than blindness to the harsh conditions they were in. In the midst of the affair, while standing on the dam, an abyss was revealed to them and clearly enlightened the questions of "Why do women conform to subordinating rules, and when is it that they burst with resistance?" For years, the women walked on the path of obedience for the reason of keeping their only breadwinning source and, more extensively, sometimes it meant saving their lives. This became a norm in the global capitalist era. Years after the affair was over, its memory was registered within various layers of the society. The public consciousness reflected through bringing up illustration from the affair that demonstrated examples of violation of gender order, women disobedience, but also the ability of marginal women to become agents and courageously take control of their lives.

What would be the theoretical lessons that this affair taught us? This research focused on the detailed account of two prominent female leaders from the margins of the economic and social ladder. The lessons should, therefore, be taken prudently before applying them to larger cases of the engendered labor market and the inference to single women who cross the lines from being "a simple employee" and the start of a struggle against the government economic policy or becomes a women CEO in the Israeli market and the larger market in Western societies. Theoretically, the study held and criticized dichotomies such as "men/women," "employers/employees," and "public /private" as organizing conservative social and gender order. In doing so, the study sharpened the problematization of dichotomous perceptions. In this respect, dichotomies that existed in the mind-set of the social order are deeply rooted in the apparatus and stand in the way of the agent who wants to motivate change. The barriers that hindered some of the actors from making the transformation and accepted the possibility that women factory workers can become good managers or householders can make significant apolitical moves were consciousness barriers. Such was the consciousness of business people, politicians, officials in governmental and nongovernmental organizations, and, most all, some of the women's consciousness who were involved in the affair. The need to break these dichotomies was crucial to change. The present research in and of itself didn't obey the standard rules of research within the standard frames of "structured interviews," "participant observer," and the like on the way to a theorization of the events. I tried as much as possible to hold the point of view of the subject of the research, following Tom Boellstorff's suggestion that distinguishes between "-emic" and "-etic" regarding methodological perspectives when treating the ties that should connect theory and practice, abstract set of thoughts, and qualitative empirical data (Boellstorff, 2010). Likewise, I followed suggestions of taking the field viewpoint presented in other studies such as Catherine Nash (2010) and Jaime Heckert (2010).

THEORIZATION AND METHODS, ETHICAL COMMENTS

The status of theory and data in this study is, thus, somewhat undermined in the face of my conscience. I moved inside and outside the empirical field and the theoretical structure and could only generalize when the events and the speakers said their words. Here again, I followed Judith Halberstam (2011) in the attempt to soberly deviate from blindly following hegemonic academic authorities and knowledge governments that tend to silence knowledge that comes from the margins, that often is delegitimized as nonsense. As much as it could appear as inconsistent—in the attempt to project the state of the affairs as they took place—the information reported within the present account is meant to serve for following studies in other fields of knowledge production. It was already possible to point out splits and fractures through which the women's hidden identities flickered, chalked, and distorted out of humiliation and oppression. Finally, it could be realized that being a worker, a women worker, was not a destiny but a hegemonic structural fixation that rigidly stood in the women's way to flexibly move to management positions and generate a dynamic and healthy reorganization. The story, as told here, thus becomes active and influential material in which Ingbar was not just the interviewee but also a creative companion to this study. Much less was the case with Vicki Knafo. I designed the study in the spirit of Madison (2011) and Mathias Detamore (2010), and I returned more than once to speak with the women, during and after the events were over. Their reflections and especially that of Ingbar enabled them to reformulate and explain their thoughts in more than one way. In doing so, I followed the suggestions of Ruthellen Josselson (2007). In spite of all these precautions, the power relation of researcher-researched will ever persist and be hierarchical. I tried to share my insights with the workers throughout the study and showed full respect to even the smallest thought they murmured. The design of the study, including its presumptions and methods, stayed in my responsibility as well as the raison d'être of the topic, as many scholars agree (Stacey, 1988; Patai, 1991; Estroff, 1995; Cotterill, 1992; Bloom and Sawin, 2009). After relinquishing the existence of one truth and the idea of (the weak) scientific objectivity, I believe it is the turn of scientific neutrality to be relinquished. This doesn't mean that power relations are neutralized; on the contrary, they are surfaced and acknowledged. The precautions that are taken along the interactions with the field actors and the empirical data collection give the parties more than one exit point. Research takes time. When interaction takes place between the researcher and the actors, both of their minds might be following an introspection, self-examination, and even withdrawal and regret. Those who are interested in critique and knowledge production take risks and know that they should reveal, at any given instance, even to the self, the study, if the field participants demand it. No matter how weak or marginal the actors in the research were when the first steps were taken, if they were not children or powerless, they have their own deliberation that is their source of making independent decisions whether to participate in the research. The ethical aspect becomes more dynamic as long as relations of the researcher and actor bring up issues regarding their relationship at any chosen moment and the value differences should remain to open discussion (Detamore, 2010). This is the sphere in which ethical relationships are prevailing without ignoring the ever-existing power relations. The research method thus designed and organized around the intimate and ideological platform and keeps relaxed communication between the knowledge producer and the knowledge provider. Krumer-Nevo et al. (2014) read these relationships as free of power relations and fantastically redeeming the interviewees by way of collecting the data from their mouths. This is clearly an abuse of power between the researcher-actor relations. Detamore suggests, more modestly, that subtle information of an intimate nature may come of this type of fieldwork (Detamore, 2010, 178). In my interactions with Ingbar where she chose to meet at times convenient to her, I made sure to accommodate myself, and when meeting, I brought up similarities and differences between her and I, including the marginal locus from where I came and the progress I made. This was of significance in building up our intimate relations, empathy, trust, and the sense of solidarity we could eventually share. This was important for the embracing moments and frustrating sentiments and the conversations brought up. I believe that thanks to this approach, Ingbar was secure enough to open her heart and tell about her deepest and most vulnerable sentiments and experiences. Here again, in opposition to Krumer-Nevo et al., it is not that the research relations could abolish the otherness feeling of the interviewees and the asymmetry of the relationship. This cannot be abolished no matter what the researcher does. The danger that the researcher will not be able to prevent her view of the subject of research as marginal and inferior exists all the time and cannot be relinquished; therefore, it should be contained and constantly reviewed rather than attempt to abolish it or play the game of bringing the interviewee to the same academic level of the researcher and, eventually, call it empowerment as Krumer-Nevo et al. suggest. The ideological view of the researcher lies all the time in the research infrastructure, and struggling to abolish it, as the Krumer-Nevo et al. approach suggests, is doomed to be defeated and is, therefore, pretentious.

One of the most challenging issues in this research was how to connect certain positions of the workers to the theoretical skeleton as I designed it on the basis of my presumptions. What was the force that mobilized the unique experience of a spontaneous burst of the rebellion? I am not sure I found the answers, but I tried to extract the materials that unfolded in front of me and register the interpretation I thought suitable for the particular part. The complexity of the reality, with its enormous number of details, was filtered according to the research goals and this, it should be noted, will never be exhausted. I further discuss this sort of problematization in relation to each case analysis.

Knafo's story tells the story of a single mother from the margins of the Israeli society who worked two jobs and raised her three children with an income that was below the minimum wage. The cuts in her wages as a result of economic policy brought her to the verge of saying "no more." She wasn't aware of what is it that she felt "no more" for but a seemingly spontaneous refusal to accept the situation and take resistant action brought her into conflict with her routine life, as it looked before the resistance. It was a life in which she consciously accepted the fate of being an oppressed and hardworking employee in exploiting labor conditions. The resistance move she took brought Knafo to a situation where she felt that she won't put up anymore with oppression and subordination. The unusual move she took—a march from her peripheral town to the capital of Jerusalem, from her life on the margins to the central metropolis—was also a consciousness march. She learned about deep-rooted obedience forces that made her accept the situation of subordination, but she also realized that the situation was political and maintained by forces of the apparatus that made them look natural and unavoidable. In the process, she learned to identify the oppressors' technologies of maintaining the relationship loop. Knafo believes in the righteousness of the democratic order, although this was etched from a patriarchal, hegemonic, Western culture, a culture which preserved women's subordination for centuries. By the same mode, the state of Israel, a national state where democratic institutions and labor unions are expected to be operating equally in favor of the workers and citizens in the society. Knafo's journey became a sobering journey of discovery that things do not work quite according to democracy and equal rights only and that there are powerful interests that conflict with those democratic principles. What she considered as sanctified by the political rhetoric unfolded in front of her as profane and mundane. Single mothers, she realized, were not equal because they were not aware of the power relations that reside in the infrastructure of gender and politics. She realized that single mothers are last in a model list that resembles the hierarchical food chain. Knafo has also realized that she shared with the hegemony the same views of the "good mother," the "good woman," and the "good worker" that served mainly the subordinators and promised her obedience to the orders, although for her it was impossible. Knafo devoted herself to a multi-functional position where she operated simultaneously as a mother, a worker, and a family under hard economic conditions. Her spontaneous rebellion began long before when her body and mind began to sense the impossibility of the situation in which she was trapped. The first to meet her resistance was herself as an obedient subject. She shifted from regular patterns as an obedient woman/mother/citizen to a disobedient subject that rebelled against oppressive authorities. She wanted to speak with the minister of the treasury person-to-person, being certain that he would listen to what she had to say, and she would certainly convince him of his lack of knowledge regarding the problems of single mothers. This may have been true that he didn't know much about what it meant to be a single mother, but she followed a mistaken, imaginary, naive picture believing that he had reasons to listen to her and to want to learn about it.

Economic cuts are taken from many positions that consider more than one social sector, factor, and state's interests. Knafo understood it as an abstract insight just as the minister of the treasury also understood in an abstract from the living conditions of the single mother. The emancipatory process that she experienced related to her consciousness rather than to her material life. The public activity in which she began to be involved exposed her to political cynicism and to the different nature of political promises and social justice activism. Lobbyists opened their hearts to her, explaining how public affairs work, and in what sense they are different from the private. This enabled her to begin seeing different codes of behaviors and to reflect on what she wasn't aware of for her entire life before. Politics began to be a personal experience. What she perceived before as "dirty business" when speaking of political business became, as she marched, substantial matter with personal angles. A faithful citizen and a devoted mother were now contradicting notions—things looked very complex from the new public perspective that she was observing. Her self-image as a good or bad mother Was familiar to her unlike her public image as a social justice activist or a politician that she never encountered. However, her personality and identity expanded while experiencing public affairs. In this respect, becoming a democratic citizen in a substantial sense extended her consciousness. Her standards as a good woman and mother and as a modest person transformed and expanded to contain much more than the regular obedient person that she was in the past, at least in her own eyes. Knafo began to question standards and origins and to reconsider her relationship with the world around her to the bottom of the psychological premordial sources in Machiavellian perceptions: class, gender, national, and ethnic relations altogether. Along with the public struggle, she was caught since she first stepped out on the journey; she has also experienced tensions and confrontations around the right strategy, the proper goals, and the true convictions with regard to her actions and agenda. Her sobering process regarding politics related to the right ways to proceed to achieve her goals, and she had to face moments of shattering of her strongest convictions, losing her innocence, and her "political virginity" confronting doubts and losing the little confidence she still had in human nature.

This process involved frustration, disappointment, and rage. Her urge to obey dissolved and evacuated conscious space that was replaced by refusal and cynicism. Knafo's expressions took the direction of apostasy and disbelief on the face of a budget allocation to settlements in the occupied territories while the poverty rate was growing and offending vulnerable populations within the green-line periphery. Knafo's trust in the government and the minister of the treasury eroded. This was the practical sense of the process of unlearning that bell hooks developed as a subversive technique of the radicalized groups. It was as if walking backwards in social loyalty direction. Knafo expressed distrust and critique that indicated that her homogeneous worldview of equality and justice as prevailing values in the Israeli society had cracked. Imagining that she could meet the minister of the treasury was reconsidered, and what surfaced from her reflections were the insights that relationship between citizens are also formed by the position where they stand and depends whether they were a minister or single mother. Her obedience stitches disentangled and voices of loyalty and citizenship commitments mixed with voices of free rider sounds around her. She could see much better the oppressive technologies and the apparatus that made them work. It was like inverting a coat and examining its inner lining, which isn't seen from the outside when wearing it. The lining exposed manipulations and false solidarity that hardly held the moment of contradicting political interests that were induced to the fields of power. Through the lenses of the methodology of the oppressed, she now realized that "one people" and "equality to women" were empty slogans, but they kept being waived by politicians. Knafo's transformation of consciousness can only be indicated from the transformation of her public expressions and her resisting actions to the common stereotypes of the righteous woman and mother. She wasn't interested anymore in the public approval of her being a good mother or worker; neither was she interested in being part of a collective. She didn't realize statements of support in the government or the public political rhetoric that repeated mantras such as "money to the poor, not to the settlements." Political actions operated within a group do not always affect the activist in a direct way. Now Knafo wanted to see the direct effect rather than change the "grand economic policy." The public and the personal interests were not one anymore, and her interest was only hers in that she cared about it most of all the people around her, no matter how supportive they were. This was a crucial political lesson: public affairs are important, but they can't be practiced as a solution to private affairs. Knafo learned a significant lesson also regarding the distance from where she was positioned, socially and politically, in relation to the center of decision-making. Her interests and those of the minister of the treasury as the person in charge of the economy of all were not the same, and she was only a small particle of an amalgam. Her gaze from the margins to the center was now mobilized, and she could understand evil and injustice not just from her perspective as a single mother. She used the public arena in which she found herself to forward the details of injustice as she has experienced it. The optimistic illusion in which she was captured dissolved as the minister of the treasury didn't respond to her request to meet and talk. She experienced political solitude of decision-makers and leaders surrounded with noisy advice. When taking pauses, she could consider binding possible personal and collective interests just to learn that they reached a point of contradiction. This moment was a differentiating moment in which she could see herself as shifting from all around her. This required a realization that she was in a writing zero degree of language for which she didn't have words yet but already experienced an autonomous action that was only hers, not an imitation of a crowd action. Her journey forward from the margin to the center was also a journey for the learning to the opposite direction backward—a desocializing direction where what was learned was dropped down in an experience of unlearning. The moves that followed this march did not ease her economic difficulties or her solitude, but she never went back to the old conventions after sobering from the political naivety, which was an irreversible move.

The birth of an autonomous action wherein women like Knafo find themselves begins, so we have witnesses, with resistance.

Bibliography

Abu-Lughod, Lila. 1985. "A Community of Secrets: The Separate World of Bedouin Women." *Signs* 10, no. 4 (1985): 637–57.

Atkinson, Simon. 2012. "Argan Oil helps Moroccan Women Become Breadwinners." *BBC News*, January 8, 2012. https://www.bbc.co.uk/news/business-16460127.

Althusser, Louis. 1970. *On the Reproduction of Capitalism: Ideology and Ideological State Apparatus*, translated by Ben Brewster. New York: Verso. https://www.marxists.org/reference/archive/althusser/1970/ideology.htm.

Anzaldúa, Gloria. 1987. *Borderlands/La Frontera: The New Mestiza*. San Francisco, CA: Aunt Lute Books.

Arendt, Hanna. 1958. *The Human Condition*. Chicago: University of Chicago Press.

Bagatz [Supreme Court Decision] 4541/94 Alice Miller vs. the Minister of Defence 49(4) P.D. 94.

Bagatz [Supreme Court Decision]153/87 Shakdiel vs. Minister for Religious Affairs 42(2) P.D. 221 (1988).

Barthes, Roland. 1977. "The Death of the Author," in *Roland Barthes*. London: Fontana, pp. 142–48.

Benjamin, Walter. 1940. "On the Concept of History," *Walter Benjamin Archives*, https://www.marxists.org/reference/archive/benjamin/1940/history.htm.

Bloom, Leslie Rebecca, and Patricia Sawin. 2009. "Ethical Responsibility in Feminist Research: Challenging Ourselves to do Activist Research with Women in Poverty," *International Journal of Qualitative Studies in Education* 22, no. 3 (2009): 333–51.

Bordo, Susan. 1994. "Feminism, Postmodernism, and Gender Skepticism," in *Theorizing Feminism*, edited by Anne Herrmann and Abigail Stewart, 458–81. Boulder, CO: Westview Press.

Bourdieu, Pierre. 1977. *Outline of a Theory of Practice*. Cambridge: Cambridge University Press.

———. 2000. *Pascalian Meditations*. Cambridge: Polity.

Charlesworth, Simon. 2000. *A Phenomenology of Working-Class Experience*. Cambridge: Cambridge University Press.

Chodorow, Nancy. 1978. *The Reproduction of Mothering: Psychoanalysis and the Sociology of Gender*. Berkley: University of California Press.

Cicero, Quintus Tullius. 2012 [64 BC]. *How to Win an Election*. Princeton, NJ: Princeton University Press.

Cohen, Gerald A. 2001. *If You Are an Egalitarian, How Come You Are So Rich?* Cambridge, MA: Harvard University Press.

Corbin, Juliet M., and Anselm Strauss. 1990. "Grounded Theory Research: Procedures, Canons, and Evaluative Criteria," *Qualitative Sociology* 13, no. 1 (1990): 3–21.

Cotterill, Pamela. 1992. "Interviewing Women: Issues of Friendship, Vulnerability, and Power," *Women's Studies International Forum* 15, no. 5 (1992): 593–606.

Crenshaw, Kimberlé Williams. 1991. "Mapping the Margins: Intersectionality, Identity Politics, and Violence against Women of Color," *Stanford Law Review* 43, no. 6 (July 1991): 1241–99.

Dahan-Kalev, Henriette and Emilie Le Febvre. 2012. *Palestinian Activism in Israel: Bedouin Women Leadership in a Changing Middle East*. New York: Palgrave MacMillan.

———. 2001. "Tensions in Israeli Feminism: The Mizrahi Ashkenazi Rift," *Women's Studies International Forum* 24 (2001): 1–16.

———. 2012. "Neither Public, Nor Private: Politics of Resistance in the Vicki Knafo Affair," In *"Where Am I Positioned," Gender Perspectives on Space*, edited by Roni Halpern, 243–82. Kfar Saba, Israel: Heinrich Boll Foundation and Beit Berl Publishers, 2012. (Hebrew)

———. 2009. "The Great Miss of Democratic Right of Protest in Israel," *Jerusalem: The Israeli Democracy Institute*, 2009 (Hebrew). IDI Publications.

———. 2007."The Achoti Movement: The Years of Labour," *To My Sister, Mizrahi Feminist Politics,* edited by Shlomit Lir, 41–62. Tel Aviv: Babel Press, 2007.

———. 2006. "Officers as Educators: The Ex-Military in the Israeli School System." *Israel Affairs* 12, no. 2 (2006): 268–83.

———. 2001. "Tensions in Israeli Feminism: The Mizrahi Ashkenazi Rift." *Women's Studies International Forum* 24 (2001): 1–16.

———. 1991. "Self-Organizing Systems: Wadi Salib and the Black Panthers, Implications of the Israeli System." PhD diss., The Hebrew University of Jerusalem, 1991.

Davis, Angela. 1983. *Women, Race and Class*. New York: Random House.

de Beauvoir, Simone, 1989 [1952], *The Second Sex*, translated by H. M. Parshley. New York: Vintage Books, Random House.

Derrida, Jacques. 1976. *Of Grammatology*. Baltimore, MD: Johns Hopkins University Press.

Detamore, Mathias. 2010. "Towards a Politics of Research Methods: Intimacy in researcher/Researched Relations," in *Queer Methods and Methodology: Queer Theories and Social Science Research*, edited by Kath Browne and Catherine J. Nash, 167–82. Burlington, VT: Ashgate.

Dochao, Rafael. 2006. "The European Commission Supports Mediterranean Women: Three Tales about Making a Difference," *AFAEMME The Association of Organisations of Mediterranean Businesswomen*, http://www.afaemme.org/studies/E3%20CM_EC%20Support_Dochao.pdf.

Douglas, Mary. 1996. *Purity and Danger*. New York: Routledge.

Drahokoupil, Jan. 2008. "The Rise of the Comprador Service Sector: 'The Politics of State Transformation in Central and Eastern Europe,'" *Polish Sociological Review* 2, no. 162 (2008): 175–89.

Ehrenreich, Barbara. 2009. *Bright-Sided: How the Relentless Promotion of Positive Thinking has Undermined America*. New York: Metropolitan Books.

Eltstein, Jean Bethke. 1981. *Public Man, Private Woman: Women in Social and Political Thought*. Oxford: Martin Robertson.

Engels, Friedrich. 1933 [1884]. *The Origin of the Family, Private Property and the State Alternate*, translated by Ernest Unterman. New York: International Publishers.

Estroff, Sue E. 1995. "Whose Story is It Anyway? Authority, Voice, and Responsibility in Narratives of Chronic Illness," in *Chronic Illness: From Experience to Policy*, edited by Carson K. Toombs and David Barnard, 78–104. Bloomington: Indiana University Press.

Fanon, Frantz. 1963. *The Wretched of the Earth*. New York: Grove Weidenfeld.

Filmer, Sir Robert. 1949 [1680]. *Patriarcha and Other Political Works*, edited by Peter Laslett. Oxford: Basil Blackwell.

Foucault, Michel. 1986. *Discipline and Punish: The Birth of the Prison*. New York: Vintage.

———. 1977. *The Archeology of Power*. London: Tavistock.

———. 1980. *Power/Knowledge: Selected Interviews and Other Writings 1972-1977*, edited by Colin Gordon. Oxford: Basil Blackwell.

———. 1983. "Qu'est-ce due les lumbers?" *Magazine Litteraire*, no. 207 (1984): 35–39 (Short extract of the January 5, 1983, class in College de France, in *Dits Ecrits* 4, no. 351.

———. 1995. "Disciplinary Power and Subjection," in *Power: A radical View*, edited by S. Lukes, 229–42. New York: Pantheon Books, Random House.

Gilligan, Carol. 1982. *In A Different Voice*. Cambridge: Harvard University Press.

Halberstam, Judith. 2011. *The Queer Art of Failure*. Durham and London: Duke University Press.

Halberstam, Judith. 1998. "Transgender Butch: Butch/FTM Border Wars and the Masculine Continuum GLQ," *A Journal of Lesbian and Gay Studies* 4, no. 2 (1998): 287–310.

Haraway, Donna. 2006. "A Cyborg Manifesto: Science, Technology and Socialist—Feminism in the Late Twentieth Century," in *The Transgender Studies Reader*, edited by Susan Stryker and Stephen Whittle. New York and London: The Transgender Studies Reader, Routledge.

Harding, Sandra. 1987. *Feminism and Methodology*, edited by Sandra Harding. Bloomington: Indiana University Press.

———. 2007. "Feminist Standpoints," in: *Handbook of Feminist Research: Theory and Praxis*, edited by Sharlene Nagy Hesse-Biber, 45–70. Thousand Oaks, CA: SAGE Publications.

———. 1986. *The Science Question in Feminism*. Ithaca, NY: Cornell University Press.

———. 1988. "Situated Knowledges: The Science Question in Feminism and the Privilege of Partial Perspective," *Feminist Studies* 14, no. 3 (1998): 575–99.

Harding, Sandra, and Kathryn Norberg. 2005. "New Feminist Approaches to Social Science Methodologies: An Introduction," *Signs* 40, no. 1 (2005): 2009–15.

Hasan, Manar. 2002. "The Politics of Honor: Patriarchy, the State and the Murder of Women in the Name of Family Honor," *Journal of Israeli History: Politics, Society, Culture* 21 (2002): 1–37.

Heckenberger, Michael J. 1995. "The Symbolic Economy of Power," in *The Ecology of Power: Culture, Place and Personhood in the Southern Amazon*, pp. 312–18. London: Routledge.

Heckert, Jaime. 2010. "Intimacy with Strangers/Intimacy with Self: Queer Experiences of Social Research," in *Queer Methods and Methodologies: Queer Theories and Social Science Research*, edited by Kath Browne and Catherine J. Nash, 41–54. Burlington, VT: Ashgate.

Hegel, G. W. F. 2008. *Outlines of the Philosophy of Right*, translated by T. M. Knox. Oxford: Oxford University Press.

Hirshi, Ayaan Ali. 2007. *Infidel: My Life*. London: Pocket Books.

Holstein, James A. and Jaber F. Gubrium. 2002. "Active Interviewing." in *Handbook of Interview Research: Context & Method*, edited by Jaber F. Gubrium, James A. Holstein, 67–80. Thousand Oaks, CA: Sage.

hooks, bell. 1984. *Feminist Theory from Margin to Center*. Boston, MA: South End Press.

Irigaray, Luce. 1985. "The Way Out of the Cave," *Speculum of the Other Woman*, translated by Gillian C. Gill, 278–83. Ithaca, NY: Cornell University Press.

Johnson, John. 2002. "In-Depth Interviewing," in *Postmodern Interviewing*, edited by Jaber F. Gubrium and James A. Holstein, 103–11. Thousand Oaks, CA: Sage.

Josselson, Ruthellen. 2007. "The Ethical Attitude in Narrative Research," in *Handbook of Narrative Inquiry: Mapping a Methodology*, edited by D. Jean Clandinin, 537–66. London: Sage.

Kandiyoti, Deniz. 1988. "Bargaining with Patriarchy." *Gender and Society* 3 (1988): 274–90.

Kristeva, Julia. 2000. *About Chinese Women*. London: Marion Boyars Publishers.

Lather, Patricia. 1991. *Getting Smart: Feminist Research and Pedagogy with/in the Postmodern*. New York and London: Routledge.

Lenin, Vladimir. 1902. "What Has to Be Done," in *Lenin's Selected Works*, 119–271. http://www.marxists.org/archive/lenin/works/1901/witbd.

Lincoln, Yvonna S. and Egon G. Guba. 1985. *Naturalistic Inquiry*. Beverley Hills, CA: Sage Publications.

Lorde, Audre. 1984. "The Master's Tools Will Never Dismantle the Master's House," *Sister Outsider Essays and Speeches*. New York: Crossing Press.

Macherey, Pierre. 1978. *A Theory of Literary Production,* translated by Geoffrey Wall. London: Routledge Chapman and Hall.

MacNay, Lois. 2000. *Gender and Agency: Reconfiguring the Subject in Feminist and Social Theory*. Oxford: Blackwell.

Mansbridge, Jane. 2001. "Oppositional Consciousness," in *The Subjective Roots of Social Protest*, edited by Jane Mansbridge and Aldon Morris. Chicago: University of Chicago Press.

Nash, Catherine J. and Alison L. Bain. 2007. "Pussies Declawed: Unpacking the Politics of a Queer Women's Bathhouse Raid," in *Geographies of Sexualities: Theory, Practices and Politics*, edited by Kath Browne, Jason Lim, and Gavin Brown, 159–68. Aldershot, UK: Ashgate.

Nash, Catherine J. 2010. "Queer Conversations: Old-Time Lesbians, Transmen, and the Politics of Queer Research," in *Queer Methods and Methodologies: Queer Theories and Social Science Research*, edited by Kath Browne and Catherine J. Nash (eds.), 129–42. Burlington, VT: Ashgate.

Nussbaum, Martha .2000. *Women and Human Development: The Capabilities Approach*. Cambridge: Cambridge University Press.

Ofir, Adi. 2015. "On Linking Machinery and Show," *Differences*, December: 54–80.

Patai, Daphne. 1991. "US Academics and Third-World Women: Is Ethical Research Possible?" in *Women's Words: The Feminist Practice of Oral History*, edited by Sherna Berger Gluck and Daphne Patai, 137–53. New York: Routledge.

Pateman, Carole. 1988. *The Sexual Contract*. Cambridge: Polity.

Popp, Gary E., and William F. Muhs. 1982. "Fear of Success and Women Employees," *Human Relation*. London: The Tavistock Institute.

Ramazanoglu, Caroline. 1989. *Feminism and Contradiction of Oppression*. New York: Routledge.

Sandoval, Chela. 2000. *Methodology of the Oppressed*. Minneapolis: University of Minnesota Press.

Seri, Bracha. 1983. "An Outsider Guest," *Kol Ha'Isha Newsletter* 19 (1983): 4. (Hebrew)

Shalhoub-Kevorkian, Nadera. 2004. *Mapping and Analyzing the Landscape of Femicide in Palestinian Society*. Jerusalem: Women's Centre for Legal Aid and Counselling.

Slaughter, Anne-Marie. 2012. "Why Women Still Can't Have It All?" *The Atlantic*, July/August 2012.

Spector, Shiri. "Polygamy among the Bedouin Population in Israel—Update." The Knesset Information Centre, October 8, 2013. Accessed March 23, 2015. http://www.knesset.gov.il/mmm/data/pdf/m03293.pdf.

Spivak, Gayatri C. 1988. "Can the Subaltern Speak," in *Marxism and Interpretation*, edited by L. Grossbury and C. Nelson, 271–316. Champaign: University of Illinois Press.

Stacey, Judith. 1988. "Can There be a Feminist Ethnography?" *Women's Studies International Forum* 11 (1988): 21–27.

Syrett, Michel, and Clare Hogg. 1992. *Frontiers of Leadership*. Oxford: Blackwell.

Turner, Bryan S. 1996. *The Body and Society: Explorations in Social Theory* (second edition). London: Sage.

Turner, Terence. 1995. "Social Body and Embodied Subject: Bodiliness, Subjectivity, and Sociality among the Kayapo," *Cultural Anthropology* 10: 143–70.

Walby, Sylvia. 1990. *Theorizing Feminism*. Oxford: Basil Blackwell.

Women's Fourth World Conference, September 1995, Beijing, https://www.un.org/esa/gopher-data/conf/fwcw/off/a--20.en.

Yuval-Davis, Nira. 2006. "Intersectionality and Feminist Politics," *European Journal of Women's Studies* 13, no. 3 (2006): 193–209.

HEBREW SOURCES

רשימה ביבליוגרפית

אכסנדרוביץ' רענן, לירן עצמור, "שלטון החוק", 2011 /https://he.wikipedia.org/wiki שלטון _ החוק _(סרט)

"הכנסת דנה בהצעות לסדר היום בנושא מחאת האמהות החד-הוריות ב-2 ביולי 2003 [...] אמהות חד-הוריות מחו על הקיצוץ בקצבאות שיזם שר האוצר בנימין נתניהו", אתר הכנסת, 16.7.2003, /www.knesset.gov.il review/ReviewPage2.aspx?kns=16&lng=1

"מימון התנחלויות בשטחים", הישיבה המאה ושמונים של הכנסת האחת-עשרה, אתר הכנסת, 24.2.1986, //:http knesset.gov.il/tql/knesset_new/knesset11/HTML_27_03_2012_05-59-19-PM/ 19860224@19860224030@030.html

"אם חד-הורית – מה מגיע לך?" פורטל זכויות עובדים, www.workrights.co.il

"ויקי קנפו: מחאה בעירום", www.ynet.co.il/articles/0,7340,L-2976935,00.html ,14.9.2004 , *ynet* http://news.walla.co.il/item/434295

אתוסר, לואי, 2003, על האידיאולוגיה, תל אביב: רסלינג, ליבידו.

באטלר, ג'ודית, 2001, "צרות של מגדר [קטע]", מכאן, ב': 202-219.

בג"צ לאה שקדיא נ' השר לענייני דתות, 153/87, 1988.

בג"ץ אליס מילר נגד משרד הביטחון, בג"צ מס' 4541/94, 8.11.1995. בית הלחמי, חנה, 2003, "ויקי, אל תעזבי, טעיתי!", 3.8.2003, www.haderech.co.il/parliament65.html

גיליגן, קרול, 1995, בקול שונה: התיאוריה הפסיכולוגית והתפתחות האישה, תל אביב: ספרית פועלים.

גרוס, אייל וזיו, עמליה, 2003, "בין תיאוריה לפוליטיקה: לימודים הומו-לסביים ותיאוריה קווירית", בתוך: יאיר קדר, עמליה זיו ואורן קנר, (עורכים), מעבר למיניות: מבחר מאמרים בלימודים הומו-לסביים ותיאוריה קווירית, תל אביב: מגדרים, הקיבוץ המאוחד, 2003, עמ' 9-45.

גרינברג, לב, 1993, ההסתדרות מעל הכול, ירושלים: נבו.

דבירי, מנואלה, "ההודנה, ויקי כנפו וימות המשיח", הגדה השמאלית, 2.8.2003, /http://hagada.org.il/2003/08 02 , וטוקבקים הע' 13, 16, 17, 20, 21, 22.

דהאן כלב, הנרייט, 2013, "שאלת ה'מה' וה'איך' בחקר משילות ומגדר", בתוך: מיה אג'אי, דפנה האקר ומיכל קרומר נבו (עורכות), שיטות מחקר פמיניסטיות, תל אביב: הקיבוץ המאוחד, סדרת מגדרים.

הסיודוס, 1956, "שירת הסיודוס", מעשים וימים, תאוגוניה, מגן הראקלס, תרגום: שלמה שפאן, מוסד ביאליק.

הקר, דפנה, לביא-אג'אי, מיה, וקרומר-נבו, מיכל, 2014, "הזמנה לדיון במתודולוגיות מחקר פמיניסטיות", בתוך: מיכל קרומר-נבו, מיה לביא-אג'אי ודפנה הקר (עורכות), מתודולוגיות מחקר פמיניסטיות, תל אביב: מגדרים, הקיבוץ המאוחד, עמ' 7-32.

ואנייה, אלן, 2000, לקאן, תרגום: עמוס סקברר, תל אביב: רסלינג

ויטיג, מוניק, 2003, "אדם אינו נולד אישה", בתוך: יאיר קדר, עמליה זיו ואורן קנר, (עורכים), מעבר למיניות: מבחר מאמרים בלימודים הומו-לסביים ותיאוריה קווירית, תל אביב: מגדרים, הקיבוץ המאוחד, 2003, עמ' 110-103.

ויקי קנפו, "שיחה עם כנפו", 15.1.2005, כנס "מזרחיות ושלום", אירגון אחותי, מצפה רמון.

כהן, רותם, "ויקי כנפו: נתניהו היה קשוב, אבל לא נתן תשובות", /www.ynet.co.il ,10.07.2003 , *ynet* articles/0,7340,L-2688536,00.html

לוינס, עמנואל, תשנ"ה, אתיקה והאינסופי: שיחות עם פיליפ נמו, ירושלים: הוצאת ספרים ע"ש י"ל מאגנס, האוניברסיטה העברית.

לורד, אודרי, 2006, "כליו של האדון לעולם לא יפרקו את ביתו של האדון", בתוך: דלית באום ואחרות (עורכות), ללמוד פמיניזם: מקראה, תל אביב: הקיבוץ המאוחד, עמ' 190-194.

ליס, יהונתן, סיני, רותי ושירות הארץ, "כנפו: האוצר מסכסך בין הקבוצות במאהל המחאה", וואלה, 21.7.2003, http://news.walla.co.il/item/416064

מירון שקד, מיכל, "כבר לא תראו את ויקי כנפו במוספים השונים של חג יום הכיפורים", 23.9.2004 , *iWomen*, כתבה וטוקבקים, www.iwomen.co.il/item.asp?aid=87564

ניטשה, פרידריך, תשל"ג, כה אמר זרתוסטרא, תרגום: אדד, תל אביב: שוקן.

סבירסקי, ברברה, 1987, נשים ישראליות בקו הייצור, תל אביב: ברירות.

סבירסקי, שלמה, "מקום מגורים ורמת שכר בישראל 1997", מרכז אדוה, אפריל 2000, תל אביב, /http://adva.org wp-content/uploads/2014/09/makom-megurim-sahar1997.pdf

סיני רותי, ליס, יונתן, "ויקי כנפו: אשבות רעב אם נתניהו לא יחדש המו"מ איתי", וואלה, 1.9.2003,

סיני, רותי, "מעקב 'הארץ' אחר המכשולים וההצלחות", הארץ, 25.6.2001, /www.haaretz.co.il/misc 1.1536966

סיני, רותי, "פרטוק יקבל שיעור בניהול", הארץ, 5.6.2001.

סיקסו, הלן, 2006, "צחוקה של המדוזה", ללמוד פמיניזם: מיקראה, תל אביב: הקיבוץ המאוחד, עמ' 134-135.

סער, צפי, "בשם הביטחון: כך פוגעים בחלשים ובנשים וזוכים בתמיכתם" הארץ, גלריה, 30.10.2012, www.haaretz.co.il/gallery/mejunderet/1.1852560

פוקו, מישל, 1996, תולדות המיניות, כרך ראשון: הרצון לדעת, תרגום: גבריאׁ אש, תל אביב: הקיבוץ המאוחד.

פרידלנדר, יהודה, תשמ"א, "'ברוריה בת רב חנינא בן תרדיון' מאת שמואׁ מולדר" מחקרים על תולדות יהדות הולנד, ירושלים: מוסד ביאׁיק, עמ' 125-163.

קוטס-בר, חן, "ויקי קנפו: גם אני מרגישה כמו עובדת זרה", *nrg*, 29.5.2010, www.nrg.co.il/online/1/ART2/113/304.html

קליין, זאב, "קנפו נפגשה עם השרים נתניהו ואורלב: 'תחזירו לי את ה-1,300 ש"ח שקיצצתם'", גלובס, 10.07.2003, www.globes.co.il/news/article.aspx?did=704668

קרומר-נבו, מיכל, סידי, מירית, 2014, "פמיניזם, כתיבה מחקרית ואחרות", בתוך: מיכל קרומר-נבו, מיה לביא-אג'אי ודפנה הקר (עורכות), מתודולוגיות מחקר פמיניסטיות , תל אביב: מגדרים, הקיבוץ המאוחד, עמ׳ 229-247.

רוזן, טובה, 2006, הצביה ציד , תל אביב: אוניברסיטת תל אביב.

ריץ', אדריאן, 1989, ילוד אישה , תל אביב: עם עובד.

שלז ג׳ולי, צברי דורון, ״דרומה״, 2000, https://www.youtube.com/watch?v=DAFZqKAmKPg

שלסקי, שמחה, אפרט, ברכה, 2007, דרכים בכתיבת מחקר איכותני: מפירוק המציאות להבנייתה כטקסט , תל אביב: מכון מופ"ת.

שנאן, אביגדור, 2004, ״שלוש נשותיו של רבי עקיבא״, מסכת , חוברת ב', עמ׳ 11-25.

שרוני, יהודה, ״ויקי קנפו לעסקים: 'מחאת הקוטג" מצחיקה אותי", *nrg*, 16.6.2011, www.nrg.co.il/online/16/ART2/250/775.html

Index

About the Author

Henriette Dahan Kalev is a professor emerita political scientist based at the Ben-Gurion University of the Negev, Israel. Critical thought and political resistance in democracies are her main fields of research. She is the founder and first chair of the gender studies program at Ben-Gurion University. Her publications, books, collections, and articles are mostly interdisciplinary and synthesize theoretical and empirical subjects. Dahan Kalev divides her time between academic research and human rights activism.